MW00366264

Black Diamond City
Nanaimo
The Victorian Era

To Gina Lehmann

With best wishes

Jan Peterson

Dec 7/02

Jan Peterson

Heritage
House

National Library of Canada Cataloguing in Publication Data

Peterson, Jan, 1937-
    Black Diamond City

    Includes bibliographical references and index.
    ISBN 1-894384-51-2

    1. Nanaimo (B.C.)—History—19th century. I. Title.
FC3849.N35P47 2002   971.1'2   C2002-910905-1
F1089.5.N33P47 2002

First edition 2002

Heritage House acknowledges the financial support for our publishing program from the Government of Canada through the Book Publishing Industry Development Program (BPIDP), Canada Council for the Arts, and the British Columbia Arts Council.

Cover design by Katherine Hale
Book design by Darlene Nickull
Edited by John Ricker

HERITAGE HOUSE PUBLISHING COMPANY LTD.
#108 - 17665 66 A Ave., Surrey, B.C. Canada V3S 2A7

Printed in Canada

BRITISH
COLUMBIA
ARTS COUNCIL
We acknowledge the support of the Province of British Columbia
through the British Columbia Arts Council

The Canada Council | Le Conseil des Arts
for the Arts | du Canada

Contents

Acknowledgements

Black Diamond City is an exploration of Nanaimo, my new home since I moved here in retirement from Port Alberni five years ago. Today it is hard to imagine the geographic impediments faced in building the city of Nanaimo, from the long finger of the original Commercial Inlet, to the rock bluff at Comox Road that had been a barrier to traffic for many years, or the bridging between Bastion and Fitzwilliam Streets. This was a company town during most of its formative years, full of young miners who had travelled halfway around the world to make their living underground digging coal. As I researched the development of the city in relationship to the settlement of Vancouver Island, the manuscript took on a life of its own.

Books are rarely the work of one person and I have many people to thank. I am especially appreciative of the Nanaimo Community Archives Society manager Christine Meutzer and her small army of volunteers who were totally supportive of my efforts and who helped in every way possible. Archive volunteers such as Daphne Paterson, Jill Stannard, Anne Royle, Florence Williams, Shirley Bateman, Ruth Tickle and Barbara Cowling, and staff Dorothy Young and Dawn Arnot, contributed greatly by providing ease of access to files and sources.

A special big thank-you to Terry Simpson who generously gave access to his personal research on his relative Adam Grant Horne. I am also indebted to the Hudson's Bay Company Archives in Winnipeg who were very supportive and who helped with information about the voyage of the *Princess Royal*. First Nation Treaty Office research coordinator, Loraine Littlefield, offered advice and information and was helpful in every way. Nor can I forget the efforts of the staff of Vancouver Island Regional Library who gallantly searched libraries across the country for information for me. I cannot begin to express my admiration for the Northwest Collection of books in the library. This collection of wonderful, old books is indeed a treasure in our community.

I would be remiss if I did not mention the work of Peggy Nicolls who researched extensively the lives of the miners from the Black Country in England and who gave permission to use this source. I also appreciated the support of the Nanaimo Historical Society and the Nanaimo District Museum staff

Other organizations who added to the depth of this manuscript were the British Columbia Archives, the New Westminster Archives, the Nanaimo Courthouse Library, the Vancouver Maritime Museum, the Vancouver Public Library and the British Columbia Courthouse Library Society.

The most important ingredient for a writer is a good support system. My husband Ray provided this in abundance. I acknowledge his patience, understanding and encouragement during the research and writing of this book. I also thank my children and their families, also my friends and neighbours for their friendship and support.

A big thank you to my editor John Ricker, publishers Rodger and Pat Touchie and their staff at Heritage House: Darlene Nickull and Linda Martin, who added their professional talent to the manuscript and gave life to *Black Diamond City*.

Introduction

The Native population, the Snuneymuxw, pronounced "snu-nay-muck," lived a life of seasonal migration when the early Spanish explored in the Nanaimo area at the end of the eighteenth century. But the first regular contact with white men came in the early nineteenth century, when the Hudson's Bay Company established a fur-trading post at Fort Langley on the Fraser River in 1827. The Snuneymuxw occupied a summer village nearby.

Later, from its headquarters at Fort Victoria, the Hudson's Bay fur-trading company sought to diversify its resources. Natives led company officials to the coal deposits at Beaver Harbour, Vancouver Island in 1835, and Fort Rupert was established. The HBC imported miners from Great Britain to work the coal deposits. And when the Natives introduced the Hudson's Bay Company to the easily accessible Nanaimo coalfield, the miners moved there and the area's future was secured for white immigration. The Hudson's Bay Company founded Nanaimo in 1852 solely to exploit coal. The HBC first christened the settlement Colviletown in honour of its governor, Andrew Colvile. It was not until 1860 that the settlement became known as Nanaimo.

The small mining community, known alternately as Colviletown, Newcastle of the Pacific Coast, and Black Diamond City, became the most important coal-producing centre on Canada's West Coast. There were already two decades of history along its shoreline when the City of Nanaimo incorporated in 1874. British Columbia was only three years old and the incorporation of Nanaimo made the city the third largest in the province with a population of 1,645. Here coal was king, and the outlook for the future seemed exceedingly bright. *Black Diamond City* is a history of the development of Nanaimo and the region.

PART ONE

HISTORIC HOMELAND

The Snuneymuxw had lived in the central Vancouver Island area for at least 4,000 years. Their territory extended from Neck Point in the north to the Dodd Narrows in the south, east to Gabriola Island and other adjacent islands, and west to the inland mountains.[1] Like many other tribes in the province, the Snuneymuxw annually travelled hundreds of kilometers, crossing the Strait of Georgia to the Fraser River and travelling as far north as Qualicum River, to fish, hunt, and gather food.

Most travel was by water. Vancouver Island's broken seacoast formed a natural highway, with the exception of a few trails that crossed the island. One trail led from the east coast at Qualicum to the head of Alberni Inlet, another from Nimpkish Lake to Kyuquot and Nootka sounds. Nearly everywhere on the island, Natives settled along the shoreline or along navigable rivers.

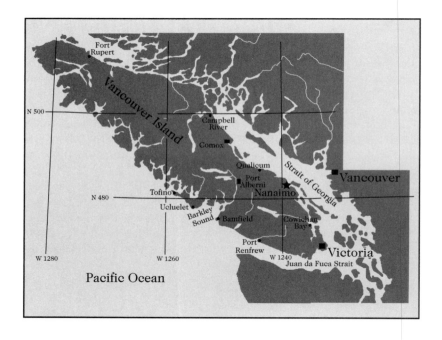

Directional map of Vancouver Island showing Nanaimo in relationship to Victoria and Vancouver.

CHAPTER ONE

The Snuneymuxw

The Snuneymuxw were part of the Coast Salish linguistic group with ties to Washington state. Their language, a Vancouver Island dialect of Halkomelem, is shared with the Nanoose, Chemainus, and Cowichan and other east coast tribes. However they may not have been the first occupants of this land. The petroglyphs, or rock art, at Nanaimo show evidence of an earlier people and culture.

Petroglyphs

Throughout the length of the Pacific Coast petroglyphs can be found along beaches or on rock faces on high ground indicating the carver wanted a view of the sea, islands, and coastal mountains. These sites may have been ceremonial, the carvings representing spirits that inhabited the place. Two miles south of Nanaimo, at a site now designated as Petroglyph Park, are many such carvings done in a style unique to southern Vancouver Island. Represented are humans, halibut and other fish, a crab-like animal and several canine figures. The site also has a large stone slat with a series of bisecting channels, some forty-five feet in length suggesting this may have been a primitive map perhaps symbolic of a spiritual journey into the land of the spirits. Other rock carvings have been found at Jack Point and Harewood, and on Gabriola Island. These ancient rock carvings give only a glimpse of an earlier people.

Interpretative drawing of petroglyphs at Petroglyph Park, Nanaimo. First seen by Mark Bate in 1860 when taken to the spot by a Snuneymuxw elder.

The Confederation of the Snuneymuxw

The five local groups formed a confederacy called Nanaimo, an anglicized version of the term Snuneymuxw. During the spring, summer, and fall, they lived in settlements along the Nanaimo River, at Nanaimo Harbour, and at Departure Bay. Before European contact their population varied from 2,000 to 5,000.

The village sites along the lower Nanaimo River were on both banks. Near the bridge where the highway crosses the river, was the village of Salaxal [xwso'lexwel]. A few hundred yards downstream from the bridge was Anwinic [enwines]. Then in order came Yicaxen [yeshexen], Tewaxan [teytexen], and Kwelsiwelh [q laisiowal].[1] The people of Tewaxan also occupied a smaller village on the Millstone River. Another group, the people of Cly-Altw, was once part of the confederacy and lived on Gabriola Island but after a battle with the Lekwiltok they moved to live near Salaxal. Their village of Tl'aa'ltxw was an important resource site on the southeastern side of Gabriola Island, on the north side of False Narrows.

Most of the people stayed together, with the exception of the Salaxal. They were the highest-ranking family and were more self-sufficient; they also controlled the only salmon weir on the Nanaimo River. All the other families moved to their winter village, Stl'ilep, at Departure Bay where they stayed from December through March, while the people of Salaxal wintered at their village site in Nanaimo Harbour, joining the other groups in the spring. Each group had house frames at their sites along the Nanaimo River, at False Narrows, and at Departure Bay. These structures were easily dismantled, placed in a canoe and transported to another site.

Families lived in longhouses, large barn-like buildings that could accommodate five or six families, or on special occasions up to a thousand people. There were no boundaries or property limits separating the houses within the villages, although individual families owned or controlled hunting and fishing sites.[2] These buildings were 100 feet long by 30 feet wide and made of split cedar boards fastened together with poles and strips of strong bark. Each family was separated by low partitions. There was no floor or windows for light other than the door when open. The wind whipped through cracks on the walls and roof. Beds were built up on platforms and the corners of the building were piled high with mats, fishing tackle and other paraphernalia. Smoke from fires circulating throughout the building finally escaped through cracks and other openings. Underneath the bunks and hanging from poles was the family supply of dried fish and berries. Dogs, cats and later chickens completed the household assembly.[3]

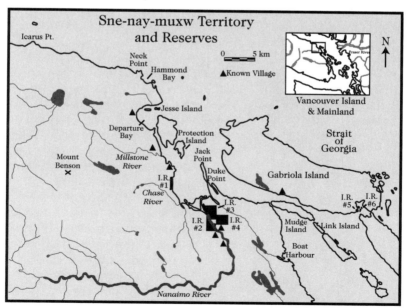

Map of Snuneymuxw territory

The Snuneymuxw and other southern tribes had the unusual custom of deforming the heads of their children, a practice similar to foot-binding Chinese children. The Flatheads compressed the foreheads of their little ones by means of boards or a hard cushion, or even a flat stone. The child was laid in its cradle or placed at one end of a narrow piece of board. At the other end another board was attached with thongs. The narrow board was pulled tight down over the child's forehead, and the head pressed gradually out of shape and the forehead flattened back.[4] This practice was discontinued in the 1850s.

Food gathering

Gathering food was a major occupation and in the case of ducks and geese, required some ingenuity. The Snuneymuxw had an unusual method of killing these birds. In the springtime, ducks and geese were abundant in the Nanaimo River estuary and swampland, or along the shoreline of Gabriola Island. About the middle of the swamp, and cutting it in two, was a series of posts about twenty feet in height and forty feet apart. Stretched between each post was a large net. At dusk, when the swamp was covered with ducks and geese the Natives would frighten them and the birds would rise in a large body with necks extending and fly around in a circle. Without seeing the net, they would push their necks through the mesh and fall back. With broken vertebrae, they would remain in a hung position until removed. The net also caught stray flights of birds during the night when the tribe slept.[5]

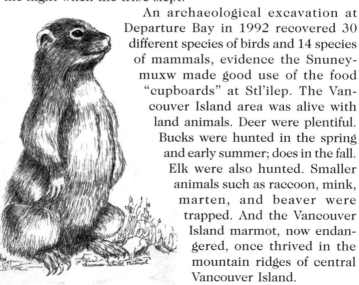

An archaeological excavation at Departure Bay in 1992 recovered 30 different species of birds and 14 species of mammals, evidence the Snuneymuxw made good use of the food "cupboards" at Stl'ilep. The Vancouver Island area was alive with land animals. Deer were plentiful. Bucks were hunted in the spring and early summer; does in the fall. Elk were also hunted. Smaller animals such as raccoon, mink, marten, and beaver were trapped. And the Vancouver Island marmot, now endangered, once thrived in the mountain ridges of central Vancouver Island.

Seasonal and daily life

In March, the Snuneymuxw began collecting food for the year with the arrival of the herring into Departure Bay and Hammond Bay. Herring in earlier times were said to be so thick at Departure Bay that sometimes they would be piled up a foot deep along the beach after whales chased them ashore.[6] A Snuneymuxw elder named Jimmy Peanuts told the legend of the herring—how the "first man" at Departure Bay had had a paddle, and how this man's use of his paddle in the water had caused herring to be created.

The spawn of herring was collected for food by anchoring quantities of cedar or hemlock brush in the spawning places. When the brush was withdrawn it was covered with a mass of eggs. The herring were secured with a rake, a stick with a row of sharp pieces of bone set in one side. In April, the tribe moved to False Narrows and Gabriola Island to dig for clams and fish for cod, grilse (young salmon), and other species, and to hunt seals and sea lions. This area had one of the most important clam beds in the region. The clams were gathered with digging sticks at low tide and were prepared for future use by steaming under a cover of seaweed and mats.

During the summer months, roots, bulbs and berries were gathered. Camas *(Camassia quamash)*, a bulbous root similar to an onion grew extensively on the bluffs of Gabriola Island and was a preferred food. It was cooked in underground ovens and provided excellent and palatable food. Later, potatoes replaced the camas bulb as the food of choice. Berries were everywhere, from wild strawberries in May, to salmonberries, salal, thimbleberries, blackberries, and bog cranberries through the autumn. Sometimes the berries were eaten fresh or dried into cakes then stored in crates made of dried alder.

In the summer camps, people sheltered under large rush mats woven by the women from tule *(Scirpus lacustris)*, or hard-stemmed bulrushes.[7] The stems were harvested in late summer or early fall, brought home in large bundles and then spread out to dry in the sun. Mats were made by laying the stems side by side, alternating top and bottom, and either sewing with a long needle or by twinning the stems together with a tough fibre such as a stinging nettle. The mats were light and insulating because of the pithy centre of the stem. These mats were quite useful; besides being used as shelter, they sometimes were placed in several layers for a comfortable bed. The tule mats were sometimes traded for mountain goat hair.

In July it was time to move to the Fraser River to fish for sockeye. Sites were located several miles from the mouth of the Fraser River, near Barnston Island. One site situated on the south shore of the river across from the island had a permanent village accommodating four hundred "Nanaimooch."[8] Here salmon was dried on open racks and stored in baskets.

The Snuneymuxw returned to their Nanaimo villages in October just in time for the run of the chum salmon, the last of the salmon species to return to the Nanaimo River.

The people of Salaxal controlled the chum salmon fishery on the Nanaimo River. The chief conducted a first-salmon ceremony that included marking a male and female chum salmon with paint and down feathers and singing a special song, after which the people were permitted to smoke-dry the salmon. This man also possessed the knowledge to paint special designs on rocks, which induced the salmon to come to the river.[9]

The most common method of taking salmon was by means of a weir placed across a river or stream. This was a fence-like structure with narrow openings, placed across the river where the water was shallow and slow moving, making it easier to catch the salmon. Weirs were used at night when the salmon could not detect the presence of the fisherman. However, fishing was most often done from a canoe, with one person steadying the craft while the other went after the fish with a long-handled net or gaff. Fishing with nets was also common.

With the onset of winter, and before the river had frozen and firewood became hard to get, families moved closer to the harbour. The islands in Departure Bay would be occupied. Jesse Island, located east from Brandon Island was once a burial site, where "Dozens of boxes were piled, one above another, moldering with age, containing the remains of Natives, there deposited."[10]

The potlatch was an important ceremonial ritual during the winter months: it was a time to share the harvest and seek spiritual renewal. The word "potlatch" means "to give," and it is usually applied to a festival or feasting in which property or goods are given away. The more that is given away, the more prestige is acquired. Missionary Thomas Crosby described one potlatch in Nanaimo whereby a man worked for years to give a great potlatch. "Everything went, including the last stitch of clothing, leaving he and his family practically naked to face the winter without any provision. His children almost starved; he contracted a cold that led to his death."[11]

With enough food stored for the winter, women turned their attention to weaving blankets and baskets. They were very proficient in weaving blankets out of a combination of a domestic dog hair and a variety of other materials such as fireweed and down from geese and ducks. Some blankets contained mixed dog hair and mountain goat hair. The Sliammon from Cortez Island were known to have bartered bales of mountain goat's hair.

The Snuneymuxw were one of several tribes who kept longhaired white dogs, which were sheared like sheep annually. There were two types of dogs in use—one a medium-sized coyote-like animal generally used for hunting, and a smaller type with prick ears, a curled-tail and long usually white hair. The latter dog's wool mixed with other hair was used to produce blankets, floor coverings, and items of clothing.[12]

The Snuneymuxw believed in the Chief Spirit, who created all things and was wise and powerful. They prayed to the sun, to the moon, and to the Great Being who provided all the fish and food. Hunters prayed and fasted to become successful hunters. Fishermen prayed for a successful catch.

The traditional enemies of the Snuneymuxw were the Lekwiltok, also known as Yucultas or Euclataws. They lived in and around Cape Mudge and were estimated to number about 4,000 at the end of the eighteenth century. When the Hudson's Bay Company (HBC) established posts in the region they noted that the Lekwiltok annually raided the southern regions of the Strait of Georgia as well as Puget Sound. They fought to control territory on the northeast coast of Vancouver Island and eventually displaced the northern Coast Salish from Qualicum Beach and Comox.

Snake Island Legends —Fear of Ling Cod

Snake Island in Rainbow Channel, northeast of the entrance to Departure Bay, was known to have snakes. The legend of Snake Island tells the story of how a teenage boy who was eating fern-roots got sick.

"Snakes were coming out of him. So he went out to the island, but still the snakes came out of him. He cut some in half with his paddle. It is said there are still snakes on this island, and some of them still appear as if they have been cut in half. Ling cod located near a reef in the vicinity of the island are said to have snakes inside them. Old-timers refuse to fish for ling cod at this location because of the legend."[13]

CHAPTER TWO

The Europeans Arrive

*T*he first European contact was made by Spanish explorers in 1791. After leaving Nootka on the west coast of Vancouver Island, Francisco de Eliza passed Nanaimo harbour naming it Winthuysen Inlet, after Spanish naval officer, Francisco Zavier de Winthuysen. The following year, two other officers from Nootka circumnavigated Vancouver Island under orders from Captain Alejandro Malaspina. Sailing the *Sutil* and *Mexicana,* Captain Dionisio Alcala Galiano and Captain Cayetano Valdes surveyed parts of the east coast and the mainland and landed at different places including Gabriola Island. They anchored at Descanso Bay where curious Natives were given beads as a token of friendship.[1] The following is an excerpt from their journal published in Madrid in 1802. The date of the entry is June 14, 1792:

> We followed the coast with the object of finding a good anchorage. We sailed straight to the Punta de Gaviola [Flat Top Island] and not finding it there, went to the Bocas de Winthuysen [Nanaimo Harbour] aided by a fresh wind from the east, which cleared the sky. We reached the east point of the entrances and passed between them and the islet [Snake Island]. On doubling the point we saw two canoes which followed close to the shore observing the movements of the schooners. On Coming abeam of them they approached very cautiously. To gain their confidence and friendship we gave those who came in them the best proofs of our intentions by throwing some strings of beads into their canoes, but we could not get them to come near. We

continued along the coast with the same object, until at last we discovered an anchorage ... we called this roadstead "Cala de Descanso" from our need of rest and our appreciation in finding it on this occasion.

The Spaniards went ashore on Gabriola Island and began to search for fresh water. Natives showed them how poor the springs were on the eastern side of the island. On their return to the beach, six Natives traded sardines for beads. Word spread quickly, and within days 39 canoes were gathered around the ship. The Spanish visitors explored for another few days before leaving on June 19.

The Spanish exploration of Vancouver Island resulted in maps, charts, and drawings about the indigenous people, their way of life, and the flora and fauna. This material is still in existence in cultural institutions in Spain and Mexico. Many of the place names now associated with the Gulf Islands and Vancouver Island are derived from these journeys.

When a Hudson's Bay Company (HBC) reconnaissance party visited the region in 1824, they reported that the Natives in the region had few European trade goods and no experience with white men. A fur-trading post was established at Fort Langley on the Fraser River in 1827. Fort Langley was close to the Snuneymuxw summer village. When the HBC schooner, the *Cadboro,* sailed up the Fraser River looking for a location for the fort, it passed the Snuneymuxw village of Nanaimooch. A number of canoes carrying 150 Snuneymuxw came out to greet them. It took several months to build the fort, and during that time many of the band came to the fort to visit as well as trade. They traded fish, caught nearby. Women traded berries for rings, buttons, and other trade goods. In later years they traded sturgeon and furs. Beaver and land otter fur could be traded for HBC "point" blankets.

Early contact with the Fort Langley employees resulted in the Snuneymuxw having no fear of the white man when he arrived on Vancouver Island. Until now they had traded fish and furs for blankets—familiar items of trade on the coast. They were encouraged to trade goods at the new Fort Victoria, but a chance encounter between a chief and a HBC employee would change their lives forever. Soon "black diamonds" would become another item of trade.

The Hudson's Bay Point Blanket

One of the trading commodities most highly prized by Natives in exchange for their beaver pelts was the Hudson's Bay "point" blanket, so named because of its size. The trading value was marked into the weave with small black stripes—three points, or stripes, equalling three beavers. There were several grades of blankets with the two-and-a-half point blanket demanding the highest number of furs. Since 1779, when the blanket was first mentioned in HBC correspondence, it has been a symbol of wealth and an important article of trade for Natives.

The blankets were manufactured in England of high quality wool that was pounded with wooden mallets to prevent shrinking, making the blankets valuable winter clothing. Sometimes they were cut into coats and leggings, their snowy colour helped hunters stalk their prey without being seen. The colourful black, yellow, scarlet, and green stripes of today were added later.

PART TWO

BLACK DIAMONDS
TRANSFORM THE WILDERNESS

The place itself appears to be a perfect "Eden" in the midst of the dreary wilderness of the North west coast, and so different is its general aspect, from the wooded, rugged regions around, that one might be pardoned for supposing it had dropped from the clouds into its present position.

—Chief Factor James Douglas
describing Vancouver Island, 1842[1]

CHAPTER THREE

The Hudson's Bay Company and James Douglas

As the new half-century approached, the United States appeared ready to take military action to secure the area between California and Alaska. There had been years of negotiations between Great Britain and the United States to decide on a common boundary west of the Rocky Mountains. These efforts had failed and the U.S. Senate declared the Oregon Territory to be American. But cool heads prevailed and in 1846 the Oregon Territory was divided between Great Britain and the United States. Great Britain obtained undisputed sovereignty to land north of the 49th parallel as well as the whole of Vancouver Island. As a result of the settlement, the Hudson's Bay Company (HBC) had to find another way to supply its interior posts. It now found itself in the unfortunate position of being subject to American import regulations. The HBC with its headquarters in Fort Vancouver requested jurisdiction over Vancouver Island in exchange for promoting colonization.

Fort Vancouver, still on the map today, was situated just a few miles north of the City of Portland, Oregon. It was here during the 1830s and early 1840s, that Dr. John McLoughlin, chief of the Columbia Department of the HBC, ruled a kingdom stretching from California to Alaska. Young James Douglas joined him at the Fort in 1830 as an accountant, and he was promoted to chief trader in 1834 and chief factor in 1839. Douglas was born of mixed parentage: his father John Douglas, a Glasgow merchant who owned sugar estates in Demerara, British Guiana, and his mother Martha Ritchie, the daughter of a black freewoman from Barbados. James was

educated in Scotland and joined the North West Company in 1819
as an apprentice and two years later went over to the HBC. He
married fifteen-year-old Amelia in 1824; she was a mixed blood
daughter of his boss, William Connolly, a company clerk.[1] It was
not unusual for an employee of the HBC to marry a Native; in fact it
was encouraged.[2] Many of the fur traders regarded these women as
temporary companions and thought nothing of moving on to other
trading posts and leaving them behind. Amelia was more fortunate
than most as she had the benefit of an Anglican marriage. She gave
birth to thirteen children. Only four survived her.[3]

At Fort Vancouver, Douglas checked the trading posts or
established new ones. In 1842, when McLoughlin became suspicious
Great Britain might yield the Oregon Territory to the United States,
Douglas picked the site of Fort Victoria on Vancouver Island as the
new fort. It was first named Fort Camosun, then briefly Fort Albert,
until finally taking the name Fort Victoria in honor of the young
queen of England. Charles Ross was charged with constructing the
fort. He died in 1844 and was succeeded at the fort by 26-year-old
Roderick Finlayson who had been with the HBC only a few years.
Under his direction two dairy farms were established and acreage
was cultivated making the HBC fort as self-sufficient as possible.
(He became one of the largest property owners in the city, and it
was under his direction as mayor of Victoria in 1878 that Victoria's
City Hall was built.)

McLoughlin ruled with James Douglas at his side. Their superior
was Governor Sir George Simpson, an energetic man, tireless and
ruthless, who swept from post to post in his state canoe, wearing a
top hat and a cloak and accompanied by his kilted piper. Born in
Rosshire, Scotland, Simpson started his professional career as a
clerk in the London firm of an uncle whose daughter he later
married. At the age of 33 in 1820, Simpson left London for Norway
House on Lake Winnipeg.

Simpson's journey up the ranks of the HBC began with the fur
trade business. He worked hard to bring about the amalgamation of
the two rival fur companies: the North West Company and the HBC.
He shot to the forefront of management in 1839 when he became
governor of Rupert's Land and was knighted for the work he had
done on behalf of the HBC and the country. He kept track of possible rivals, such as McLoughlin, whom Simpson described after
their first meeting as "such a figure as I should not like to meet in a
dark night in one of the bye lanes in the neighbourhood of London."
However, he liked James Douglas, as he was "a stout powerful man
of good constitution and respectable abilities."[4]

Andrew Colvile & Colviletown

Colvile was a successful London sugar-broker and a powerful figure in the Bay hierarchy. His name is historically associated with Nanaimo as the first name given to the town. Colvile was born in 1779 and rose to be governor of the HBC from 1852 to 1856. He had been deputy-governor since 1839. During his tenure, the town of Nanaimo was officially named Colviletown. For a time maps and charts showed Colviletown, but the name was not officially removed until August 1860.[5] Simpson had at one time expressed his desire to have Colvile named his successor but when his will was read, Colvile's name had been deleted with no reason given.

Hudson's Bay Company granted Vancouver Island

Great Britain was opposed to restrictive trading monopolies and saw no value in Vancouver Island apart from that of furs.[6] On January 13, 1849, it relieved itself of direct responsibility for Vancouver Island. By Imperial letters patent, Queen Victoria granted to the HBC "the Island called Vancouver Island together with all royalties of the seas upon the coasts thereof and all mines royal thereto belonging."[7] The island was handed over to the HBC for ten years subject to several conditions; one was the right of the Crown to re-purchase the island from the HBC on the termination of the trading licence that would expire May 30, 1859. Also the HBC was required to develop and settle the island. The HBC could keep 10 percent of all the money it received from the sale of lands, coal, or other minerals, but it was obligated to spend the remaining 90 percent on surveys, roads, bridges, churches, and schools plus any other amenities for the settlers. In 1849 James Douglas moved to Fort Victoria. Great Britain retained civil authority by appointing a governor.

The first British governor Richard Blanshard was an inexperienced young lawyer who arrived in the spring of 1850. He soon discovered he was a governor of a colony without colonists. In dispatches to London he complained of the HBC monopoly of land and prices, and that there were only three settlers on the island. When he accepted the appointment, he failed to ask if he would receive a salary. He soon found that there was no wage or expenses for his services. Great Britain expected him to govern the colony at his own expense.[8] He also discovered to his dismay, there was no accommodation for him. Feeling he had been tricked by the HBC, he complained bitterly to London.

Coal discovered at Fort Rupert—miners arrive

Until this time, sailing ships navigated the waters of the Pacific and Atlantic oceans. Soon the age of steam revolutionized not only transportation on land as well as sea, but also the whole basis of industry. Coal was required to manufacture steam for railway engines, factories, and shipping. The steam engine had an obvious attraction for ship owners: it could provide a steady output of power even in a flat calm. Its initial disadvantage was its appetite for coal. Many ships played important roles in the HBC history. They maintained order and carried on trade with Alaska. On the West Coast those most familiar were the steamer *Beaver* and the schooner *Cadboro,* both armed with cannon. The *Beaver* became the flagship of the HBC's western fleet and was the first to fly the HBC flag. The *Cadboro* sailed up the Fraser River carrying tools to build the post at Fort Langley.

Coal was first discovered on northern Vancouver Island at what is now known as Beaver Harbour in 1835. Kwagiulth Natives visiting Fort McLoughlin on Milbanke Sound, near Bella Bella, watched the HBC blacksmith at his forge. When asked where he got his "black stones," he told them that they came from far across the sea. The Kwagiulth told him that similar stones were available closer to home, on Northern Vancouver Island. Company officials sent aboard the Beaver investigated and found a considerable amount of coal near the surface. The location took the name of the ship.[9] The north island coalfield extended to Port McNeil, fifteen miles to the south. Only when the Royal Navy vessels converted to coal fuel was interest aroused in the coal deposits there.

The first shipment of coal from this north island post was made in 1846 when the steam sloop H.M.S. *Cormorant* took on coal at Suquash, six miles from the site of Fort Rupert. Here Natives simply dug the coal from the surface with trade axes. Although the fort was primarily built to develop the coal industry, it was also designed for trade, to

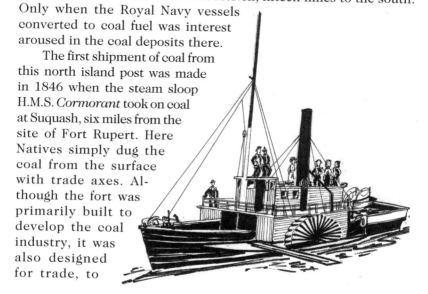

replace Fort McLoughlin that had been closed in 1843.[10] The HBC had already discovered there was valuable timber in the area suitable for ship spars, and logging began almost immediately. The Royal Navy ship H.M.S. *America* returned to England in 1845 with a supply of spars for testing. The timber was found to equal anything on the world market. The export of shingles followed.

Fort Rupert was established on the south side of Beaver Harbour, about half way between present day Port McNeil and Port Hardy.

Ships approached Fort Rupert from the open Pacific, along the west coast of Vancouver Island, by the northern straits because it would have been more difficult to travel the inside straits. Seymour Narrows, the narrow passage between Vancouver and Quadra islands, and the dangerous Ripple Rock stood in the way. There was no easy access or deep-sea harbour, only a stretch of shallow beach to be crossed before

Fort Rupert's Name

The fort was named for the first Governor of the HBC, Prince Rupert of Rhine whom author Peter Newman described as "a latter-day Renaissance man."[11] Rupert was an artist, an inventor, a chemist, and an entrepreneur. He invented the first primitive torpedo; designed many surgical instruments, and worked on a process of painting on marble and drawing buildings in perspective. Many consider him the scientific equal of Sir Isaac Newton.

This remote location named for such a distinguished person had been the home of the Kwagiulth for thousands of years. They first viewed the newcomers with caution and curiosity, and perhaps thought they would benefit through trade. The HBC negotiated a "deed of conveyance," the legal language for a written agreement giving the right of occupancy.[12] Before their eyes the fort was constructed and Scottish miners began to arrive.

loading. A Native trail led to the West Coast of the Island and it was thought the HBC might have established a west coast base there, but this never happened.[13] There was a decided advantage to having coal available from Vancouver Island instead of having it transported from Wales, or Scotland, as was the case with the Pacific Mail Steamship Company that contracted with the HBC to supply coal for its steamers. Experienced miners were recruited from the coal mines in Ayrshire, Scotland.

Royal Navy Commander R.C. Mayne described Fort Rupert as "the best built station of the Hudson's Bay Company I have seen." He noted the similarity of it to other company forts, "it is stockaded, and has its gallery and bastions. It stands almost in the middle of the Indian village."[14] The stockade was eighteen feet high. Great care had been taken in the fort's design so it could be defended by a handful of employees. The most impressive piece of architecture was the fort's main gate, which was positioned directly above the entranceway so as to overshadow all activity there.

Captain William McNeill, a former captain of the *Beaver*, was placed in charge of Fort Rupert. At first the HBC used what labour was available—local Kwagiulths and Hawaiian Kanakas brought over on HBC ships. Although some coal was produced, it soon became evident that shafts would have to be sunk, and a more elaborate mining operation would need skilled labour. The Scottish-recruited miners were among the first settlers on Vancouver Island.

CHAPTER FOUR

Hudson's Bay Company Ships Bring Miners and Settlers

*A*lthough the HBC was a land-based company, its trade depended on ships to transport furs and keep its forts supplied with goods. Several sailing vessels ran from Gravesend, on the River Thames, England, via the Orkney Islands off northern Scotland, to posts on Hudsons Bay.[1] Each time a ship docked at the Orkney Islands, the ship's captain hired ten or twelve men to work at the HBC's various posts.[2] The HBC liked Scottish workers; they were hard working and cheap. John Nixon, an early HBC governor at Fort York, reflected the thinking of the time:

> If England can not furnish you with men, Scotland can, for that countrie is a hard country to live in and poore-mens wages is cheap. They are hardy people both to endure hunger, and could, and are subject to obedience, and I am sure that they will serve for six pound pr years and be better content with their dyet than Englishmen.[3]

Usually the ships arrived the first week of June and stayed for several weeks giving enough time for loading, visiting ashore, or signing up new recruits. Eventually permanent recruiting agents were stationed in the towns. The Orkney Islanders were poor and relied heavily on agriculture and fishing. When other British colonies like Australia also began attracting immigrants it became more difficult to lure workers to Vancouver Island. Land became the added incentive. Who could resist such an opportunity?

Aside from the need for workers, the HBC was also motivated to recruit immigrants to fulfill its settlement obligations or lose the right to run the colony. When experienced miners were needed for the coal-mining operation at Fort Rupert, the HBC looked to Ayrshire to find the expertise. Ayrshire is a busy and prosperous county in the Lowlands of Scotland, and once the heart of the coal mining industry. Miners were recruited from towns like Kilmarnock, Riccarton, Irvine, and Muirkirk, and the neighbouring county of Lanarkshire.[4] The success of the Scottish mines rested squarely with men who faced the coal pits in semi-darkness with lamp-lit tunnels. Often entire families worked in the pits, including children. Children started work at age ten and often worked their way up to full collier. No one got rich working in the mines. Coal-mining families were usually poor. Their homes were owned by the proprietors of the mine and located in or near the colliery yard.

The HBC offered financial inducements including a grant of land after the miners had completed their contracts, or return passage to Scotland. Those recruits were young and adventurous and probably thought this was a way to better their lives and perhaps increase their social status. In Scotland, they would unlikely have been able to afford land, or gain a foothold on respectability, or provide a better life for their children. On Vancouver Island they would have more land than any had ever dreamed possible. The Ayrshire miners boarded ships like the *Pekin*, the *Tory*, and the *Harpooner* to come to Vancouver Island. The Orcadians arrived on the *Norman Morison*, the *Harpooner*, the *Tory*, and the *Golmeza E.*

The Harpooner

On November 29, 1848 the first of the immigrant ships, the HBC barque *Harpooner*, sailed from London. On board were the Muirs and McGregors, Ayrshire families bound for Fort Rupert, with contracts for three years. The Muir family included 49-year-old John Muir, his wife Ann and their four sons Andrew, John, Michael, and Robert, and their cousin Archibald Muir. Michael Muir celebrated his fourteenth birthday at sea.[5] John Muir, Sr., was hired as oversman, or manager. Also included were Muir's daughter Marion Turner, a widow, and her two young sons John and William Turner. The McGregor family included 40-year-old John McGregor, Sr., his wife Mary, and their three young children John, Archibald, and Mary. Another miner, John Smith and his wife Marion also accompanied the group. Also on the voyage was 35-year-old Dr. Alfred Robson Benson, a doctor who is remembered for his service in Nanaimo. An Act of Parliament compelled the HBC to carry surgeons on immigrant ships.[6] The ship's arrival was duly noted: "The *Harpooner* arrived in Fort Victoria on May 31, 1849, with eight miners, eight workingmen, a shipwright, and several carpenters and bakers."[7]

Aboard the ship was the first independent settler, the colourful Captain Walter Colquhoun Grant, the son of the Duke of Wellington's chief intelligence officer at Waterloo and late of the Scots Greys. Captain Grant, 26-years old and 6 feet 2 inches tall, was penniless when he convinced the HBC he was a competent land surveyor and was appointed colonial surveyor. He brought with him the necessities of a colony gentleman: eight labourers, coaches and carriages for non-existent roads, and sets of cricket equipment for non-existent playing fields. He also had one distinct disadvantage for the job— he lacked a sense of direction and got lost on several occasions. He did, however, manage to complete a few surveys, but they were noted for their lack of accuracy. Grant settled in the wilderness at Sooke, about twenty miles from the fort. He named his homestead Mullachard after his ancestral home in Strathspey, Scotland.

The Fort Rupert mining experience

The miners were detained in Victoria until August 1849 as the post at Fort Rupert was not yet complete. During this time they worked as labourers, digging a well and blasting rock for a dockyard.

Nostalgic for Scotch Broom

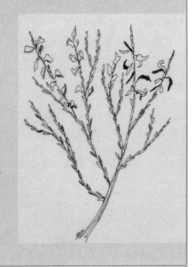

Fortunately or unfortunately for Vancouver Island, Captain Walter Grant has the distinction of being the person who introduced the Scotch broom (*Cytisus scoparius*) to the province. In October 1850, he sailed for Hawaii with the hope of selling his lumber there. While in Honolulu, the British Consul presented him with some broom seeds. On his return to Sooke, he planted the seeds outside his home. After a short stay, he sold his property to John Muir, Sr., for $4,000 and returned to England. When the Muirs took over the property they found broom plants growing. The men wanted to pull up the plants but Ann Muir found the broom plants reminded her of home and demanded they be left.[8]

On August 27 they boarded the brig *Mary Dare,* and after what Andrew Muir described in his diary as "a hard tedious passage"[9] they arrived at Beaver Harbour on September 24.

The Fort Rupert experience would be an unhappy one for the HBC and for the miners. The HBC hierarchy at Fort Rupert knew little of mining. Chief Trader Captain William Henry McNeill would have been happier at sea than in the land-locked fort he was assigned. He was a difficult man with a bad temper, but a well respected disciplinarian. The children of Victoria loved him for importing firecrackers from Hawaii. His assistant was his son-in-law George Blenkinsop, a young good-natured Cornishman, and Blenkinsop's assistant was Charles Beardmore, a loyal company employee. None were equipped to handle the labour troubles ahead.

The Muirs and McGregors were experienced miners who took great pride in their work and who did not take well to doing the mundane chores they were assigned at Fort Rupert. Living conditions were not what they expected from their contract, and the coal proved to be inferior. They were also apprehensive about the large Kwagiulth village of Ku-Kultz nearby. Their fear may have arisen from their first impression at Fort Rupert. For the day after their arrival, a raid had just been completed on a neighbouring tribe. Sixteen war canoes were drawn up on the beach and sixteen poles erected. Each pole had a human head displayed: trophies from their earlier encounter. Ann Muir, the older woman in the group, was the first white woman seen in the area. She was shown great respect by being offered a choice of any two of the sixteen heads.[10]

The Scottish miners had come out to find a working mine, even a workable seam, instead they found neither. Difficult working conditions continued until the spring of 1850.

The Norman Morison

On March 24, 1850 another ship arrived at Fort Victoria with more immigrants. The *Norman Morison* "the nearest thing to a *Mayflower* in British Columbia' history."[11] Aboard were 80 immigrants including miners and their families under contract and destined for Fort Rupert. Their arrival almost doubled the population of Vancouver Island. One of the newcomers was Dr. John Sebastian Helmcken, a man who would make a mark on British Columbia political history. He was the second doctor to arrive in Victoria, the first being Dr. Alfred Benson. Dr. Helmcken claimed he was "the leading physician from San Francisco to the North Pole, and from Asia to the Red River."[12] This had been a difficult voyage due to a smallpox outbreak. The ship was quarantined for three weeks while Dr. Helmcken treated six cases of smallpox. The one unvaccinated man died at sea. Passengers were glad they had had the good doctor aboard to tend to their medical needs.

Dr. Helmcken had signed on with the HBC for five years in 1849 as a surgeon and clerk at a salary of 100 pounds sterling per year. This included room and board, instruments, and a free passage home. He was London-trained but with a German background and became known to generations of Victoria children as "Dr. Heal-my-skin."[13] Dr. Helmcken was first appointed colliery doctor at Fort Rupert and with the new recruits, joined the other Scottish miners at the northern island fort.

The miner's strike at Fort Rupert

Before long the Scottish miners staged a strike, the first such labour unrest in British Columbia's history. Andrew Muir wrote in his diary about the problems he experienced. The strike erupted when he and John McGregor were ordered to dig a drain. The men asked for clarification of their contract. If they were to be used as labourers, then the contract should state this, and they would do it. Blenkinsop took the offensive position, threatening the men with sword and pistol. McGregor and Muir reluctantly went back to work on the drain. Four days later Andrew was charged with neglect of duty and fined 50 pounds. Since no one seemed to please management, the miners decided to stop work until the matter was settled.

There were pleas from McNeill and Blenkinsop for the men to return to work. But Andrew and John refused and were placed in irons where they remained for six days without a bed or clothing to keep them warm. Governor Blanshard heard of the problem in Fort Victoria and appointed Dr. Helmcken as a justice of the peace. The dispute escalated and when the barque *England* arrived to take on coal, the miners had decided they would head for the California gold mines if they could be released from their contract. When this was refused, they slipped away from the fort and boarded the ship. Only John Muir, Sr., his son Michael, and their families were left behind until they were transferred to work the coal in Nanaimo. Muir and McGregor went to San Francisco but within a year they returned to Victoria. Andrew Muir was made the first sheriff of Vancouver Island and John McGregor became the chief inspector of mines. In 1852, the HBC welcomed them back to Nanaimo.

Helmcken submitted his resignation to HBC Chief Factor James Douglas in 1850 claiming there was too much trouble at Fort Rupert, and he feared for his life since there was no protection against the

3,000 Kwagiulth in the area. He threatened to leave the HBC's service unless he could be moved.

Visiting ships provided the only relief and amusement for the isolated fort. One crew of a visiting American ship conferred on Dr. Helmcken the humorous title of honorary member of the "Independent Order of Antediluvian Eccentrics" under the name and title of "Superannuated Rhubard."

Helmcken got his wish and was transferred back to Victoria.[14] His place was secured in the HBC hierarchy when he married Douglas' daughter Cecilia in December 1852.

Much to Douglas' dismay, the Fort Rupert experience had been less than successful. When news of the labour trouble reached headquarters in London, Douglas received a letter severely reprimanding the actions of Captain McNeill and other officials there.

The Tory

Still more miners continued to arrive on the *Tory* in the spring of 1851. Douglas' letter to the HBC in London, advising that the coal venture had failed, arrived too late to prevent the *Tory* sailing. There were 125 labourers and their families aboard. They had been recruited before the trouble in the fort escalated. This ship brought eighteen recruits from the Orkney Islands; two brought wives. A number of the men were sent to farms and eight went to Fort Rupert to assist the mining operation. They included Mary and Andrew Hunter, a steam engineer from Kilmarnock, Ayrshire; James Sabiston and John Malcolm, labourers from Stromness. (Sabiston's other two brothers, John and Peter, sailed on the *Norman Morison*.) Other Orkney recruits were James Stowe a labourer and shipmaster; William Isbister, a stonemason; Peter Papley, a blacksmith (whose brother Alexander came on the *Norman Morison*), and Margaret and John Work. Also aboard were Adam Grant Horne, from Kirkwall, who would play a major role in the exploration of the central island, and Charles Alfred Bayley, who became the first teacher in the new fort at Nanaimo.

The Pekin

Back in Scotland, on December 5, 1850 the HBC signed up more Ayrshire miners: Boyd Gilmour and John Bryden from Riccarton; Gilmour's nephew Robert Dunsmuir; the James Dick family from Kilmarnock; and the brothers Archibald and Adam French, from Muirkirk. The news of the unfortunate circumstances at Fort Rupert also came too late for these new recruits who had already signed their contracts. The ship, the *Pekin* sailed two days later with their wary passengers. The two wives, Joan Dunsmuir and Jean Gilmour, together had a total of seven children: Jean's five, ranging in age from two to fourteen; and Joan's two little girls.[15] It was a difficult voyage as both women were pregnant. On June 20, as the ship edged its way up the Columbia River towards Fort Vancouver, Jean gave birth to a son, naming him Allan Columbia Gilmour. The *Pekin* arrived June 29, 1851 in Fort Vancouver where Joan gave birth a son named James on July 8.

Fort Vancouver was the largest of the HBC forts in the west; but it did not impress the crew, for like their passengers, they were tired and weary after the long voyage of 191 days. With a shortage of food and low wages, and sick with scurvy, most of the ship's company deserted and headed for California seeking their fortune in gold.

On July 18, the Dunsmuirs and Gilmours sailed aboard the *Mary Dare* for Fort Rupert. The trip around the northern tip of Vancouver Island lasted three weeks. They finally reached their destination in August, eight months after leaving Scotland. Fort Rupert would be their home until transferred to Nanaimo.

The decline of Fort Rupert

It has been estimated that approximately 10,000 tons of coal were mined at Fort Rupert between 1846 and 1854.[16] Not a large production considering Douglas' expectations. Still the HBC was successful with furs and shingles. In 1853, 500,000 shingles were shipped to Victoria. As a HBC fort, Fort Rupert had a lingering death. The mining operation was eventually abandoned, as the coal was judged unfit for commercial purposes. Douglas then decided it was time to investigate reports of "black diamonds" at Nanaimo.

Governor James Douglas rules

Governor Blanshard was frustrated at every turn. He had difficulty from the start as chief factor Douglas controlled everything that happened in Victoria. After less than a year in office, he resigned and returned to England taking with him a petition containing fifteen names of settlers, including six of the Muirs, asking for a legislative council.[17] Perhaps adding salt to the Blanshard wound, Douglas was appointed governor.

Colonization of Vancouver Island advanced slowly. The project was doomed from the start. Initially the HBC decreed no colonist could settle within the Fur Trade Reserve, twenty square miles containing the best land surrounding Fort Victoria.[18] Advertisements were placed in English and Scottish newspapers, but these met with little response. The HBC wanted to establish a social structure similar to that of England. No doubt the working class were to be properly relegated to their particular station in life. Encouraged were British gentlemen of substantial means who could afford passage, land purchases, and labourers to work their property. Those who did respond did not have money to invest in land and just wanted a chance in a new land. Getting here was also difficult. The long voyage around Cape Horn took five months. Douglas once warned, "the first settlers in this country will have many difficulties to contend with, first the scarcity and quality of food, the want of society, exposure to the weather, and generally, the absence of every thing like comfort."[19] Historian Jean Barman noted only three independent purchasers of over a hundred acres actually settled on Vancouver Island under the HBC, and none of them profited from their interest in land.[20]

Life in Fort Victoria in the early 1850s was rather pleasant. Douglas sat supreme in his dual capacity as governor and HBC chief factor. He carried his role in the HBC with due pomp and circumstance giving every appearance of being pompous and over-bearing. Old Square-toes, as his detractors nicknamed him, had a fondness for gold-braided military uniforms, and was often seen around Victoria accompanied by a sword-bearing bodyguard. The uniform may have been worn to throw fear into the Native people and suggest a power system.

Occasionally a British Royal Navy ship called in at the port of Esquimalt. The white settlers were mostly British and though there were definite divisions in class between those who worked for the HBC and those who did not, most managed to accommodate different lifestyles. Most company officers came from Scotland. They usually joined the firm as clerks and were trained on the job under watchful eyes of post managers. The profit-sharing chief factors and chief traders occupied the upper echelons of the officer class. Collectively these men shared 40 percent of the fur-trading profits of the HBC.[21]

At Fort Victoria there were occasionally clashes with the Songhees, usually over conflicting views of property. Roaming cattle were regarded as wildlife available for the taking. Residents were also alarmed when large numbers of Haida and coastal Tsimshian visited Victoria annually to take advantage of new markets and to find work. Feelings ran high against all Natives making it quite uncomfortable for Douglas' wife Amelia who was subjected to insults from prominent white women.

First Native Land Treaty—the Songhees.

James Douglas negotiated the first land treaty with the Songhees of Esquimalt on April 29, 1850. Nine purchases were made around Victoria that year. It seemed to be HBC policy to recognize a claim by the Native people despite the company holding title from the Crown. For a payment of 371 blankets valued at 17 shillings each, he persuaded the chiefs to show their approval by making their signs on the bottom of a blank piece of paper. Douglas then wrote to the London office asking for a text. He was supplied with a copy of the New Zealand Land Company legal document used to buy tracts from the Maoris. Douglas copied the wording and added local details. Such was the first treaty on the Pacific Coast. Other treaties would be signed at Fort Rupert, Saanich, and Nanaimo.

It was obvious Douglas intentions were honorable. He probably never envisaged that reserves would become a permanent feature of the landscape. He thought of them more as "cultural way-stations where missionaries and others could teach the residents Christianity and the practical skills they would need to survive in the new economic order."[22] Thinking perhaps that most Native people would eventually make it on their own away from the reserves, he gave them the same rights to settle off reserve lands as white settlers.

CHAPTER FIVE

Nanaimo Coalfield

The Hudson's Bay Company entered a transition phase in the middle decades of the nineteenth century. What had traditionally been a fur-based economy expanded to include new commodities and market conditions. The Pacific Coast offered new possibilities to exploit the area resources and open new markets for the commercial enterprise. Although fur trade remained part of life in the far-flung forts of New Caledonia, it would be coal that would change the economic outlook on Vancouver Island.

Fort Rupert may have been the first location on the island where coal was mined, but it would be the Nanaimo mines that would enrich the HBC.

Che-wich-i-kan meets the blacksmith

A chance encounter between Snuneymuxw Chief Che-wich-i-kan (Ki-et-sa-kun) and a blacksmith in Victoria, set the wheels of development in place in Nanaimo. Che-wich-i-kan, historically referred to as "Coal Tyee," had gone to Victoria to have his gun repaired. At this time he commented about black stones being plentiful in his area. When this conversation was repeated to HBC authorities, the chief was invited to bring some of his black stones to Victoria. In return he would get a bottle of rum and have his gun repaired free.[1] The date was December 1849. However, the chief was ill during the winter. As nothing more was heard from him, it was assumed the story was untrue, until the following spring when Coal Tyee returned with a canoe laden with coal. It was tested and found to be of excellent quality. A company clerk, Joseph William McKay, was quickly dispatched to Nanaimo.

Bronze bust of Coal Tyee (Ki-et-sa-kun) unveiled at Mark Bate Memorial Tree Plaza, June 29, 2002. Sculptor: Dorothea E. Kennedy.

The McKay explorations

Joseph William McKay was born at Rupert House, Hudson Bay, on January 31, 1829 to William McKay and Mary Bunn. His family was large—nine sisters and two brothers.[2] McKay was first posted to Fort Vancouver in 1844 when he was fifteen-years old, and then two years later to Fort Victoria where he clerked for Chief Trader Roderick Finlayson. In early May 1850, McKay outfitted a prospecting party and began searching for coal in Nanaimo. He found what became known as the Douglas vein at the spot from which Coal Tyee had taken his sample. He also explored the beautiful countryside between Nanaimo and Victoria, finding several large tracts of land suitable for settlers. There were also some indications of gold but nothing to warrant extensive prospecting.[3]

The post at Nanaimo was sheltered from the weather by Newcastle Island to the north, Protection Island to the east, and the smaller Cameron Island in the harbour. Further to the east was Gabriola Island. Within the geographic configuration at Nanaimo were two deep-sea harbours: one at Departure Bay further north and west of Newcastle Island; and one at Nanaimo Harbour, earlier known as Wentuhuysen (or Wenthuysen) Inlet. Both harbours provided safe anchorage for visiting vessels. Forests thick with Douglas fir and cedar covered the steep slopes from the shoreline west to Mount Benson. When McKay first arrived, scattered along the rocky foreshore were the longhouses of the Snuneymuxw families. Running parallel to shore was a piece of land several hundred yards wide separated by a narrow passage of water later given the name Commercial Inlet. It was here the Douglas seam was uncovered and where the first log cabins were built.

Pemberton and Pearse surveys

The Nanaimo district was next surveyed by Joseph D. Pemberton and his assistant Benjamin William Pearse, from a base known for many years as Pemberton's Encampment at the mouth of the Millstone River, earlier called Millstream. Pemberton, a 30-year-old civil engineer from Dublin and a former professor of engineering and mathematics at an English agricultural college, became the colony's official surveyor in 1851, replacing Captain Grant. Nineteen-year-old Pearse had some previous training as a civil engineer in Devonshire, England, before he joined Pemberton as his assistant the same year. A preliminary survey of the east coast of the island was made, and by November a survey of the "fur trade reserve," was completed. This was the property in and around Victoria that the HBC wished to retain. Over the next few years the surveyors explored and mapped Saanich, Cowichan, and the Nanaimo district.

Pemberton's accomplishments during his first years on the island were highly regarded by the HBC. When his contract expired in June 1854, Douglas recommended it be extended. The surveyor was as much an explorer as a surveyor. He explored central Vancouver Island from Qualicum to the Alberni Inlet and Barkley Sound. He was also interested in politics and served as a member of the House of Assembly of Vancouver Island, and was a member of the executive council. After leaving the HBC in 1858, he became the Colony of Vancouver Island's surveyor-general and held this post until 1864 when he resigned after injuries suffered following his being thrown from his horse. These injuries affected him for the rest of his life. On one of his many trips back to England he met Teresa Jane Grautoff whom he married and brought back to Victoria. There he built their dream home "Gonzales," a twenty-room mansion.[4] Pemberton settled down to raise Clydesdale horses and shorthorn cattle, and died in 1893. Pearse paid tribute to his old friend of 42 years, noting their friendship was "never strained or disturbed by a word of thought of difference."[5]

Douglas seizes control of the Nanaimo coal beds

In August 1852, Douglas personally made a canoe trip from Fort Victoria to Nanaimo accompanied by Joseph Pemberton, John Muir, Sr., and Douglas' secretary, Richard Golledge. The expedition explored the area of the Cowichan River. The cultivated fields of potatoes particularly impressed Douglas. To the north they explored the mouth of the Chemainus River before proceeding to Nanaimo where the coal deposits were examined.

It was important for Douglas to prove to the HBC that his coal-mining dream on Vancouver Island could be a reality, and Nanaimo offered a chance to blot out the failure at Fort Rupert. He found the Snuneymuxw were "very friendly, and disposed to give every information we desired," and noted three coal beds cropping out in different parts of the inlet. The three included the original site at Nanaimo Harbour, another on Protection Island, and the third at Midden Bay on Newcastle Island.

Douglas wrote of his journey:

> I rejoice to say that our journey has been productive of very satisfactory results; as we have had abundant evidence to prove that the mineral wealth of Vancouver's Island has not been over rated. This discovery has afforded me more satisfaction than I can express.[6]

It was on this trip that Douglas was startled to find that the maps of Vancouver Island were wrong, that they showed islands such as Galiano and Valdes as being part of Vancouver Island.[7]

Douglas formally appointed McKay on August 24,1852 to be the HBC representative in Nanaimo. With the appointment came instructions:

> You will proceed with all possible diligence to Wentuhuysen Inlet commonly known as Nanymo Bay and formally take possession of the Coal beds lately discovered there for and in behalf of the Hudson's Bay Company.[8]

He was to stop anyone from working the coal beds unless so licensed by the HBC, and to those duly licensed, to ensure they paid a royalty.

Mining begins in Nanaimo—the McKay journal

The journal of Joseph William McKay, recorded in the HBC Nanaimo daybook, documents the day-to-day struggle of establishing the

Hudson's Bay Company at Nanaimo. McKay encountered such immediate problems as getting enough food, shelter, and equipment, while at the same time trying to avoid getting embroiled in tribal conflicts so common in early Vancouver Island history. His first journal entry is dated August 24, 1852, when he received written instructions from Douglas to go to Nanaimo and take charge of the coal beds. He was advised to sell the coal to any vessel calling for $10 per ton.[9]

McKay next met with the Snuneymuxw who traded some large mats, some salmon and potatoes, and 300 feet of cedar planks. He began building the first hut on August 27. Correspondence between Douglas and McKay supplement the journal entries and show how Douglas dictated almost every aspect of the initial coal mining operation. Douglas informed McKay he was first sending John Muir, Sr., and his sons Robert and Archibald, and John McGregor, Sr. Instead of rations, these men were to be allowed one shilling per day, and would provide their own provisions. Douglas, knowing how difficult it was to find food, pointed out to McKay this "will save you much trouble." When the Snuneymuxw Chief Wun-wun-shum arrived at the site on September 1, McKay thought he was "impertinent in his behaviour." The Chief argued the coal was worth one blanket for five barrels of coal, and he would not listen to any proposal to allow the whites to work the coal. Whereas the Snuneymuxw had freely shown the seams of coal to the HBC and assisted in their arrival, it was clear now they wisely wanted to garner some benefit from the coal extraction.

The Muirs, McGregor, and blacksmith Camille Raymond arrived on the *Cadboro* on September 3 "after a tedious passage of seven days," from Fort Rupert. Their first order of business was to make a pig sty then land four pigs and one sheep from the ship. The first farm animals had arrived in Nanaimo. Cows were added to the list of animals brought to the village. The docile cows were easy game for one astute Snuneymuxw who boldly slaughtered one and sold the meat as venison to unsuspecting housewives.[10] The men built their own log hut "lined and covered with cedar bark." Raymond made a shed for his forge and complained that the HBC had sent the wrong bellows. Natives brought more food to the fort to trade. McKay asked Douglas for some light pick axes for the Snuneymuxw miners, "as they waste a great deal with their axes." Some were hired to work in the newly discovered salt spring.

On September 9, 1852 the *Cadboro* sailed with the first 480 barrels of coal. The Snuneymuxw had mined and loaded the coal—twenty barrels for a two-and-a-half point blanket and other goods.

The Salt Spring on the Millstone River

Salt was manufactured for a short period of time from the saltwater spring on Millstone River (at the site of the present day Tally Ho Hotel–Howard Johnson). The salt was an excellent quality and was recovered through evaporation. A shed was constructed and evaporating pans installed. The salt was principally used for preserving game and fish. In a letter to McKay in 1853, Douglas acknowledged receipt of Nanaimo salt. "I received the Salt which appears to be of good quality though rather rusty in consequence probably of the pans not being Clean but I have no doubt your next samples will be in better condition. The dried codfish was also received and proves to be an excellent article. Cure as many of them as you can."[11] Salt was being put to good use in 1856; "Finley, Rich and Isbister engaged salting herrings, which we trade off the Indians at a rate of five barrels for a blanket.[12]

The saltwater spring was abandoned in 1862 when the HBC holdings were sold to the Vancouver Coal Mining and Land Company (VCML).[13]

McKay advised Douglas that Pemberton had almost completed the survey of the Wentuhuysen Inlet, and he had commenced running lines inland.[14] Douglas was obviously pleased and sent his compliments to Pemberton.

The Snuneymuxw remained adamant they would not allow other tribes to work the coal; this was their domain. However, a week later, a group of Sno-who-mish and Sheshalls [Sechelt] arrived wanting to get into the shingle business. They brought samples of split cedar shingles to trade, but McKay noted "they asked extravagant prices." The small fort also had a visit from the Cowechin Chief, Tsaw-si-ai, who arrived with 40 armed people in four canoes. In his letter to Douglas he explained why the show of strength.

On coming alongside the *Recovery* I invited the Old man on board treated him to some victuals and enquired of him his intention in coming here in such a warlike manner. He informed me that he had just returned from the Fraser River and that he had come over from his village which is about fifteen miles distant on a complimentary visit to the Nanaimo Indians who were his relations and friends. On leaving the harbour they shot an Indian Collier. The excitement occasioned by this occurrence has nearly died away and the coals are coming in this morning as usual.[15]

Again McKay asked Douglas to send more axes, iron wedges and shovels for the Snuneymuxw miners. On September 30, The *Recovery* sailed for Victoria with 1391 barrels of coal. McKay advised that a Sno-who-mish man had been murdered at Nanaimo eight days ago by a Snuneymuxw in revenge for three killed by the Sno-who-mish last winter.

Douglas was anxious to find out if his experiment of coal mining at Nanaimo would be profitable and asked McKay on October 27 if the miners had reached the seam of coal:

> My chief anxiety is to have that question solved, for as soon as that takes place I will address the HBC on the subject of sending out an additional body of miners and such other assistance as may be required from England.[16]

The journal continues, noting Raymond the blacksmith had a bad leg and was receiving medical care. Michel Le Fleur was sent to replace him until he recovered. On November 8, 1852, the fort traded 200 bins of potatoes from the Chemainus tribe, 13 deer from the Sheshalls, and 300 salmon from the Snuneymuxw. Venison, salmon, and potatoes would be the fare for some time to come. Natives of the Cowichan and Chemainus valleys had grown potatoes since their first encounter with the HBC at Fort Langley. Surplus potatoes became an item of trade, second only to salmon.

The Christmas Hill murder

On November 13, McKay first indicated his knowledge of the Christmas Hill murder of HBC shepherd Peter Brown, on November 5. Natives told him that Sque-is, son of Thum-thum-a-liked, a Cowechin, accompanied by a son of a Snuneymuxw chief, was accused of murdering Brown at the sheep station near Victoria. A week later, the Cowechin Chief Tsaw-si-ai brought dispatches from Victoria that confirmed the report of the murder. McKay was ordered to stop the sale of all ammunition at the fort.

On December 6, McKay had a visit from the accused and indicated he did not want to get involved. He wrote:

> the Nanaimo murderer waited on me accompanied by a party of Nanaimo braves for the purpose of exculpating himself from the accusation of being concerned of the murder of Peter Brown. I told him that I had no right to examine depositions on such subject and referred him to the legal authorities at Victoria.[17]

The murder of the shepherd was an early turning point in Douglas' relationship with the Natives. He wanted to show the strength of the HBC and perhaps show himself as a forceful person who would not stand for the willful murder of company employees. This incident also showed the strong character of Douglas. The two young men accused of the murder had fled to their tribal homes. Douglas marshalled a party of armed forces and a local militia group, the voyageurs, on board the steamer *Beaver* that had in tow a second vessel, the *Recovery,* carrying four naval officers and eighty bluejackets. Behind the *Recovery,* completing the tow, were the launch, a barge and pinnace of the H.M.S.*Thetis* carrying artillery.

The voyageurs were an elite group of expert canoeists and company servants. Their clothing was as colourful as their exploits. They wore moccasins, long worsted stockings, buckskin trousers, sky blue coats with brass buttons over red-and-black flannel shirts, caps, and broad red belts. These colourful scouts earned a dollar a day and rations. Failing to find the murderers at the Saanich Native village, the punitive armada left Victoria for Cowichan Bay where Douglas arranged a parley and landed his forces. He pitched a tent on a little hill, sat down on a stool in front of his troops, and lit his pipe.

Soon a flotilla of canoes, filled with Cowechins in war paint and beating drums, appeared from the river and moved along the shore past the troops. They were "whooping like demons" and beating with their paddles against the sides of the canoes. Douglas kept on smoking. They landed below his post. Then, the whole mob, yelling and brandishing spears and guns rushed up the incline. Except for an order to his men not to fire, Douglas sat there stolidly. The warriors, baffled by his indifference, stopped.

Douglas raised his hand and said:

> "Hearken, O Chiefs! I am sent by King George who is your friend, and who desires right only between your tribes and his men. If his men kill an Indian, they are punished. If your men do likewise, they must also suffer. Give up the murderer, and let there be peace between the peoples, or I will burn your lodges and trample out your tribes."[18]

After more negotiations and Douglas' promise to give the accused Native a fair hearing at Nanaimo, the Cowechins surrendered a man thought to be the accused, Sque-is. The man who was actually delivered was a slave, offered instead as compensation. Douglas may have known of the deception but accepted the man possibly to avoid hostilities. He was placed aboard the *Beave*r and the expedition continued to Nanaimo. The other accused Native, Siam-a-sit, the son of Tche-whe-tum, a powerful Nanaimo chief, fled to his home. McKay's journal documents the hunt and capture:

> January 10, 1853: His Excellency the Governor opened negotiation with the Nanaimos for delivery into the hands of justice of Siam-a-sit, a son to Tchewhetum and Leamtum, being accused of having participated in the murder of Peter Brown at Victoria.

Douglas demanded his surrender. The Snuneymuxw Chiefs offered to pay indemnity according to their custom. This was refused. The McKay journal gives the sequence of events as they unfolded:

> January 11: Indian captured today by a reconnaissance party.
> January 12: the Snuneymuxw who promised to deliver the murderer assembled round the *Beaver* armed but not having the murderer with them Tchewhetum was seized and detained by a pledge for the delivery of his son into custody.
> January 13: Chief Wun-wun-shum promised to deliver into the hands of justice the Nanaimo murderer.
> January 14: The Nanaimo murderer was brought to the Bay astern of the *Cadboro* but succeeded in making his escape. An armed party of men of war went up the Nanaimo River to attack and take possession of the village.

Sailors, voyageurs, marines, and a posse of miners followed the wanted man up a small stream, now known as Chase River after the infamous chase. He hid in a hollow tree trunk. It was snowing and had he remained quiet he might have escaped, for his footprints had been obliterated; but seeing his pursuers approach, he tried to shoot one. A flake of snow fell into the firing-pan of his musket, and it dampened the priming charge. He was detected and captured:[19]

> January 15: The Nanaimo murderer was today captured near the mouth of the Nanaimo River and put into safe custody on board the *Beaver*. The party of men of war was recalled from the Nanaimo River.
> January 17: Two men were tried for the murder of Peter Brown and they were found guilty, condemned and executed at Tide Staff Point.

The trial aboard the *Beaver* on January 17, 1853 was the first trial by judge and jury under English law. In Douglas' words:

> "The two Indians now in custody were brought to trial and found guilty of willful murder, by a jury composed of the officers present." [The two were hanged] "in the presence of the whole Nanaimo tribe, the same appearing to make a deep impression on their minds."[20]

The sentence was carried out on Protection Island at a site originally called Execution Point, today know as Gallows Point.

> January 18: The steamer *Beaver* sailed with the Governor and suite. The *Recovery* left in tow of the *Beaver*.

The Snuneymuxw mourned the death of Siam-a-sit the young Native who was hanged. The tribe viewed his hanging as a great injustice. His widow was nicknamed the "Gallows Widow," and after a suitable period of mourning, she married her husband's brother, a practice of levirate that was common with the Coast Salish people.[21] Somehow the miners put all the excitement aside and returned to work.

More miners arrive from Fort Rupert

Another ten miners had arrived December 9, 1852, from Fort Rupert, in two large canoes manned by twelve Kwakiutl [Kwagiulth]. Later the same day, the *Beaver* brought Boyd Gilmour, Robert Dunsmuir, and their families, plus three other miners. They had the same food conditions attached as the previous miners, for on December 17, McKay noted Gilmour had traded six deer from the Snuneymuxw. More men arrived in April from Fort Rupert. Included were Jean Baptiste Fortier, Adam Grant Horne, William Isbister, Andrew Hunter, Henry McNeill, also surgeon Dr. George Johnstone. Adam Grant Horne was on the sick list.

Building the Bastion

On February 3, 1853, Joseph Robilliard and Versailles began squaring wood to build the Bastion, a project that continued for some time. The Bastion was completed in 1854 and partially eased the fears of the white community against possible marauding Native attacks. The fear was not from the Snuneymuxw but from other northern tribes who arrived in their large canoes and were enemies of the local tribe.

The Hudson's Bay Company Bastion built between 1853 and 1854 is now a Nanaimo landmark.

The Bastion was constructed with 16-inch squared timbers fitted together without the use of metal nails. The first floor was used as a jail. Historians have credited the building of the fortress to two expert axemen, French Canadians Leon Labine and Jean Baptiste Fortier, but there were others who squared the timbers and assisted in the construction. William Isbister, the stonemason from Orkney, laid the foundation. Two cannons were placed in front of the building, more for ceremonial use than defense. Sometimes a fusillade of guns was fired to impress the Natives. They did however provide Douglas with the mandatory seventeen-gun salute when he visited the fort. The HBC red ensign flag was unfurled over Nanaimo for the first time.

Douglas to McKay, May 20 1854:

Mr. Gilmour does not appear to be very successful in his researches for coal and moreover appears much dissatisfied with his lodgings, and his treatment generally. He evidently considers himself slighted, a circumstance which I much regret, and trust you will give him no cause of complaint. He has written to me, respecting his position at Nanaimo.

Boyd Gilmour, first hired in Scotland as mine foreman, or oversman, was a man a little over his head. He had struggled at Fort Rupert having trouble controlling the men working under him. Douglas brought him to Nanaimo hoping for better results. McKay had discovered outcroppings on Newcastle Island and speculated the Douglas seam extended under the sea to the island. Gilmour was set to work assessing the Newcastle seam. On April 10, 1853, McKay noted Gilmour had altered his opinion regarding the coal on Newcastle Island and had left home for Victoria, possibly to complain to Douglas. The Newcastle Island site would baffle many because of the faulted nature of the coal seam. A few days later he was back in Nanaimo, only this time he had moved to a coal outcrop at Chase River, a few miles south. His third exploration was an outcrop found among the trees of Commercial Inlet, and as successful as this was, it would be Robert Dunsmuir who would be given the task of directing the bore. Douglas was not impressed with Gilmour and his search for coal.

More housing was needed for the new arrivals. Building continued throughout the months of May and June 1853. Several entries note Robert Dunsmuir refused duty. On July 4, McKay put Adam Grant Horne to work on "such light jury as calculated to do him no injury." There seemed to be no shortage of food:

> Large quantities of salmon were brought in, more than before. The venison was in bad condition because of the warm weather, and the hunters were often wind bound in crossing the Gulf of Georgia.

On July 17, McKay advised two births had been recorded in the small community. "Mrs. Dunsmuir and the Native wife of John Malcolm, a labourer." Malcolm was another recruit from Orkney. The Dunsmuir child, Alexander, was born in a small log cabin, the first white boy born in Nanaimo.[22] Mary McGregor had the distinction of giving birth to the first white girl, Margaret, on March 16, 1854.

Another 40 Scottish miners recruited for Nanaimo sailed on the *Colinda* in August 1853. Douglas asked "every possible exertion must be made to prepare house accommodation for them on their

The Oxen Round-up

Oxen were brought to the village in September 1854. The animals were necessary for the logging operations. A team of oxen yoked together could haul logs from the forest along greased skid roads. The animals were strong, slow, and stupid, and they required constant supervision. At first they roamed freely about the village and often wandered into the woods, until a fenced pen was made to contain them. Snuneymuxw young men were sent to find the strays. The animals also required shelter, so a shed was built.

Then came the arduous task of breaking in the oxen to perform the heavy work. This job was assigned to Thomas Quamtomy. Finally the oxen were trained to haul logs. This small act must have seemed like a giant step forward.

To feed the oxen, John Malcolm and William Weston would go up the Nanaimo River to cut the hay. Joseph Robilliard built a hay shed to store the fodder. Finally the Snuneymuxw agreed to allow the hiring of a number of Quackholds [Kwagiulths] to do various tasks, such as carry hay from the river. Every job required extra work; nothing came easy.

arrival." Unknown to Douglas these miners never did arrive in Nanaimo; they mutinied in Valparaiso, Chile, after running out of food on the voyage. Nevertheless, more house-building required more lumber. Francis Cote was contracted to build the houses, and Douglas instructed that while he was not to hire Natives, McKay could give him any Native assistance he required, charging him the cost. Cote had to feed and pay his own expenses, but he could have "provisions at servant's prices." Douglas estimated Cote could build at least six houses by spring. The shingles were to come from Fort Rupert. The Snuneymuxw, who were also essential in the early logging operation, would deliver the logs. John Malcolm used horses to haul the logs to the small water-powered sawmill erected on Millstone River. Later oxen were brought to Nanaimo to use for log hauling.

Joseph McKay recommended that the sawmill on the Millstone River be converted to steam-power and use the steam-power for both mining and milling:

> "A circular saw may be worked by the steam engine with apparent little extra trouble. As a great deal of lumber is required for building, the circular saw would be a great acquisition, the more so as our sawyers with three pit saws, are barely able to supply the increasing demand for sawn lumber in the coal mines.[23]

Although the steam plant was built, it lay idle. When Mark Bate arrived in 1857 the mill was still water-powered.

The Nanaimo Coal Company

The coal-mining operation evolved into a separate organization known as the Nanaimo Coal Company.[24] Joseph McKay initially oversaw all aspects of the Nanaimo coal operation. The Snuneymuxw eagerly accommodated the HBC, pointing out exposed seams in the region. In the first few years, they dug surface seams and traded several thousand tons of coal with the HBC.

Native women worked alongside men, loading coal from canoes to the ships. The process was very labour intensive. The coal was hauled in baskets from the pit site to the weigh station. Then it was transferred to the canoes and then to the ships to be stored in barrels. The women received tickets for every tub of coal they carried. These were exchanged for trade goods.[25]

There was no great rush to develop the Nanaimo mines. The HBC had only furs in mind when it came to the economy; coal was just another commodity

Joseph McKay was transferred to Fort Simpson when the Crimean War broke out in 1854.

The Muir and McGregor families leave Nanaimo

The first miners who contracted with the HBC in 1848 to work the coal beds at Fort Rupert and then at Nanaimo also moved from the area. For the Muir family this move was permanent, but the McGregors would return.

The mining contract of John Muir, Sr., as oversman, expired in 1854, and he moved his family to live permanently in Sooke where he operated the small sawmill previously owned by Captain Grant. His stay in Nanaimo had been brief and troublesome, since he and Boyd Gilmour had disagreements over the coal-mining operation. His son, Andrew Muir, the fiery young rebel at Fort Rupert, married Isabella Weir. Their married life was short; she died following the birth of their daughter. He died two years later, in 1859. Despite the exodus of the family from Nanaimo, Andrew's cousin Archibald Muir remained living there. He would marry Julia Bevilockway, a daughter of a *Princess Royal* pioneer family.

John McGregor replaced John Muir, Sr., as oversman, but he too had difficulty working with Boyd Gilmour. After Gilmour returned to Scotland. George Robinson became resident manager. When Robinson had an altercation with McGregor it was the latter that was sent to Victoria.

The Russian Threat and the Life of Joseph McKay

At the outbreak of the Crimean War, Great Britain, France, and Turkey took up arms against Russia. Governor James Douglas received orders to provide sanctuary for any French ship that might be in danger from Russian warships. Douglas did not regard the Russians as a threat but saw this more of an opportunity to move north and by force of arms, add Alaska to the British Empire. To defend the entrance to Victoria harbour, he asked for arms and men and for a detachment of the Pacific fleet to be stationed at Esquimalt. His request was rejected. He was told the Russians were unlikely to attack so unimportant a place as Fort Victoria and that Great Britain did not want any territorial gains in the war with Russia.[26] Douglas did, however, receive funds to construct three hospital buildings, known later as the "Crimea Huts." They included an operating room and surgeon's quarters.

Still McKay continued to record in his journal the daily happenings in the small community for several more months before his transfer to Fort Simpson at Chatham Sound on the north Pacific Coast. McKay's previous experience working with Natives was relied upon to prevent the Tsimshian at Fort Simpson from falling under Russian influence.[27]

He returned to Victoria in 1856 and represented Victoria District in the House of Assembly of Vancouver Island for three years. He married Helen Holmes of Lancashire, England, in June 1860, a union that produced four daughters and one son.[28] McKay was a man with many outside business interests. Nevertheless he continued to serve various other HBC posts in the interior until released by the company in 1878. Then he became a cannery manager and later an Indian Agent. At the time of his death in 1900 he was assistant superintendent of Indian Affairs in British Columbia.

John McGregor purchased land in the Metchosin District. Three more children were born there: James, Agnes, and Kate. The McGregors returned to Nanaimo in the early 1860s, and John returned to the mines. He died on January 12, 1866.[29] Mary and the children continued to live in Nanaimo. After the death of their father, nineteen-year-old John, Jr., and eleven-year-old William followed in their father's footsteps and began working in the mines. John died in 1873 after a long illness. William became manager of the largest mine, the No. 1 mine. He married Amanda Meakin whose parents, John and Mary Ann Meakin, were *Princess Royal* pioneers.

Two sisters married two brothers. Margaret married Thomas Watson Glaholm, a local merchant.[30] They had five children. Her sister Kate, married Captain John William Glaholm, and they had three children. Margaret and Amanda McGregor were very good friends and visited each other regularly. McGregor Park, near Pioneer

The McGregor family: Margaret, Mary, Kate, and child. Margaret was first white girl born in Nanaimo.

Plaza, on the waterfront, commemorates this family and other Scottish pioneers.

The McGregor's daughter Margaret, who grew up in Nanaimo, recalled how time was measured during her childhood in the small mining village:

> "Noon and suppertime were announced from the Bastion by beating a suspended crosscut saw with a triangular piece of steel. Later a man beating a brass tambourine gave the time at regular intervals as he marched along the winding paths. Still later again the Hudson's Bay Company imported a bell from England and the settlers turned out en masse to see it installed on a thirty foot scaffolding in front of the HBC's store."[31]

Robert Dunsmuir stays on

The contracts signed by Dunsmuir and Gilmour expired in August 1854. They could choose to stay and sign new contracts, or return to Scotland. Coal mining prospects did look good in Nanaimo and that bode well for increased earnings, but their living conditions were little better than in Fort Rupert. The men were discontented. Gilmour told Douglas he wanted a raise if he were to stay. Douglas informed him that the *Princess Royal* had already sailed from England with new miners and their families, and he refused to entertain any suggestion of a wage increase. The Gilmour family decided to return to Scotland. Boyd Gilmour's nephew, Robert Dunsmuir, stayed on.

Tribal warfare—Chief Wun-wun-shum's sacrifice

The Snuneymuwx were at first accommodating but when outside tribes were given work the local tribe could have done, they began to see their employment and trade opportunities slipping away. One incident in 1854 unsettled many in the small community. Snuneymuxw Chief Wun-wun-shun, respected along the coast for his wisdom, put his own life on the line to save his tribe and to avert war. The incident happened when several of the Lekwiltoks were hired to cut logs to build new homes for the *Princess Royal* miners. Edward Walker was in charge of the loggers.[32] The Snuneymuxw objected—they considered the town their preserve and were fearful the visitors would cut into their employment and trade with the whites. They warned the Lekwiltoks to leave, and when they refused, they killed three of them.

For a time nothing happened, then one day the Lekwiltoks arrived in force. At first the white settlers were not too afraid. They usually stayed out of tribal disputes and knew the authority of the HBC protected them. From around Protection Island's southern point came more than 100 Lekwiltok canoes. Nanaimo residents watched in horror as the harbour filled with canoes full of painted and menacing warriors. This was no skirmish; it was a full-scale war. Captain Stuart ordered the women and children to the Bastion, knowing the town might be attacked. He knew it would take time to alert Fort Victoria about the invasion, and the invaders would be long gone before the gunboat arrived.

The Snuneymuxw paddled out from their village to meet the enemy fleet head on. With sinking hearts the whites counted only 40 Snuneymuxw canoes. Defeat seemed inevitable. The two sides observed each other across the harbour. Tension ran high as the chief of the Lekwiltoks rose in his canoe demanding reparation. Snuneymuxw Chief Wun-wun-shun acknowledged the justness of the demand. This put the angry chief at a disadvantage. He thundered, "Three Lekwiltoks have died. Three Snuneymuxw must die! And there must be reparation as well."

Chief Wun-wun-shun agreed. A silence fell over the group. Who would the three Snuneymuxw be? No one offered to sacrifice himself. If he chose someone and they refused, the Lekwiltoks would attack. This was no time for discussion.

The wise old Chief knew he had to do something to avert a massacre. He rose slowly in his canoe and with dignity addressed the hostile visitors. He told them who he was and they listened with respect. Was he not a great chief? Was he not a warrior famous along the coast? After telling them of his prowess he ended by saying, "Surely I, the great Wun-wun-shun, am worth three common men! If you agree, kill me and let our people be friends."

There was whispered conversation between the Lekwiltoks and then the commotion ended. The northern chief stood and accepted the offer. The Snuneymuxw sat in stunned silence as Chief Wun-wun-shun stood up in his canoe and faced his executioners. Twice they fired to wound. He made no move as the musket balls tore at his flesh. Then a third shot was fired. The ball struck him between the eyes. Chief Wun-wun-shun had brought peace to Nanaimo.[33]

CHAPTER SIX

The Princess Royal *Voyage*
—a Chronology

*I*n the fall of 1854, another shipload of miners arrived to establish new lives in Nanaimo. The arrival of the *Princess Royal* pioneers is still celebrated today. The ship was described as a "fine new ship" replacing the unwieldy old *Norman Morison*. The ship was only four years old and was built of oak and teak by Green & Co., Blackwall of London. She was 120 feet in length, and 700 tons with a 36-foot beam.

George Robinson was hired as manager of the Nanaimo coal operation and was directed to hire about twenty colliers, married and preferably with families to accompany him on the voyage. "The theory was that family men would not be restless or tempted by the California gold rush."[1] Meetings were held in the "Black Country," for those willing to embark on such an adventure as moving to Vancouver Island. The Black Country is an area roughly ten miles square to the northwest of Birmingham, England. Those recruited miners came from Brierley Hill, Dudley, Bromley, Wordsley, Pensnett, and several other villages in the region. In 1850 the region had become the most densely populated and economically prosperous part of the industrial Midlands; it was also blackened with heaps of waste from primitive iron-smelting methods. The area earned a gritty reputation. It has been described as:

> The Black Foundry, black by day and red by night, cannot be matched for vast and varied productions by any sphere of equal radius on the surface of the globe. The furnaces roar and glow by night and day, and the great steam hammers thunder.[2]

The recruiting center was at the Brierley Hill Colliery in Staffordshire, England. The Staffordshire miners signed a 5-year contract that stipulated they would be paid 78 pounds sterling a year to produce 45 tons of clean coal a month, and at the end of the 5 years they would receive 25 acres of free land.

For the voyage, George Robinson listed the miners, their wives, and children, but did not list his own family, which included his wife Ann and their two children Amanda Theresa and Victor Ernest. Only one family came from London: they were John and Mary Ann Meakin and sons Frederick Charles and John William. John, Jr., later claimed he learned to walk on the rolling deck of the ship. They were the last family to board.

Charles Gale's Princess Royal *Log*

The *Princess Royal* log made by first mate, Charles Gale, described the voyage as "a gloomy history of death, misery and dissatisfaction."[3] Gale noted, "the steerage passengers consists of 23 miners and their families, numbering 83 persons." Also included were ten Norwegians and a "Mrs. Laing and her five children who were on their way to join her husband on Vancouver Island." The Norwegians were hired for "general service to be employed where they may be most required." Steerage was in the badly lit hold of the ship. The first night, beds were made up on the deck, or on planks crudely fastened to the ship's sides. Belongings were close at hand, unfastened and hazardous in rough seas.[4] This would be a difficult voyage few would forget. Robinson and his family shared a cabin with Mr. and Mrs. Clarke and their baby. Clarke, who became the schoolmaster at the new Craigflower School, conducted school classes for the children on the voyage. Robinson's maid and four other women travelling to join their husbands shared intermediate accommodation.

On June 3, 1954, the ship was towed from London down the River Thames to Gravesend where it began its journey down the English Channel out into the Atlantic Ocean. From the beginning there was trouble with the crew. On the afternoon of the first and second day the steward was found drunk. He refused to work until Captain David Wishart came aboard on the third day. Others in the crew did not want to go to Vancouver Island. The miners were expected to work during the voyage as part payment for the fare. "Thomas York and John Malpass were assigned to serve out stores with the third officer. William Harrison and Daniel Dunn assisted the cook, George Bull helped the steward, and Jesse Sage attended to the stock." Others took turns on the watch. There were no idle hands aboard this ship.

By June 11 all the passengers were seasick from the motion of the ship as it heaved and dipped in the Atlantic Ocean in bad weather. Few made it on deck for several days. "All the passengers during the gale has been in a dreadful state of sea sickness, scarcely one of them able to come on deck the last 5 or 6 days past." The pumps were attended to every two to four hours as the ship took on more water. The log noted on June 13, the ship made about "an inch of water an hour over twenty-four hours." The weather improved by June 17.

On the morning of July 1, there were light squalls, calm sea, and the temperature was very hot. Gale documented the death of the first child on the voyage:

Mrs. Clarke, wife of the teacher who was to be stationed in the vicinity of Mr. McKenzie's farm [Craigflower] lost her baby July 1, and the child was buried at sea the evening of the same day.

A week later, on July 7, a Danish seaman named Schmidt died. He had been ill for eighteen days.

A hospital was constructed for another woman about to give birth. John Baker's wife Isabella, who was pregnant, became ill during the church service on July 16 and had to be carried out. The Bakers were the youngest couple aboard the ship, only twenty years old. They travelled with John's brother George Baker and his wife Mary Ann and their daughter Ester Elizabeth Ann.

Towards the end of July, the weather again turned stormy. The ship tossed and turned in gale-force winds. The pump continued night and day. A small mutiny erupted when the men complained about the condition of the rice served. They refused to work. Captain Wishart examined the rice and ordered it cooked in a different saucepan. He said he did not want the passengers eating bad food when there was good food on board. The bad rice was fed to the pigs. Only the Norwegians went back to work. When the other men still refused to work, the Captain mustered all aboard and lectured on the consequences of their action. He advised in the future he would be guided entirely by the Passenger Act and their conduct would be reported to the HBC on his arrival on Vancouver Island. He did not want any more grumbling or swearing, and they must return to work on their watches as normal. If these conditions were met, he would return them to their full allowance.

The Passenger Act governing the "Carriage of Passengers by Sea" is dated June 30, 1852 and outlines the penalty for refusing to observe the rules and regulations:

any Person on board who shall neglect or refuse to obey any such Rules or Regulation, or who shall be guilty of riotous or insubordinate Conduct, shall be liable for each Offence to a Penalty not exceeding Two Pounds Sterling, and in addition thereto to be confined in the Common Gaol for any Period not exceeding One Month, at the Discretion of the Justices who shall adjudicate on the Complaint.[5]

Seventeen miners refused to work and had their names duly recorded: "George Baker, John Baker, Matthew Miller, John Meakin, William Incher, Joseph Webb, Richard Turner, Richard Richardson, John Richardson, Thomas Jones, Elijah Ganner, John Thompson, Thomas Lowndes, Thomas Hawkes, Joseph Bevilockway, John Biggs, and Edward Gough."

The law stated a copy of the Passenger Act must be posted on the ship for the passengers to peruse. If it had been posted, some of the miners may still have been unable to read its contents, as evidenced by the agreements they signed.[6] Few of the miners could read or write; many signed an "X" mark to their indentures. However, those who could read no doubt advised them of the document and understood the implications because soon they were back to work.

The log continued with the day-to-day operation of the ship, the labour trouble now settled. On August 8, George and Ann Bull's second daughter eighteen-month-old Susannah died after a month's illness, leaving their oldest child five-year-old Sarah Ann. The child was buried at sea that evening.

Bad weather was a constant problem as the ship rolled in heavy seas. Carpenters and the sailmaker were kept busy with ship maintenance.

By mid-August the log recorded for the first time that a sickness had overcome many. "Cake Fever is raging very bad on board. We have 7 or 8 layed [sic] up with [it] now and that Mr. Thomas,"[Gale calls him the 'Juvenile Doctor'] is more like a nurse for them than a doctor." This illness continued to be a problem throughout the voyage.

There were many uncomplimentary remarks recorded in the log about Dr. Thomas. At one point Gale suggested it would be much "more to the advantage of the ship to have a more practical person on board or none at all." Gale's feelings towards the doctor may have had more to do with the distribution of liquor than his medical skills. Thomas distributed the brandy, rum, gin, or wine, as medicine if someone was ill, and seemed to have been liberal with the "spirits and double allowance [of] meat."

Also for the first time, there appeared to be dissatisfaction with the Robinson party. Gale described them as "a dirty lazy dissatisfied set and Mr. Robinson himself is worse than his people, if it can be possible." More complaints were recorded on September 18 about the family when Mr. Robinson felt his party should have extra provisions sent to their cabin.

Besides what they eat at the cabin table, the captain allows Mr. Robinson oatmeal, rice, sugar, molasses and flour. Besides that the steward is authorized by the Captain to make fresh bread for the wife and children twice a week and still he grumbles and finds fault.

Robinson claimed to be a teetotaler, but Gale complained, "every day he took wine, brandy and gin to his berth."

Water from a leak on deck flooded the forehold and damaged a bale marked for James Douglas. The damaged item caused some consternation especially as the bale was addressed to the Governor. Captain Wishart duly inspected the bale and had others who examined it sign a written statement to that effect.

Samuel Gough, son of Edwin and Elizabeth Gough, celebrated his fifth birthday on the voyage with his three-year-old sister Amanda Theresa. Later in life he recalled a childhood memory of how frightened he was of the rough seas when the ship rounded the Cape Horn, with hatches battened down and all belongings on the move, and many seasick passengers. He said it was the worst part of the voyage.[7] However, not all his memories of the voyage were negative, for he fondly remembered an old sailor who took particular care that the children received full rations of plum duff and other delicacies that were served in first class.

Yet another death was recorded September 21, when John Benjamin, the son of Lavinia and John Malpass, died. He and his sister Eliza had became ill with a throat ailment. Only Eliza, recovered.

Four days later Isabella Baker gave birth "in very great haste" in the morning. The young mother had been on deck washing and by afternoon she gave birth. The child lived only a few weeks. When it appeared the child would not survive, the Bakers requested their child be christened into the Church of England. The baby was given the name Anne Marie in a service conducted by the Captain. Two more Baker children would be born in Nanaimo.

On September 30, a son named George was born to Mary Ann and Jesse Sage, a brother for William and Selena. Mary Ann gave birth amidst a terrific storm as the ship rounded Cape Horn. They were within sight of the barren and desolate coast of Patagonia.

Passengers later claimed that two sailors were washed overboard in this storm. Research has shown this incident may have happened on the 1862 voyage of the *Princess Royal*. From the diary of William Cartwright:

> Shortly after rounding Cape Horn in a gale, the *Princess Royal* lost her second mate and an able seaman. They were engaged in taking in the job when the vessel pitched forward heavily and when she recovered the men had disappeared.[8]

As Mary Ann Sage and her baby George did not go ashore until their arrival in Nanaimo, Nanaimo was considered his birthplace. Normally a birth aboard ship is recorded as at the registration place of the ship, which in this case would have been London. It bothered George Sage later in life that people referred to him as, "the man without a country," because of his birth at sea, and that they did not consider him a "native son" of Nanaimo. The 1891 census does not give him a place of birth, it just states "at sea."[9]

The *Princess Royal* was now safely around Cape Horn with pleasant weather ahead. But still troubles persisted with the crew; the second and third officers could not agree and were constantly swearing at each other, and the steward was found drunk on more than one occasion. "The ship is getting too small for them," noted Gale. Men were employed scrubbing paintwork inside and out and with general maintenance. The weather warmed as the ship neared the Sandwich Islands (Hawaii).

In Gale's opinion Robinson continued to be an irritant. He hoped Robinson would be better in the mines than he was aboard the ship. The supply of liquor had been depleted, an "unfortunate occurrence" noted Gale, as it was used for medicinal purposes.

On October 20, pilots boarded the ship and eased it into Honolulu harbour. The sight of this pleasant land was tinged with sadness as Thomas Lowndes died. He was one of the Staffordshire miners who had been ill almost since the ship left London. The Lowndes couple was the oldest aboard: Thomas was 37 and Charlotte 33. She accompanied her husband's body ashore for burial. A few days later, two other men were taken to hospital in Honolulu.

Five-year-old Eliza Malpass recalled the stopover in Hawaii. She saw:

long tables standing under thatched roofs, spread with coral and fancy shells for sale. Even then the tourist trade was not overlooked.[10]

The ship took on meat, vegetables, bread, and water supply. On Sunday, October 22, all passengers and crew were allowed ashore for leisure activities. During the next few days the crew discharged and stored cargo. The Robinson party refused to work and continued to complain about their food. Their servant asked to stay in Honolulu, but Captain Wishart tried unsuccessfully to persuade her to stay with the ship, so hired a police officer to guard her day and night. When some of the miners refused to work, eight Chinese were hired to work each day discharging goods.

More passengers, including John Richardson, the brother of Richard, fell sick, and a doctor was brought aboard. John's wife Seadonah and their daughter Hester (Esther) Ann watched over him until he recovered. Seadonah gave birth to Benjamin a month after their arrival in Nanaimo. Another couple had a closer call: Ann and Joseph Bevilockway gave birth to their daughter Julia just two days after their arrival in Nanaimo. Julia joined her brothers George Louis and Louis Moses, and her sister Margaret Catherine, also known as Kate.

William Incher's wife Sarah became very ill and died in childbirth on October 28. The child lived for a short time. William was left to care for their three other children. Also six-month old Samuel, the son of Frances and Elijah Ganner died about the same time. The Ganners had five other children with them on the voyage: sons Joseph, William Henry and Elijah, and daughters Hannah and Sarah. A carpenter came aboard and made coffins for the two bodies that were buried ashore in Hawaii. Five men went ashore for the service.

The log noted Robinson was distraught over the death of Sarah Incher, as she was well liked. As the ship readied to leave Captain Wishart ordered all crew and passengers to return to ship. However, the lack of wind delayed departure. During this waiting period, three more of the crew deserted. The following day, the Captain had read the logbook and became extremely upset at the comments made by Gale about the passengers. Gale was told to keep "absurd comments" as to what may or may not have occurred on board, or his opinions of the captain or the passengers, out of the book. For most of the remainder of the voyage, Gale failed to keep his recordings strictly to the ship's operation and weather conditions.

The ship left Honolulu October 31. However, the tragic chronicle of deaths continued through to the very end of the voyage. Sarah Incher's baby died on November 8 and the body, Gale noted, "was thrown overboard and no more notice taken of it than as if it had been a dead cat." On November 13, Mary, daughter of Richard and Elizabeth Richardson, died in her mother's arms at 5:30 p.m. Ten hours later she was buried at sea. "The usual cerimoney [sic] performed by the Captain."

A winter gale was blowing as the *Princess Royal* entered the Strait of Juan de Fuca on November 22. Again the steward was found drunk. The weather was so bad Captain Wishart could not see land. The guns were charged with powder to announce their arrival but were not fired. It was three days before the ship finally anchored in Esquimalt Harbour. Governor Douglas came alongside but did not board. Captain Wishart left with him probably to report on the voyage.

Douglas wrote of the arrival of the vessel. "It was safely at anchor, the weather being dreadful and they being glad of a shelter in any secure place." He added she had made "a remarkable expedition voyage having been little over 5-1/2 months from Gravesend." This was considered a relatively fast voyage from Great Britain.

On November 24, the sails were dried and put away, and all gear was tallied and put below deck. While passengers loaded their luggage, boats were lowered ready for unloading. "Mr. Clarke, the teacher, and Robinson's servant were landed." Craigflower School was not yet completed when Clarke arrived. The school opened in March 1855, and Clarke remained as teacher until the fall of March 1859 when he resigned and returned to England.[11]

Another day passed before the weary miners and their families were transferred to the *Recovery* that brought them to Nanaimo. At 11 a.m., on November 27, 1854 they came ashore at Pioneer Rock, near Cameron Island. Joseph McKay and the Scottish miners warmly welcomed the newcomers. Most stories are embellished over time, and this one takes on an almost biblical proportion. It was said that the sun broke through the clouds at the moment the first miner set foot on land.[12] After such a horrific voyage the *Princess Royal* passengers may have thought they had arrived in paradise.

Meanwhile back in Victoria the ship was prepared for its return voyage. The *Otter* eventually towed her into Victoria Harbour where guns were fired in salute, one for the HBC and eleven for the government. The fort returned the welcome. Over the next few days bales of furs were loaded before she set sail for the long journey back to England.

Those not mentioned on the voyage

There were other passengers on the *Princess Royal* whom Charles Gale did not mention in the grueling narrative of the ship's log. They were: Richard Turner and his daughter Christianna. His wife Sarah had remained behind in England. Richard was described as a "good workman, seldom missed a day of labour, but was something of a miser."[13] Daniel Dunn was assistant cook on the voyage.

Thomas and Anna Maria York and their daughter Phoebe who did not stay long in Nanaimo. But Thomas has his place in British Columbia history. Discontented in Nanaimo he left with other dissidents for Bellingham. He liked the area and settled there for a short time and is credited with contributing to the layout of the town. The lure of gold attracted him to Fort Yale where he operated a miner's hostel. His son Thomas Fraser was born there on October 21, 1858. The family next moved to Spuzzum, several miles north of Yale, where he and his partner operated a ferry until the Alexandra suspension bridge was built. York moved yet again, this time in 1865 to the Sumas Prairie where he ran a store. But he saw yet another opportunity, that of farming. He applied for a land lease of 2,000 acres, then started a dairy farm. Thomas died in 1893.[14]

William and Ann Harrison and their daughter Ann also did not stay long in Nanaimo. Harrison was another of the dissident miners who left for Bellingham. He did return to the Nanaimo mines for a short time but under what he considered unfavourable conditions, so he left the area permanently.

Joseph Webb's wife Naomi chose not to travel with her husband in 1854, as she was pregnant with their first child David. She arrived on a later voyage.

There is little mention of John and Jane Biggs in the log, so it would appear the couple's voyage was as uneventful as it could be under the circumstance, although John was one of the "bad rice" mutineers. John was a carpenter so he would have been kept busy on the voyage. His first home was in a row of three houses on what is now Chapel Street. These later became known as the Biggs cottages and served as a hospital for a number of years.

After he completed his HBC contract, he pre-empted land outside the HBC holdings, at Biggs Point, across Nanaimo Harbour. In 1860, he and Edwin Gough had their own contract to mine at a level to the east of present-day Bastion Street. Mark Bate described Biggs as a "frank conscientious man who would not knowingly do wrong himself nor failed to express the utmost indignation for those who did."[15] The Biggs raised a large family in Nanaimo, and descendants still live here today.

The Biggs family: Eliza, Sarah, Henry, Louisa, Elizabeth: Front row: Maria, Ann and John Biggs.

Matthew and Caroline Miller and their two daughters Elizabeth and Sarah Jane were also on the voyage. Matthew brought with him a violoncello, his prized possession. Not only did he entertain the passengers on the long journey but he also played for the Sunday services conducted by Captain Wishart.[16] His talent would have been welcomed in early Nanaimo.

Thomas and Mary Hawkes brought their two children, one-year-old James and three-year-old Jane Ellen. Thomas was a coke-burner by trade, and had a reputation as a good miner and was never afraid of hard work. He became known for his tremendous strength.

John Thompson and wife Elizabeth were newlyweds, married just before they boarded the ship. Nineteen-year-old John ferried the passengers ashore on their arrival in Nanaimo. John was a restless man, mined for a number of years then bought a farm where he raised pigs. He shared the first slaughtered cow with other families. And he loved apples, so much so that he had them shipped from Washington state. Later he bought ten acres on Newcastle Townsite from the Esquimalt & Nanaimo Railway and divided this into town lots. On one, he built the Mount View Hotel. His wife Elizabeth was well liked in the community, as a nurse and counsellor.

Thomas Jones, from Wales, was unsuited as a miner. Shortly after arriving in Nanaimo he got into trouble by running up a debt at the HBC store. Then he deserted with another miner, also in debt; the two were caught and put in jail only to be released when they agreed to work off their debt. Jones paid off his debt, saved some money, then left for the Cariboo. He did return to Nanaimo and opened a small store, but he eventually returned to the interior where he gained a reputation as a mining promoter.[17]

The "juvenile doctor" referred to in the log was Dr. Thomas, who remained in Nanaimo as the colliery doctor until replaced by Dr. Benson in 1857.[18]

All played an important part in the development of the mines and the town. There would be many more voyages of the *Princess Royal* bringing others to Nanaimo. However, the voyage of 1854 is remembered as a milestone in the early history.

Governor James Douglas ordered more houses built to accommodate the new miners and their families. There were 20 duplexes measuring 40 by 25 feet, four rooms to each with a central chimney. Mark Bate described the homes:

> The houses were primitive and looked dreary on the outside and had cramped space inside, with no spare rooms. Wind blew between the logs and poles that were plastered up with clay or stuffed with moss. The interior furniture consisted of benches, boards and bunk-like bedsteads. A community Dutch Oven was used for baking and cooking. The floors were covered with rush mats or rugs made in part of dog hair. Photographs of loved ones were displayed on the walls, or illustrations from newspapers. Despite the simple home visitors were always made welcome. When a white tablecloth materialized and was spread over a painted board, it showed a measure of warm hospitality extended to the visitor.[19]

The Lavinia and John Malpass family shared a crowded duplex with the Jane and John Biggs on Chapel Street. Their daughter Eliza recalled,

> Here they seldom allowed the central fireplace to go out, banking it with coal each night. There was usually a pot boiling over the fire. Water was carried in powder cans up the steep banks of the gully for her father's bath when he came home at night from the mine. The spring at the ravine became a popular place for the young people to meet, and several romances began when a boy offered to carry the girl's pail up the bank.[20]

The families welcomed the accomodation in these modest homes.

CHAPTER SEVEN

Nanaimo—from Outpost to Company Town

In 1854, the Hudson's Bay Company still had five years remaining in its trading licence agreement with Great Britain, and it was important for the company to fulfill its obligation in the Colony of Vancouver Island. Part of that agreement was to establish "settlements of resident colonists," preferably from Great Britain. Therefore bringing in indentured miners to work the Nanaimo coalfield was in fact aiding settlement. The village of young Scottish and English miners had all the ingredients necessary for it to become a town with a future. But first the HBC had to come to an agreement with the Snuneymuxw to ensure the coal reserves would remain in company hands.

The Nanaimo treaty

On December 23, 1854, Governor James Douglas signed a treaty with the Snuneymuxw, the last of the 14 treaties negotiated on Vancouver Island between 1850 and 1854.[1] Eleven were near Fort Victoria, one in Nanaimo, and two at Fort Rupert. The wording of each was identical and fairly straightforward:

> The condition of or understanding of this sale is this, that our village sites and enclosed fields are to be kept for our own use, for the use of our children, and for those who may follow after us; and the land shall be properly surveyed hereafter. It is understood, however, that the land itself, with these small exceptions becomes the entire property of the white people for ever; it is also understood that we are

at liberty to hunt over the unoccupied lands, and to carry on our fisheries as formerly.[2]

In Nanaimo, the area of negotiation extended "from Commercial Inlet 12 miles of the Nanaimo River ... made by the Parlequun Tribe before Squoniston & others."[3] While the other treaties were signed to fulfill the HBC obligation to colonize Vancouver Island, the Nanaimo incentive was not only land, but to formalize the HBC ownership of the coal deposits. Until this time the Snuneymuxw had worked in the mining operation, services for which they had traded for goods.

James Douglas was instructed by the HBC management to extinguish "the Indian claim to the coal district."[4] The treaty listed 159 names of Snuneymuxw men with 160 "X" marks. The Snuneymuxw had an oral tradition therefore the "X" marks were an affirmation of the agreement. Douglas signed the document with three other HBC employees; Charles Edward Stuart, Richard Golledge, and George Robinson. At the bottom of the document is written "636 white, 12 blue and 20 inferior," referring to the number of blankets distributed by Douglas.

The issue of land ownership would come back to haunt government for many years to come. When Douglas signed the treaties there were few settlers on Vancouver Island, and Natives roamed freely over the unoccupied land, carrying on hunting and fishing without hindrance. He believed that all cause for discontent would be removed if he gave as much land as they requested. His policy was to give the Natives whatever plots of land they chose and as much acreage as they requested. Not being farmers, they asked for little, in no case more than ten acres per family. Douglas did not think there was any point in moving them away from white settlements, believing that close contact between the races would help to advance the Natives in civilization.

Those who came after Douglas thought his reserve policy had been too generous and soon cut back land on many of the reserves.

The First Nanaimo Census

Governor James Douglas ordered the first census of the colony be taken at the end of 1854. It recorded the white population to be 774, of which 151 lived in Nanaimo and 232 lived in Victoria. Nanaimo had 52 dwelling houses, 3 shops, 6 outhouses and 1 school with 29 regular students.[5] There was no breakdown by occupation, though there was a very detailed account of the number of horses, cows, sheep, and poultry in each area. Nearly half the population was under 20 years of age; only 15 people were over 50, and no one at all was over 60.[6]

Native Elder Dick Whoahdum
Recalls Treaty Discussion

During the Royal Commission on Indian Affairs meetings with the Snuneymuxw in 1913, an elder named Dick Whoahdum recalled the treaty discussion. At 83, he was only one of ten Snuneymuxw still alive who discovered coal. Che-wich-i-kan, or Coal Tyee, the man who originally discovered coal, died in February 1881, at age 75.[7] Whoahdum noted his people lived at different places depending on the season:

> They draw the salmon from the Nanaimo River, and they go to Departure Bay for curing the herrings. I told Sir James Douglas that these three places [the other place being Gabriola Island] were our land. Sir James Douglas said, "I don't take any land away from you at all. All these three places where you live at different times are yours."[8]

> Whoahdum said the promise had been broken, and they were pushed off their land and had even been stopped from cutting wood and taking fish. Much of the land allocated by Douglas was taken away. When it came to the allocation of land, Natives and Europeans were not treated equally. On the reserves that were set up, families were given a maximum of 10 acres, whereas Europeans could pre-empt 160 acres, then purchase another 480 more.

Douglas busied himself with a round of official duties intent on developing the resources of the island and making certain that the HBC retained all its powers and privileges. So the HBC added more land to its Nanaimo coal operation on May 7, 1855, by purchasing 6,193 acres of Crown land at a price of one pound sterling per acre. The property included Cameron, Newcastle, and Douglas [Protection] islands. In addition, another 1,074 acres were reserved: 724 for public use, 100 acres for roads, and 250 acres for "the future benefit of the Indians."[9] So what had begun as an amicable arrangement in trading for coal between the HBC and the Snuneymuxw now alienated the latter from ownership of the coal resources and from much of the land.

Douglas only had to answer to Governor Simpson or the British Colonial Office. Without long-distance telephones or telegraph he used his own best judgement when an emergency came up, then reported afterwards. Democracy was not one of his strong points. But times were changing.

The Haida & the Dead Dog.

The Haida incident revolved around George Baker, the owner of the Dew Drop Hotel on Haliburton Street. In the summer of 1858, a large number of Haida visited Nanaimo. They prowled around the streets picking up anything that looked interesting. Several passed Baker's door and were snapped at by the family dog "Lady." One man picked up a piece of rock and hurled it at the small dog and killed her. Baker was away at the time, down the Nanaimo River gathering a scow load of hay. On his return, Mary Ann Baker told her husband of the dog tragedy. Baker promptly went to the Haida encampment intending to chastise the offender. The Natives surrounded him menacingly and refused to allow the guilty person to be harmed.

George Baker, the owner of the Dew Drop Inn (now called the Patricia Hotel).

Baker reported the incident to Captain Charles Stuart, who sent a force to arrest the accused. The Haida were prepared for this; they were armed with knives, guns, iron bolts, bars, and bludgeons, and showed every intention of fighting. They refused to permit the accused to be arrested. George Mitchell, the gunner at the Bastion, fired a few charges near the encampment to show they meant business unless the man surrendered. The shot tore things up effectively, and soon the Haida was arrested and taken to Captain Stuart for punishment. As magistrate, he ordered the man flogged with the cat-o'-nine-tails. The mess steward, George Mills, carried out the sentence.[10]

The schoolteacher insisted the boys should watch the flogging, believing it would set a good disciplinary example. John Meakin who was then a five-year old, remembered it as one of his most unhappy memories of his school years.[11]

Captain Stuart, the Hudson's Bay Company new officer-in-charge

Captain Charles Edward Stuart, from Bristol, England, succeeded Joseph McKay at the Nanaimo post as officer-in-charge on July 6, 1855.[12] Stuart was highly regarded by the HBC, having served on several of the company vessels, the *Cadboro, Vancouver, Una,* and the *Beaver.* He soon won the confidence of the community, and as law enforcement officer, often he was called upon to administer justice.

Nanaimo—the Hudson's Bay Company mining village

In 1854 mining began in earnest and within ten years, several mines were started in the area bounded by present day Wharf, Front, and Commercial streets. These included the No. 1 pit, the No. 3 pit, the Douglas mine, the Newcastle mine, plus other minor workings.

Boyd Gilmour's find on Commercial Inlet evolved into two small mines, the Park Head Mine and Dunsmuir's Level-Free Mine. Gilmour had been convinced the Level-Free Mine was played out, but his nephew Robert Dunsmuir thought otherwise. He asked Douglas for the chance to operate the mine, hire his own people, use his own money, and then sell back to the coal company all the coal he mined. To do this he needed an advance for start-up costs, which he assured Douglas, would be paid back when the mine produced coal. Douglas was a little taken aback by the proposal and could not decide how to handle the situation of an independent collier. The HBC Nanaimo daybook in 1855 recorded the outcome of Douglas' decision.

The Bastion and Nanaimo Harbour showing an earlier time when sailing ships anchored in the harbour.

"Dunsmuir commenced working on his own account."[13] The mine was successful and gave Dunsmuir his first taste of management. In October 1855, Dunsmuir and Edward Walker were granted the first free miners' licences issued by the HBC.

The mining village gave every appearance of a small company town. The HBC sawmill at Millstone River produced lumber to build homes and supply the mines, and the HBC farm supplied fresh produce and feed for the livestock. The influence of the HBC was everywhere—from the homes in which the miners lived to the store where they purchased their goods.

The company store

At the HBC store in Nanaimo, Adam Grant Horne, assisted by John Malcolm, traded with the Snuneymuxw for furs and salmon. Prime furs valued up to $100 were traded for a twist of tobacco or some other trade goods. Work tickets awarded for every tub of coal carried were traded for blankets, beads, shirts, or other items.[14]

Horne traded HBC blankets for land otter and beaver skins.

Malcolm issued miners' rations until this was replaced with the allowance of a shilling per day in lieu of rations. Malcolm seldom smiled, but he was known as an honest man.[15]

The company store had the only liquor supply, and this was dispensed from a rum jug into any utensil the customer happened to bring along. Horne annually applied to Victoria to renew the Nanaimo liquor licence.

The store where the miners were expected to spend their wages was located at what was later the parking lot of the Canadian Imperial Bank of Commerce on Wharf Street. Adam Grant Horne Lane in that vicinity is named in his honour, as is Horne Lake, west of Qualicum.

Rebellious miners

Not all the miners were happy in Nanaimo and they looked to the Puget Sound Coal Mine at Bellingham Bay to better their situation. Recruiters were sent to Nanaimo to lure the new miners to their operation. In 1855 a number of the *Princess Royal* miners broke their contract with the HBC and left for Bellingham. Leaving their wives and families behind, these rebellious miners included John Thompson, John Baker, Joseph Webb, Joseph Bevilockway, William Incher, William Harrison, Thomas York, George Baker, Daniel Dunn, and John Meakin. The coal operation in Bellingham was not what they were led to believe, and before long they trickled back home to Nanaimo. The HBC reinstated them on "less favourable terms."[16]

More mining families arrive

More mining families arrived from Great Britain in 1857. Even with the inducement of the land, the HBC still had difficulty finding unskilled workers for its mines; therefore the Snuneymuxw were still essential in the mining operation. Sometimes the HBC store ran out of trade goods to pay them. Loading coal onto waiting ships was hindered when the Snuneymuxw moved to their autumn fishing sites.[17]

To guarantee trade goods as well as labour, the HBC endorsed intermarriage between Snuneymuxw women and HBC employees. These marriages had distinct advantages, almost guaranteeing work for the immediate family and other Snuneymuxw.[18] And there were now a number of children in the community from mixed marriages. Their lives would bridge two cultures.

The growing number of children requiring schooling in the community concerned Governor Douglas. In 1853 he transferred the first schoolteacher Charles Alfred Bayley from a day school in Victoria to Nanaimo. In addition to his teaching duties, he served as the village postmaster. Many of the children of the immigrant families attended their first school under Bayley.

After Bayley left, Christopher Finlay, the HBC accountant, taught the children for two years. Finlay was very strict and frequently administered physical punishment.

Nanaimo in 1859

In Nanaimo it was "black diamonds" that was the driving engine of the economy. Commander R.C. Mayne described the city in 1859: "Along the shore are the colliery buildings and about a dozen remarkably sooty houses, inhabited by the miners and a few Hudson's Bay Company officers here."[19] Surveyor Pearse, however,

---

The 1857
Nanaimo Census

Enumeration on February 1, 1857, showed the population of Nanaimo consisted of "51 males, 20 females, 2 Kanakas, 5 Iriquois. Children: 26 boys, 28 girls - total 132." Their ethnic origin was: "91 English, 37 Scotch, 2 Irish, 1 Welch, 3 French Canadian, 1 Norwegian, 5 Iriquois, 2 Kanakas."[20] These figures did not include the Snuneymuxw population at this time. However, a census taken three years later showed a population of 399 that included 50 old men and women, 211 young men and women, and 138 children.[21] Since the census was conducted during the summer months when many were away fishing, the figures may have been low.

Charles Bayley–Nanaimo's first schoolteacher.

Charles Alfred Bayley had come to Vancouver Island on the *Tory* with his father who was to manage the HBC's new Uplands Farm at Cadboro Bay, Victoria. The young Bayley had signed the five-year HBC contract as a labourer in 1850, but James Douglas found him unsuitable so appointed him schoolmaster for children of the HBC's "labouring class" in Nanaimo.[22] His salary was 40 pounds sterling a year. Parents added another pound for each child and supplied books and paper.[23] Bayley's school was established in a small log building provided free by the HBC.

During his stay in Nanaimo he married fifteen-year-old Agnes Hunter; he had boarded with Andrew and Mary Hunter and their family when he moved to Nanaimo. An entry in Adam Grant Horne's diary of December 23 notes: "Mr. Bayley married at 7 p.m." The Hunter family had also been on the *Tory*, the same ship that brought Horne to Canada in 1851. Bayley and Agnes Hunter were married aboard the *Sir James Douglas*, in the Nanaimo harbour, the first recorded marriage in the mining village. The couple would have six children.

Bayley's appointment to Nanaimo was less than satisfactory. Unhappy with the lack of supplies and salary, he fulfilled his contract with the HBC then returned to Victoria where he opened a store selling supplies to gold miners.

presented another view of the coal mining community. In the General Report on the Country around Nanaimo, dated July 11, 1859, Pearse noted the town had about 200 inhabitants and how friendly the Snuneymuxw were:

> Indians, though numerous, are perfectly peaceful, are made use of by White farmers as plowmen, servants, voyagers. In fact do all kinds of labor but receive little pay and rations. When kindly treated and properly supervised the results of their labour are profitable to the employers.[24]

The Nanaimo mines continued to develop despite setbacks such as flooded shafts and mechanical breakdowns. A wharf had been built the previous year but it was still not suitable for all ships. Also the primitive method of loading coal from canoe to ship limited the export of large quantities. Snuneymuxw women carried the coal to the ships in canoes. "It was a curious sight to see the string of Natives working like ants in one continuous line over the trail to where they deposited their loads."[25] By November 1859 only 25,398 tons of coal had been exported.[26] Improvements such as a coal tramway and another steam engine helped double production.

CHAPTER 8

Nanaimo Pioneers

N anaimo pioneers were just ordinary men who sought to build for a better future despite the hard work and setbacks they would encounter along the way. The storekeeper–explorer, the mine manger–mayor, the schoolteacher–minister, and the doctor–coal mine owner, all had a strong sense of community. Their success rested with individual effort. Their family ties were strong, and they were happy in the belief they could improve the situation for others. These men paved the way with courage, determination, and purpose.

Adam Grant Horne & his explorations

Adam Grant Horne was twenty years old in 1850 when he signed on as a labourer with the HBC at Kirkwall, on the Orkney Islands. Initially he was sent to Fort Rupert but was transferred in 1853 to Nanaimo and was put to work in the new HBC store. The young highlander was a tall good-looking man, with dark red hair, about 6 feet 3 inches tall and weighing 200 pounds. He spoke with a quiet firm voice and although poorly educated, what he lacked in knowledge he made up for in many other ways. He became a skilled trader, was fluent in several different Native dialects, and could communicate with most island tribes. He earned their respect, and he helped them when asked. Sometimes he was required to be a doctor, a dentist, or a barber, and on occasion he even repaired boots and shoes. His job required him to be versatile and able to cope under any situation.

Journey across Vancouver Island

Horne gained a reputation as a fair man and is remembered for his exploratory trek in 1856 across Vancouver Island, from Qualicum into the Alberni Valley. HBC chief factor Roderick Finlayson asked him to find a trail he suspected Natives used to cross the island that was thought to start near Qualicum Creek emerging somewhere at the head of the Alberni Canal. Horne was instructed to open trade for furs and establish friendly relations with the west coast tribes.

The HBC Nanaimo daybook recorded Horne's departure:

Saturday, May 10, 1856, 2:30 p.m. Toma Ouatomy [Quamtany] left here on an expedition across the Island, accompanied by three Indian men and one Indian woman. Mr. Horne also left with him with instructions not to proceed further than the high mountain beyond the large lake in the interior but if the interior tribes be peaceable he may proceed to the Alberni Canal.

Finlayson also sent along Cote, the French-Canadian hired to build the miner's cottages. Cote was considered, "a good canoeman and someone who knew the coast well,"[1] and invaluable in a crisis and knew no fear. Horne thought Cote was a peculiar character. He had a head of wiry curly hair that hung in ringlets about his shoulders, and he swore in French! An interpreter named Lafromboise was also sent along.

Horne gave the following account of his expedition in an interview in May 1883 with Dr. William Wymond Walkem, the surgeon at East Wellington Colliery. The story first appeared in Walkem's 1914 book *Stories of Early British Columbia*. (Walkem's brother George was premier of B.C. from 1874 to 1876.) The following is a brief excerpt from that account.

One-armed Toma—Iroquois Guide

Thomas Quamtany, also known as "One-armed Toma" and Thomas Anthony, was an Iroquois employed by the HBC. He joined the Horne expedition and was considered an excellent guide, interpreter, and sharpshooter, although he only had one arm. He lost his arm in an altercation with a rival Cowichan young Native over a young woman both were courting. Toma was seriously wounded in an ambush and only by receiving immediate attention did he survive.

Governor James Douglas considered him his personal servant. He would not obey anyone unless ordered by the Governor. When Douglas heard of the attempt on Toma's life he sent a force of 400 men into the Cowichan Valley to hunt down and capture the would-be assassin. The Cowechan, Tathlesit, was captured, given a brief trial and hanged on the spot.[2]

Toma also assisted the Vancouver Island Exploring Expedition of 1864.

The Horne expedition left Victoria in a Haida canoe furnished by the HBC. It was roomy and light and behaved well in heavy seas. The first night they camped at Salt Spring Island then continued on the next day passed Nanaimo until they were within a mile of Qualicum.

The Qualicum massacre

As the expedition approached Qualicum, a large fleet of Haida canoes approached the creek and disappeared behind the brush that bordered the banks of the river. Before long they saw thick volumes of smoke rise from the creek. Horne's party lay hidden and waited patiently to see what would happen. Several hours later they were horrified to see Natives manning each canoe standing upright holding a human head by the hair.

As the wind started to blow from the north, the prows of the Haida canoes were turned south and mats were hoisted as sails. Within an hour they were out of sight. The Horne party remained hidden for another hour before venturing up the creek. The rancherie, or Native village, was still hidden from them, but smoke continued to rise from the point of land covered with heavy timber. Horne described the scene: "What had evidently been a rancherie was now a blackened heap of burning timbers. Naked bodies could be seen here and there, but not a living being was in sight." He walked to where the bodies lay. Each one was headless and mutilated. They searched for survivors without success. Some in the party wanted to return to Fort Victoria but Horne refused. He had been sent to do a job and he would do it. Since there were no Qualicums to lend assistance in finding the trail they would have to find it themselves.

To Horne's great surprise, only a few yards along the creek, beneath an overhanging maple tree, they found a naked elderly woman moaning, chanting, and bleeding and her face pale. She looked at the strangers; they were the first white people she had ever seen. They gave her some rum and water, and with the aid of the interpreter she told them what had taken place.

The Haidas had crept into the rancherie where the tribe slept. Most were killed before waking. Others were outnumbered and stood no chance. The old woman was wounded with a spear and had fled to the creek. The Haidas had carried off two young women, four little girls, and two small boys. This massacre had been to avenge the killing of a Haida at Cape Mudge where a warrior had attempted to carry off the daughter of the Euclataw chief. The Qualicums were an Euclataw sept so the Haidas took their revenge on them. The old woman died as Horne and his party looked on.

Encounter with the Nuu-chah-nulth.

The Horne expedition continued on the journey across Horne Lake, and down the mountainside into the Alberni Valley where contact was made with a tribe recognized as belonging to the Nootkan group—known today as the Nuu-chah-nulth. The expedition had been told that the majority of the Natives of Barkley Sound had never seen a white man, and consequently they might be difficult to approach, or even be hostile, unless the group succeeded in gaining their confidence and friendship. The initial encounter was tentative. Horne gave a knife and offered biscuits and mirrors. With the help of a young Songhee boy captured years before by the tribe and the expedition interpreter Lafromboise, the expedition made its intentions known. Horne explained about the HBC trading posts and how the company would like to trade blankets for furs. With great ceremony, the chief was given a HBC blanket. He in turn was pleased and gave Horne two otter skins. When the young Songhee asked for his freedom. Horne offered more blankets for his release. After some difficult negotiations, release was eventually granted.

Spearing a codfish

In the evening, Horne watched a Native spear codfish. The man had a wooden block carved into the shape of a boy's spinning top and decorated with feathers resembling a shuttlecock. He placed the shuttlecock at the end of a pronged spear and pushed it into the water. Then he withdrew the spear and allowed it to come slowly upwards in front of the shuttle as bait. After withdrawing the spear he plunged it quickly downward again, then withdrew a struggling gray cod.

Return via Qualicum

On the return journey they cautiously approached Qualicum to make sure the Haidas had not returned. The buildings were still burning and the headless bodies had been partly devoured by wild animals. Seeing no canoes in sight, they continued on towards Nanaimo. As they turned into the mouth of the Nanaimo River, the Snuneymuxw gave them a friendly reception. The next day Horne continued on to Fort Victoria to report the expedition findings and received the "commendations of the chief factor."

The HBC Nanaimo daybook noted Horne returned May 18, 1856 and had traded a quantity of beaver and marten furs. It was learned later that a young boy of the massacred tribe had escaped unharmed into the forest and was found two days later by friends. As an adult he lived in a little cabin by the mouth of Qualicum River and became known as Qualicum Tom.

Horne's autumn journey

This same year Horne took an autumn trip into the Alberni Valley. His 1856 diary stated he left on September 10, with Thomas Mills, William Rich, Alexander Papley, a man named McArthur, another named Tahua, plus three Natives and their women. Again he took the Qualicum–Horne Lake route into the Alberni Valley where his party now received a warm reception from the tribe. For the next two days they shared an offering of salmon and potatoes with "Chief High-in-ulith and Chief Cacupet" and their people and were entertained that night with singing and dancing. The latter may have been Ka-koop-et, also known as Mr. Bill and having the honourable title of "Keeper of the Songs." He was present during the Anderson Sawmill period in Alberni (1860–1864)[3]

Horne thought that the warriors were a pretty sight, dressed up in their new HBC two-and-a-half point blankets with feathers on their heads. Following a salute of twenty guns in honour of the head chief, Horne was presented with the largest canoe he had ever seen. Two of the chiefs accompanied Horne back to Nanaimo, but along the way one changed his mind and wanted to return home stating he was ashamed to continue on because he had no sea otter skins to give the chiefs of Nanaimo. Horne promised to keep him safe, and the party arrived back in Nanaimo on September 20 without incident.

Horne settles down

Horne continued to operate the HBC store and serve as postmaster in Nanaimo, but the arrival of the *Princess Royal* on January 18, 1857 with more immigrants to Victoria also brought his future wife Elizabeth Bate. She came with her brother Mark, who would become the first mayor of Nanaimo. Two years later she and Horne were married. A brief entry in Horne's 1859 diary reads: "February 22: I was married by the Reverend Dossen at Nanaimo in the school room to E. Bate." The wedding ceremony was in fact conducted by the Reverend Richard Dawson and witnessed by Captain Charles Edward Stuart plus family members and friends; Caroline and George Robinson, Dr. Alfred Benson, Mark and Sarah Ann Bate, and Cornelius Bryant. Captain Stuart presented the newlyweds with a family Bible in which he inscribed "to my friend Adam Grant Horne on the day of his marriage with best wishes for his health and prosperity, A. D. 1859, Feb. 22, Colvile Town, Nanaimo, Vancouver Bible, as well as the demise of two girls and a boy who died before their eighth birthday. The remaining children were Adam Henry, Ann

Elizabeth and Adam Grant Horne with children Annie, Sarah, Bert, Tom and baby Lucy. Circa 1872.

Elizabeth, Sarah Maria, Herbert Lewis, Thomas Charles, Emily Maude, George Grant, Lindley Dallas.

The first family home was at the southeast corner of Bastion and Commercial streets. When the HBC disposed of its interests in Nanaimo in 1862, Horne opened his own store. He built a wooden-frame building (opposite today's Dorchester Hotel on Front Street) with access to the ramp leading to the old wharf. The building was later used as a police station and as the first courthouse.

Two years later Horne rejoined the HBC service and was posted to Fort Simpson (at Chatham Sound) with Elizabeth and their two small children. Two other daughters were born here.

Horne's next posting was at Comox in 1868 where he operated another small store.[4] The Comox area was largely undeveloped and its population scattered. The first settlers had arrived about six years before. The store was strategically located near the foot of Comox Hill to attract customers from the general area. The Horne family spent the next ten years here before returning to Nanaimo.

When the HBC store in Comox closed Horne returned to Nanaimo and again opened his own store A.G. Horne & Son, on Victoria Crescent. His older sons worked in the store while the youngest delivered goods with a horse and buggy. The store gave credit to the miners and their families, allowing many to buy goods when the mines were idle and to pay the bills when they worked.

Horne the mine owner

For a time in 1879 he was in partnership with Peter Sabiston, Jacob Blessing, and John Dick in a mining enterprise in the Mountain District west of Nanaimo. The Minister of Mines report for 1879 noted: "A first-class seam of coal was found under the estate of Messrs. Sabiston and Horne by Mr. John Dick. This very valuable property is within

Horne Sews on the Scalp

Family members have many stories to tell about Horne's exploits in Nanaimo and Comox. His granddaughter Carrie Brown Doney, of Seattle, wrote about one incident that showed his ability to adapt to a variety of situations:

> One night there was a lot of noise at the gate of the fort. Grandfather went out to see what was wrong, and there stood a huge Indians with an oatmeal sack in his hand. He said the Indians had all been fighting and the chief had been scalped and grandfather was to go sew the scalp on him. They were all very upset about this. Grandfather refused to do it at first, and tried to get rid of him. He had a medicine chest that he used for small wounds but he had never done anything like that before. The Indian persisted and grandfather was afraid he would stick a spear in him, so he went.
>
> The chief's hide was so tough that grandfather had to take his shoemaker's awl and make holes in his head and also through the scalp to sew it on. The old chief was so drunk that he could not feel a thing. Grandfather thought he would be dead by morning anyway, so he just sewed it on. But in the morning he was very much alive and lived to be an old man.[5]

Some time later, when Doney's mother was married and living in Union Bay, an old man came to the house with a bucket of clams. He began talking to her mother in the kitchen, and then suddenly lifted his hair up and there were the scars where Horne had sewn on his scalp many years before. "Every stitch had grown together perfectly."

two miles of Nanaimo Harbour."[6] The mine proved a success, and the partners divided the profits equally. The story passed down through the family relates how Horne sold the mine to Earl Westwood for $500 because he wanted to buy a "real nice present" for his wife Elizabeth. She was quite upset at this turn of events and told Horne he did not get enough money for it. The mine was eventually sold to Robert Dunsmuir for more than $30,000.

Mark Bate—Nanaimo's future and durable mayor

Mark Bate first heard of Nanaimo from his Uncle George Robinson who was manager of the mining operation in Nanaimo. Sadly Robinson's wife Ann died in 1856 shortly after the birth of her third child who also died six weeks later. Robinson wrote to his sister Maria inviting her to come to Nanaimo to help care for his other two children. Maria agreed and brought with her three cousins, Mark and Elizabeth Bate and their cousin Cornelius Bryant. They boarded the *Princess Royal*, in London, in August 1856 and landed at Victoria on January 18, 1857.

Mark Bate was twenty years old. No doubt his vision of the new colony was coloured by stories of the gold rush from his Uncle George who had told of how a French Canadian had brought gold dust to Nanaimo, and some predicted that New Caledonia would become a second California.

Mark was born in Birmingham on December 11, 1837, and educated at Dudley Grammar School in Worcestershire, England. He left school at age seventeen to work in Bramale, Cochrane & Co. where his father was a partner. There he remained for two years learning all aspect of business until deciding to come to Vancouver Island. On the day of his arrival in Victoria he wrote in his diary:

> Sunday morning the 18th, we were towed by the *Beaver* into Fort Victoria harbour. We fired our guns at noon and the Fort returned the salute. Went ashore with Drs. Benson and Johnson and to church in the afternoon.

His cousin Cornelius Bryant wrote of attending services conducted by the Reverend Edward Cridge, the colonial chaplain who interviewed and recommended him for the position as schoolteacher for Nanaimo. The HBC chief traders and staff welcomed the newcomers.

Bate meets Victoria personalities

During Bate's twelve-day stay in Victoria, he met many of the early personalities of the fort including John Work, Sr., whom he described as "covered with a heavy Inverness cape and carrying a skukum walking stick. He was rather kindly inquisitive and agreeable always."[7] Work, an Irishman now retired, had spent his entire adult life working for the HBC. He purchased 700 acres that made up Hillside Farm and devoted his life to raising fruits and vegetables. His daughter Sarah married Roderick Finlayson and another daughter Jane married Dr. William Fraser Tolmie.

Bate also had tea with Judge David Cameron and his family at Belmont, Esquimalt. Cameron was chief justice of Vancouver Island and the first judge of the Colony, and also brother-in-law to Governor James Douglas. Cameron

Mark Bate served 16 terms as mayor of Nanaimo.

Island in Nanaimo takes its name from the judge although he never lived nor held office there. Bate explained the connection:

> He was the bookkeeper with the help of a clerk for the Nanaimo establishment. The books were sent by canoe from N. to E. [Nanaimo to Esquimalt] to be written up. My first job in the office of the HBC was copying Mr. C. books for transmission to England.

He described Victoria as he saw it in 1857:

> I saw the country around Victoria in all its pristine beauty and grandeur. The picnicy looking spaces between the oaks here and there struck me as charming spots which I had not expected to see in this far off land. I went to the farms, the Governers, Langfords, Skinners, McCaulys and to Craigflower; saw the school house and school master.[8]

Bate welcomed to Nanaimo

After meeting officials, the newcomers sailed on the *Recovery* arriving in Nanaimo on February 1, 1857 where Bate began work as clerk of the Nanaimo Coal Company. He was also impressed with the beauty of Nanaimo and of his warm welcome. As the ship rounded Lighthouse Point, now known as Jack Point, he saw a row of small whitewashed houses on the hillside overlooking the harbour. "The grassy slope between the buildings and the harbour looked as fresh as spring." A heavy cloud overshadowed Wakesiah Mountain (Mt. Benson). He noted that the dark green of the forest gave the place

> a rather weird aspect. The shadows of evening were coming on when the *Beaver,* after dropping the *Recovery* in mid-harbour, slowly and cautiously made her way to an anchorage near the entrance to Commercial Inlet.[9]

All the village residents, including his Uncle George Robinson, welcomed the new arrivals from the hillside. Bate gave an inventory of the village as it existed on his arrival:

> Forty-five buildings, with one exception, constructed of hewn and round logs, including the Bastion, a sawmill store and warehouse, two carpenter shops, a blacksmith shop and stable.

The exception he referred to was "the Stone House" built in 1852 by William Isbister: "A curiously constructed tenement said to be the first stone building erected in the Colony, as strongly built as a fort, walls 3 feet thick."[10] The building, used by the HBC officer-in-charge, was constructed of stones from the beaches and lime made from crushed clam shells to form the walls. The Snuneymuxw called the house, the "Tyee House."[11]

The settlers had arrived to "the wilds or dense wilderness." Bate noted how the houses were roughly constructed but despite these modest surroundings, he found "there was a brightness, a warmth of feeling in every abode."[12]

Bate enjoyed writing and throughout his lifetime in Nanaimo he wrote for various publications. Here is an excerpt from a poem in which he gave his impression of Nanaimo:

> Since first Nanaimo shores I sighted
> With what a fierce and fearless thread
> I on the rugged beach alighted
> A landing place to step upon
> Nor wharf at which to tie
> The *Beaver* anchored in the stream
> Off Cameron Isle nearby
> Kind hearts and hands e'en then were here
> To greet a stranger who had come to stay
> Of the whole souled folk he then did meet

The Bate family settled into their new surroundings. Mark became familiar with the workings of the mine operation while taking an active interest in the affairs of the town. In 1859 he married Sarah Ann Cartwright. They had ten children: Mark, Jr., Thomas Ezra, John Augustus, Emily, Sarah Ann, Lucy Alicia, Mary Beatrice, Elizabeth Ada, George Arthur, and William Charles.

News from home

Bate soon discovered getting news from home was very difficult. When mail arrived, after their being cut off from the world for weeks at a time it became a cause to celebrate. Mail arrived via *the Sir James Douglas* taking days to come from Victoria. Bate reminisced: "Postage of a half ounce letter to the old country [cost] 30 cents, and yet how gladly was an opportunity embraced to send a letter off and with what ecstasy a letter or newspaper was received."[13] When mail arrived from England six months late, it would be addressed to the designated person, care of Colviletown, Nanaimo, Colony of Vancouver Island. Also a letter sent to Ottawa had to have an American stamp beside the British Columbia one, otherwise the Postal Service in San Francisco would not accept it. "It was humiliating and unfair."[14]

More Bate family members arrive

More members of the Bate-Robinson family arrived in Nanaimo in 1862. They also travelled aboard the *Princess Royal*. This would have been the fateful voyage when two men were lost at sea rounding Cape Horn. The passenger list included Mark's sister Lucy, Miss Robinson, Joseph Bate, and William Cartwright—Sarah's brother who settled in Victoria. Lucy Bate married Peter Sabiston who had arrived on the *Norman Morison* in 1851 from the Orkney Islands. The Sabistons built a home in the Mountain District west of Nanaimo, and it was here that coal was discovered in 1879. After the successful mining venture, Sabiston managed several hotels.

George Robinson remarried, this time to Caroline Dakens in San Francisco. Now George's sister Maria was free to pursue her own career as a dressmaker in Victoria. She married John Spence, and when he died she married Harvey Snow. Mark Bate referred to Maria as his Aunt Snow.

The Robinsons returned to England in 1859, then came back to Victoria in 1864 where George pursued another career as a photographer at George Robinson's Photographic Studio. He had taken photographs in Nanaimo, but had done it quietly for "He did not think his employees would think it very proper for him to be using such fanciful equipment."[15] In 1871 he again changed career direction and studied dentistry in Olympia, Washington. The following year he finally settled in England.

Cornelius Bryant—teacher and minister

Mark Bate's cousin Cornelius Bryant replaced Christopher Finlay as the schoolteacher in Nanaimo. Bryant was a tall man with flaming red hair and beard, who loved reading and music and had a fine voice.

Teaching days

A large house had been provided for the young schoolteacher. Bryant's progress is noted on January 1858 when Governor Douglas visited during a school student examination.

> He expressed his pleasure in witnessing the proficiency and clean appearance of the children. I saw him again in the evening when he again expressed his gratification on seeing the general progress of the scholars.[16]

Despite his enthusiastic beginning as a teacher, Bryant, like his predecessor, often complained about the slow payment of his salary.[17] He was also confounded by the difficulty in getting the children to attend school, especially the young boys:

> Miners considered it more important to get a meal than an education. Sons went into the mines and daughters were expected to get married.[18]

He also deplored the way the miners lived and worked. He did not drink and was dead set against alcohol and preached against it, something that probably did not go down well with the hard-working young miners. And he also argued against "squaw men," those who took Snuneymuxw women as wives. Community leaders did not escape his criticism whom he observed as riding "their fast horses and some of them [he feared] having their fast habits also." Profanity appalled him, especially from children. Sin was sin and must be condemned.

Bryant's HBC contract was short-lived. When the Colony of Vancouver Island was transferred to the Crown, he was informed that the HBC would no longer pay his salary and that he must give up the house he had occupied. He would, however, be allotted two rooms at the end of a larger house where his Uncle George Robinson had been living.

In addition to being school-teacher and postmaster, he had also made out the accounts for the miners' wages. For this service he had received six pounds sterling a year. He continued to teach school and serve as lay minister until 1870 when he resigned to give full time to the ministry.

Bryant, the Exhorter

Bryant had been an Anglican until he met Arthur Browning, a Methodist who came to Nanaimo in 1859. Bryant subsequently converted to the Methodist church.[19] In 1864, he married Elizabeth Murdow and continued to work

Cornelius Bryant, schoolteacher.

with the miners and the Snuneymuxw. In 1867, he was appointed Exhorter to the Nanaimo Wesleyan Mission and the following year was licensed as Local Preacher of the Nanaimo circuit. He left Nanaimo for New Westminster but missed his home and returned several times. In 1875 he was ordained as a minister of the Canadian Methodist Church.

On November 11, 1877, Bryant conducted the wedding ceremony of Samuel Gough and Emily Elizabeth Woodward. Samuel was superintendent of the Wesleyan Methodist Church Sunday school and played the church organ his family had brought around Cape Horn. The church was located on Front Street, near the present Globe Hotel. Often the organ was loaded on the back of Joseph Ganner's wagon for Samuel to play at church picnics. "Samuel continued to ring the church bell for fifty years, calling the congregation to services, or for weddings and funerals, and for fires until the fire hall was built. He and Emily often supplied the church with flowers from their garden."[20]

After his wife Elizabeth died, Bryant lived in retirement with his son Wesley in Vancouver. On May 14, 1905 he died during a session of the British Columbia Methodist Conference. He was buried beside his wife in "poor black Nanaimo."

Dr. Alfred Robson Benson—frontier doctor

Dr. Alfred Benson, from Whitby, Yorkshire, spent fourteen years (1848-1862) with the HBC, and four years (1857-1861) in the HBC service in Nanaimo. Dr. Benson arrived in Victoria with the first group of Scottish miners aboard the *Harpooner* on June 1, 1849.

Dr. Benson at Fort Victoria

As the first medical officer at Fort Victoria, Benson was known to be a "sterling, honest, kind-hearted, upright man, always ready to do good." Others viewed him as "an idler, a grumbler, a political radical and rather slovenly."[21] Medical advice and medicines were free of charge and given to all in the town. He was seldom seen without a pipe in his mouth, and his rooms in Bachelors' Hall, Fort Victoria were crowded with Native artifacts, geological specimens, and books in no particular order. As well as tending to his medical constituency, he was also required to attend inquests and coroner's duties.

His college friend Dr. John Sebastian Helmcken first met him in London, England, where Benson was nicknamed "the Commodore" because he had once commanded a ship. Their meeting was a memorable one. Benson had been invited by the London Medical Society to give a report at which time his friend noted his punctuation, like his appearance, was casual. The two men next met in Fort Victoria in the spring of 1850. Benson, whose neglected appearance had been a source of consternation to his London colleagues, stood out even in a cultural backwater such as Fort Victoria. "His slovenly outfit was aggravated by a pair of seaboots, one trouser leg tucked in, the other out." Helmcken, however, was always respectably dressed. But Benson assured him that before long he would adapt to the ways of the frontier.

Dr. Benson in Nanaimo

Nanaimo was Benson's second assignment for the HBC. He arrived on December 17, 1857, and moved into the former home of Dr. Thomas, and next door to Eliza and Daniel Dunn. Eliza was a herbalist and often helped Benson.[22] The HBC Nanaimo daybook noted the departure of Thomas on February 20, 1857: "Dr. Thomas left on the steamer *Otter* having been relieved by Dr. Benson who remains surgeon at Nanaimo."

On December 19, 1860 Benson married Ellen Philips. They were together only two years when she died.

Eventually Benson left the service of the HBC and became surgeon for the Vancouver Coal Company before opening his own medical practice. When he returned to Great Britain in 1862, he was a highly respected Nanaimo resident.

Mark Bate noted:

> ## Fort Victoria—the Benson Tour
>
> Dr. Benson invited Dr. John Sebastian Helmcken on a tour of Fort Victoria. It was no more than a cluster of log buildings within a stockade and the Songhees encampment beside the harbour. Helmcken failed to notice that Benson had both pant legs tucked inside his boots, while he, Helmcken was decked out in the latest of London fashion with polished shoes.
>
> The two men set off. Benson kept a brisk pace while Helmcken struggled to keep his shoes from being sucked into the mud. The more he struggled the filthier he became and the louder Benson laughed. By the time they reached today's Beacon Hill Park, Helmcken had abandoned any hope of saving his suit. Then Benson suggested a short cut through a swamp. Deep into the bog Benson announced that he had lost the way, all the time jumping from "hillock to hillock" safely inside his boots, as his friend floundered. Finally Benson tired of the sport and with a final laugh and "I told you so!" led the way back to the fort. They were just in time for dinner with Douglas who was always punctual. They had no choice but to enter the dining hall as they were.
>
> James Douglas disapproved of Benson's political leanings and was not amused by his antics, and he soon banished him to Fort Vancouver, in the junior Helmcken's place. Benson was a man who cared little for diplomacy or rules of conduct and enjoyed a good joke. Once while having a stimulating dinner conversation with Douglas, Benson was asked by the governor why so many HBC men were bald, obviously expecting a medical answer. Instead Benson replied, "they'd sent their furs home!"[23]

It was not uncommon to meet the Doctor with his coat buttoned over by the first button through the second buttonhole, or even a more ludicrous hitch, than that … with one leg of his pants inside and the other outside his boots. He never had bottles in the surgery. When patients required medicine his first inquiry generally was "Got a bottle, eh?" or, "Go and get a bottle." He owned a sharp little Irish Terrier named Bizzie. On one occasion Job Langston was about to enter the surgery when Bizzie, who was curled up on the doormat, bit him on the leg. Langston responded with a vicious kick and Bizzie went yelping away. The Doctor came to the door and was told the trouble. Langston also explained his business, which was to have a tooth extracted. While the operation was being performed, Langston yelled a little—the lance was being rather freely applied. He continued to cry out in pain, "Oh, Oh!" The Doctor, apparently taking sweet revenge, said, "Kick my Bizzie, eh, eh; kick my Bizzie!"[24]

Benson became impatient with the tree stumps he bumped into when walking around the town after dark, so on his days off, he hacked away at the obstacles while attempting to straighten a path to his house. He soon gave up in disgust and decided it would be easier to carry a lantern after dark.[25]

The doctor also had a hobby few knew about—photography. When Francis G. Claudet, a chief assayer, visited Nanaimo in 1860 he met Benson who soon learned that Claudet was the son of A.F.J. Claudet, one of England's distinguished photographers. Francis told him the had been taught a great deal about photography from his father. When Francis said he'd left his equipment in Victoria, Benson offered to lend him his. Later Francis said,

> I paled at the sight of the doctor's equipment, did not wish to hurt his feelings that this kind man had offered me. I made the excuse that I was too busy.[26]

He regretted later that he had not asked Benson how or where he had obtained all the bulky equipment required in those early days of photography. Claudet returned to England after the assay office in Victoria closed in 1873.

Benson's coal venture

After expiration of the HBC lease, it became possible for any company to acquire property rights outside the HBC's claim. Dr. Benson had discovered coal near Chase River, south of Nanaimo and in 1863 applied to lease 3,000 acres. He was informed he could only lease the land after he had formed a company. When he was about to throw up his hands in despair at the bureaucracy, along came a wealthy Englishman, the Honourable Horace Douglas Lascelles, seventh son of the third Earl of Harewood, to his rescue. He commanded the gunboat H.M.S. *Forward* out of Esquimalt and was known to be a kind and generous man.

Lascelles established a small house on the Esquimalt Road where several young penniless Englishmen could stay. Victorians liked Lascelles, perhaps because he liked to spend money, but also because he "never made any virtuous pretensions, nor posed as a moral man."[27]

Lascelles was just what Benson needed: he was rich, sporting, and enjoyed a drink. Benson invited him to his cabin and after a few drinks asked him to become a partner.[28] The Harewood Coal Company was formed, and Benson applied for 9,000 acres of land. The Harewood Coal Company received 8,962 acres and was then in business.[29]

Mountain Named for Dr. Benson

During the summer of 1859, hydrographer Captain G.H. Richards, RN, and the officers of the survey ship H.M.S. *Plumper,* spent a week on top of Wakesiah Mountain making observations. Before leaving, they placed a large Union Jack flag at the peak, which could be seen from town until a winter storm destroyed it.[30] Richards noted that when comparing his survey notes by sea, with those of Pemberton and Pearse who had surveyed by land years before, he found an error of less than 50 feet in 100 miles.[31] The mountain was renamed Mt. Benson in honor of the colliery doctor who served the community and who figured prominently in their early memories.

The area had been known as "Pearses Plains" from 1852 when the two surveyors did their topographical survey of the district. The Snuneymuxw knew the land as Wak-Siah, a Chinook word meaning "far away." The valley at the base of Mount Benson was a traditional hunting ground for the tribe.

In order to make the mine operational Benson and Lascelles needed someone with mining expertise. Benson persuaded his old friend and neighbour Robert Dunsmuir to leave the Vancouver Coal Company mining operation and join the new enterprise for a share of the profits. After a year of trying to make it profitable, Dunsmuir realized it was a futile exercise unless he could get the coal to the ships in the harbour, something the Vancouver Coal Company could easily do being close to the water.

Dunsmuir left the troubled company, and the mine was sold to Captain Thomas A. Bulkley. It was under his direction that the aerial tramway was completed in 1874, and the Harewood Coal Company was able to compete with rival markets.

Harewood Mine Tramway

The aerial tramway of the Harewood Coal Company was an amazing sight and a bit of a novelty to the coal miners of Nanaimo when it first became operational on March 21, 1876. The owner, Captain Thomas A. Bulkey, hoped the tramway would solve his problem of getting the coal to the harbour quickly and efficiently for shipping, something that had plagued the Harewood Coal Company when Robert Dunsmuir was in charge.

The aerial tramway, the wharf, and coal bunkers were completed in November 1876. The first coal was extracted on November 1 with an output of 50 tons a day. The mine employed 53 men, of these 13 were Chinese. The latter were paid $1 per day whereas the white miners were paid $2 per day. The distance from the mine to the shipping point at Cameron Island was over 3 miles. Two hundred buckets, half of them filled with coal, travelled 4 miles per hour at a rate of 10 tons per hour over the elevated line. Four-legged tripods, ranging from 10 to 50 feet in height, supported the cable that was powered by a donkey engine at the mine.[32] Coal was shovelled into the buckets attached to the cable that was in continuous motion.

Samuel Thompson worked in the mines from age nine when he first loaded cars for his father. He escaped death three times in different mine explosions when others perished, so he felt particularly lucky. For a time he worked at the Harewood Mine, a mine with a reputation for having no gas and never having had an explosion. Like other miners, he wore a kettle-shaped lamp filled with fish oil on the front of his cap. Light came from a cotton wick emerging from the kettle spout. Although it was against company rules, Samuel occasionally took a quick ride to town in a coal bucket.[33]

William Flewett was in charge of the tramway. He saw an opportunity of using the tramway to communicate with staff at the base, so he installed a wire on the trestle of the tramway then ran it all the way down to the harbour. This became Nanaimo's first telegraph line.

Unfortunately the aerial tramway was a one-year wonder. Plagued by mechanical problems and lack of parts, it took a team of men to keep it operational. The tramway closed, as did the mine, but the tripods remained standing for another twelve years until the Vancouver Coal Company purchased the Harewood Coal Company lease in 1884 and had them taken down.

Stranded in a Coal Bucket—in Mid-air

The first person to ride the buckets was Captain Jemmy Jones, the skipper of the schooner *Industry* that transported the first Harewood Mine coal from the Cameron Island bunkers to San Francisco. While waiting for the schooner to load one day, he walked to the mine. On his return journey he decided to ride the buckets. Unfortunately for him, the engineer shut down the system for a lunch break, leaving Jones stranded between two tripods at the intersection of Albert and Wallace streets. Several young people saw his predicament and vulnerability and started taunting him. He in turn threw chunks of coal at them hoping they would go away. The police arrived and ordered Jones down. He continued to throw coal. When the buckets finally arrived at the Cameron Island bunkers, he was arrested. Jones was fined after the magistrate berated him for behaving in a way unbecoming a ship's master.[34]

CHAPTER NINE

Two Colonies—Vancouver Island and British Columbia

In 1856, Governor James Douglas was ordered to introduce an elected assembly at Vancouver Island, one of the stipulations in the original HBC grant. He knew little of electoral law or parliamentary procedures but gamely went about trying to fulfill the wishes of the Colonial Government in London. The proposed electoral qualifications, ownership of twenty acres of land, would have disenfranchised nearly everyone in Victoria and certainly in Nanaimo. The solution was to change the property requirement and give the vote to every freeholder of property worth 300 pounds sterling, thus excluding the Native population entirely.

The First House of Assembly of Vancouver Island

Four electoral districts were established with the following representatives: Sooke, John Muir; Esquimalt, Dr. J.S. Helmcken and Thomas J. Skinner; Victoria, Captain E. E. Langford, Joseph D. Pemberton, and James Yates; and Nanaimo, Captain Charles Edward Stuart. Only one complication marred the inauguration: Captain Stuart and Captain Langford lacked the required qualifications. Joseph W. McKay, now chief trader, filled the Victoria vacancy and Dr. John F. Kennedy represented Nanaimo.[1]

The seven members of the House of Assembly of Vancouver Island sat for the first time on August 12, 1856 in the Bachelors' Hall in Victoria. Chief Justice David Cameron swore them in and Dr. Helmcken was elected Speaker. Almost all the members were HBC employees. These were the men who drafted the first laws governing the Colony of Vancouver Island. While Governor James

Douglas congratulated the colony on its "slow but hardy growth,"[2] he retained a veto over all legislation.

Helmcken recorded his impressions of a few of the first members:

> Jos. Pemberton, Surveyor General, who always endeavoured to induce both sides to agree! In medio tutissima his motto. Jos. McKay, lively and active, who knew everything and everybody. The patriarchal Muir, one of the led, who had been in the Hudson's Bay Service at the coal mines at Fort Rupert—who said Aye or Nay when present. Dr. Kennedy, who voted; and last, J.S.Helmcken, innocent and ignorant of "politics," a London sparrow, too fond of nonsense and cigars.[3]

Influence of the Fraser River gold rush

Great Britain began to take notice of this far-flung colony on the West Coast when prospectors raced to the goldfields. There had been rumors of gold finds along the Fraser River as early as 1856 and on the Queen Charlotte Islands even earlier in 1851. The latter find was of little consequence, but the find on the Fraser River changed the fate of the Colony of Vancouver Island. This was the river that lured men north and east into unexplored territory.

In 1858, Victoria was still just a sleepy HBC trading post. Life however was about to change. With the California goldfields almost depleted, prospectors headed north for the Fraser River strike. The first contingent arrived in Victoria on April 25, 1858. The *Commodore* with 450 adventurers almost doubled the population overnight. Over the next few months Douglas found the settlement overrun by a torrent of some 20,000 experience-hardened men who knew no law except survival. They were anxious to get to the goldfields and wanted only supplies and transportation. Overnight Victoria became a tent city; land values skyrocketed.

Thomas Crosby, the young Methodist missionary who started his work in Nanaimo teaching Snuneymuxw children, happened to be travelling to Victoria during this gold rush period. He noted thousands of men filled the streets of San Francisco nearly all bound for the Fraser River or Cariboo:

> The steamboats, some of them not very sea-worthy, were all overcrowded, bound north. A short time before the old steamer *Republic* with eight hundred passengers, and the old *Sierra Nevada,* with nine hundred, had gone "up." And now another old coffin, the *Brother Jonathan,* which had

passed the Customs to carry only two hundred and fifty, took on eleven hundred men and was still selling tickets.[4]

The miners, he noted, "were stowed away like pigs, two in a bunk, and they did not dare to leave their bunks for fear they would lose them." They were on the steamers for eight days. There were others who ventured out in small boats and canoes and were either lost or wrecked on the Strait of Georgia. Others went overland from California by way of Whatcom and Sumas, or by the Columbia and through the Okanagan Valley.

Nanaimo also had its share of gold diggers on their way to the Fraser River. Mark Bate described the shipping schedule during the gold rush period:

> The *Beaver* came along about every six months, the *Otter* more frequently, and an Express canoe occasionally. But ere two summers had passed what a change? Toot, toot, toot! We were suddenly enlivened after what seemed the quietude of years. Ocean steamships *Commodore* afterward called *Brother Jonathan*: river steamer *Surprise* and *Seabird* three or four times a week with hundreds, yea thousands, of eager gold seekers on the way to Fraser River. This was the period of the Fraser gold excitement with all its attendant affects, when hardy pioneers of California and an impetuous host from other countries made a rush from the placer diggings of New Caledonia.[5]

Governor James Douglas, always the opportunist, took the situation in hand. He issued a proclamation similar to one issued earlier during the Queen Charlotte Island gold strike. The document stated no one could disturb the soil in search for gold "without having been duly authorized in that behalf by Her Majesty's Colonial Government."[6] Every miner had to have a licence, priced first at 10 then later at 21 shillings a month. The licensing was all quite illegal for Douglas had no jurisdiction over the mainland (New Caledonia) other than as head of the HBC. All ships entering the Fraser River without a licence or clearance from Victoria customs would be seized. To enforce regulations he placed H.M.S. *Satellite* at the mouth of the Fraser. Meanwhile, in Victoria, the money kept rolling in.

Colony of British Columbia created

Great Britain responded to the gold rush by declaring its presence in the region. On August 2, 1858, the new colony was established in London. New Caledonia could not be its name because the French had a colony with that name, instead Queen Victoria chose the name British Columbia. The HBC exclusive trading licence was revoked.[7] The Crown Colony did not, however, include Vancouver Island. James Douglas became governor of both colonies on the condition he sever all ties with the HBC. He resigned as chief factor and disposed of all his interests with the HBC to govern the two new colonies for a six-year term. He was required to establish a council and hold elections for an assembly.

Responding to a request from Douglas for a naval or military presence in the region, London sent to British Columbia a company of Royal Engineers under the command of Colonel Richard Clement Moody. They arrived in Esquimalt on Christmas Day 1858, and Moody immediately assumed his duties as commissioner of Lands and Works, lieutenant-governor, and commander of Her Majesty's land forces for both colonies. The military presence was further enhanced at Esquimalt the following spring when 160 marines arrived from Hong Kong.[8]

Moody was charged with selecting the new capital and chose Queensborough, a year later renamed New Westminster. Douglas was dismayed the capital city was not Victoria. In order to maintain Victoria's presence in the region he made Victoria a free port, ensuring that all deep-sea shipping stopped there. All the banks and major marketing enterprises would be in Victoria.

On a cloudy wet day November 19, 1858 at Fort Langley, the HBC red ensign came down, and the British flag was raised signifying the formal inauguration of the new Crown Colony of British Columbia. As the flag went up, the *Beaver* gave an eighteen gun salute.

New administration and arrival of Judge Begbie

There was a new arrival at the ceremony: Chief Justice Matthew Baillie Begbie who had been offered 800 pounds sterling a year to become chief justice in the new colony. Begbie, a tall Scot like James Douglas, had his own share of tenacity. He was born in 1819 and educated at Cambridge. As a barrister he had specialized in contract law and interpretation of wills and trusts, but he had never argued a criminal case before he received this appointment.

He became a colourful figure in the history of British Columbia, gaining a reputation as a "hanging judge" from his tenure in the Cariboo, although very few hangings actually took place in this period.

He sported a wonderful Victorian beard, shiny boots and a great wardrobe. He loved his magistrate's outfit, flashing the red cloth and white fur as he walked. He peppered his talk with French and Italian phrases.[9]

With him, justice came swiftly and in a no-nonsense manner:

My idea is that if a man insists upon behaving like a brute, after fair warning, and won't quit the Colony: treat him like a brute and flog him.[10]

He was often called upon to settle disputes in the Nanaimo mines.

At the ceremony in Fort Langley, Douglas administered the oath of office to Begbie and installed him as chief justice of British Columbia. Begbie in turn administered the oath of office to Douglas and pronounced him governor.

"Gold had been the midwife for British Columbia's birth. Gold continued to nourish the infant."[11] Within four months, $750,000 worth had been shipped out of the Fraser Valley.

Great Britain sent some civilians to help out in the new colonies; W.A.G.Young was appointed Colonial Secretary; George Cary became attorney-general and Wymond Hanly, inspector of customs. Captain W. Driscoll Gossett was appointed treasurer; the harbour master was James Cooper, and the inspector of police was Chartres Brew. These people helped Douglas govern and draft legislation.[12]

Alexander Grant Dallas—the new HBC boss

Now that James Douglas had retired from the Hudson's Bay Company to take on the new position as the governor of the two colonies, his son-in-law Alexander Grant Dallas was appointed head of the HBC western department. Dallas was born in Scotland. And he started his career in China with the powerful trading house Jardine, Matheson & Company before joining the HBC—where he invested much of his wealth accumulated in the Far East.[13] He has been described as "a capable if colourless businessman."

Although Dallas often had differences of opinion with his father-in-law, they usually reconciled. Dallas was a little annoyed when Douglas declared Beacon Hill a public park. He said that property belonged to the HBC, and Douglas had no right to give it away. The two men, however, showed respect for the other. Jane's marriage to Dallas produced nine children; they even named one son, James Douglas, after his grandfather.[14]

Unfortunately Dallas did not share Douglas' enthusiasm for the coal-mining operation at Nanaimo and instituted a new management style. Until this time two men had shared the duties; George Robinson had managed the coal operation, while Captain Charles Edward Stuart had been the HBC officer-in-charge of the town. Robinson returned to England at the end of his contract and Stuart was fired. In their places, Dallas hired a man with no HBC experience: Charles S. Nicol, who became general manager and superintendent of mines.

The management of the coal operation was now concentrated in Nanaimo. Nicol as general manager, James Farquhar the accountant and bookkeeper, Adam Grant Horne the clerk and storekeeper, and Dr. Alfred Benson, colliery surgeon.[15] This initial attention to Nanaimo was only preliminary, for Dallas never for a moment believed the coal operation could make a profit. He suggested to the HBC that the its future rested in commercial ventures, not in coal. This observation perhaps paved the way for the department stores that are scattered throughout Canada today.

Advice to migrants in the 1860s

In the 1860s, settlers began arriving in British Columbia, and not all were miners. The Overlanders made their historical trek over the Canadian prairies and across the Rocky Mountains into British Columbia. Others made the land journey through American territory into California and Oregon, then sailed up the coast to Vancouver Island. Those coming from Great Britain relied on Alexander Dallas—a considered authority on Vancouver Island—for advice on how to get to the island.

> Spring is the best season in which to arrive. The shortest route is by the Isthmus of Panama, which can be reached via New York, or by the West India steamers to St. Thomas's. The latter route ought to be adopted only in winter and spring, as the emigrant may be detained some days both at St. Thomas's and Panama, waiting for the connecting steamers, and both those places are subject to the visitations of yellow fever. St. Thomas's has been much maligned for its heat and insalubrity, but I heard a Glasgow skipper say it was the finest climate he was ever in, as he was "aye drinking and aye dry."
>
> Whether by St. Thomas's or New York, no emigrant need calculate on reaching his destination under fifty or sixty pounds. The voyage around Cape Horn can be made for thirty pounds, or even less, but generally occupies five or six months. As the passenger is fed and lodged for such a period,

some may consider this an advantage, and in comparing the voyage with the shorter one via Panama, and the cost, be of the same way of thinking as the Highlander, who complained of a professional dentist, that he charged him half-a crown for pulling out a tooth, which was done in a second, while a blacksmith dragged him all around the smithy for a quarter of an hour and charged only sixpence.[16]

Dallas also gave his opinion of the type of person needed for the Colony of Vancouver Island in this article from the *London Times,* January 1, 1862:[17]

This is not the country for broken-down gentlemen or "swells." Washing costs 72 cents per dozen. You cannot get your boots brushed under a shilling; servants' wages are five to eight pounds per month. This is enough to dismay a professional man with a family, but it is good news for the washerwoman, the shoe-black and the servant of all work. Single men can generally rough it out, and the restaurants, generally kept by Frenchmen, are far better than they are in London.

Women wanted for the colonies

Dallas complained about the lack of women in the colony, being only "one to every one hundred men at the mines." He said he did not believe any man could settle in a country without the benefit of the fairer sex, and suggested those of the "weaker sex" could easily get employment as a domestic servant with the certainty of marriage in the future. After all, he said, miners were not too particular. These women could be "plain, fat, and 50," but good-looking women would be prized.

An immigrant of such character would be a great boon to the colony as I am sure it would be to many under-paid and over-worked women who drag out a weary existence in the dismal streets and alleys of this metropolis.

No doubt his article prompted many young women in England to take a chance of a new life in the colony.

In 1862 the British Columbia Emigration Society was formed to bring women to the colony, no doubt to accommodate the young miners. The previous year, the first bride ship left for Victoria and after having stopped in at San Francisco, the women aboard were persuaded to stay in the United States. There were a few disappointed males waiting in Victoria.

In June 1862, another 60 women, with a matron to watch over them, made the same voyage aboard the *Tynemouth,* only this time they made it to Victoria. There was great excitement when the ship arrived at Esquimalt. The *Colonist* of September 11, 1862 reported that "men from every profession and trade vied for a vantage point to view their possible future companion." Most of the women were between 12 and 18 years of age.

The following year another 36 young women arrived.[18] Many of the women married and found happiness in this new land and left their mark on the history of the province.

CHAPTER TEN

Changing Players in
the Colony of Vancouver Island

The next few years were a time of great change in the twin colonies.
Queen Victoria would have been happy with her new British Empire
acquisitions. The HBC no longer held the power and control over
the everyday life of the settlers. But Governor James Douglas, whose
heart was still with the HBC, had difficulty resolving the divisions
between the young colonies he governed. Nanaimo's rich coal
resource enabled it to hold its own between the dueling colonial
governments in Victoria and New Westminster.

In September 1860, Sir George Simpson, the head of the HBC
operations in North America, died at the age of 73. He had been
active in the affairs of the company until the end. Only a few
days before he had entertained the Prince of Wales—later to
become Edward VII. Alexander Grant Dallas became head of the
empire. The family relationship between Dallas and his father-
in-law James Douglas and their allegiance to Great Britain and
the HBC must have had some difficult moments. The conflict
between the two men over the land at Beacon Hill Park shows
the complexity of their business and personal life. Dallas sued
his father-in-law in his capacity as HBC representative, claiming
that the land belonged to the HBC.[1]

Pressure for Governor James Douglas to retire

The HBC grip on Rupert's Land began to slip and there was growing
pressure on Douglas to retire. The government in New Westminster
did not like having an absentee governor of British Columbia
seconded in Victoria.

A petition circulated calling for his removal. Leading this movement was Amor de Cosmos and his *Colonist* newspaper in Victoria and John Robson with his *British Columbian* newspaper in New Westminster. Robson dismissed Vancouver Island as that "insignificant little Island which forms the natural breakwater to British Columbia." Amor de Cosmos, originally from Nova Scotia, adopted this bizarre name instead of his birth name of William Alexander Smith. Who could have foreseen that both these men would one day be premier. A Canadian politician, the Honourable Malcolm Cameron, presented the petition to the Colonial Secretary in London. This together with discussions with the Duke of Newcastle laid the groundwork for Douglas' exit from public life.

Sir James Douglas

In 1863 Douglas was knighted for his service to the British Empire. Throughout his term in office James Douglas used his own brand of authority, having little to do with democracy. Still he managed to keep a good relationship with the Native population. And it is to his credit that he handled the influx of miners during the Fraser River gold rush, reminding all that this was and would remain British territory. Sir James Douglas had been the right man during the early years of the province, but not for the years ahead.

The citizens of both colonies had a love-hate relationship with their governor The Duke of Newcastle advised him about the movement to unite the two colonies under one government. Douglas had ruled Vancouver Island for twelve years, twice the usual period for a governor, and since the Duke did not think Douglas would want to live in New Westminster as the Governor of British Columbia alone, he advised him that he intended to relieve him of both governments.[2]

Creating a new British Columbia

Now there were demands for a British system of representational government. Finding a constitution was not difficult. Great Britain had many to choose from among its colonies around the world. The best it seemed was that of Ceylon, which provided for a legislative council of five heads of governmental departments, five magistrates, and five elected representatives.

On January 21, 1864, Governor Sir James Douglas opened the first session of the new Legislative Council of British Columbia, partly elected, partly appointed—representing the union of the two colonies. He spoke of the importance of roads and the need to promote settlement. At Victoria he was honoured with a grand testimonial dinner.

In the spring, Douglas left on a European holiday. Douglas retired at James Bay, enjoying a fortune built up during his half-century in the fur trade. Following Douglas' death on August 2, 1877,[3] the *Colonist* expressed public feeling: "Today a whole Province is in tears. The country has sustained an almost irreparable loss in the death of this great and good man, who has gone to the grave full of years and honours, leaving a bright and imperishable record behind him."[4] Amelia Douglas lived until 1890, while the last of their thirteen children lived on until 1933.

New governors of Vancouver Island and British Columbia

Douglas' successor as Governor of Vancouver Island was Arthur Edward Kennedy, who was sworn in on March 26, 1864. Kennedy, "an Irish gentleman of a good type," who preferred a man to be "decidedly wrong than undecidedly right,"[5] was a former captain in the British Army who had first entered the civil service in Ireland during the great potato famine. He later served as governor of Sierra Leone and then of Western Australia.

This was the first time Kennedy had worked with an elected assembly made up primarily of men (from Victoria) who viewed government as an arm of business, especially their own. These men disliked Kennedy because he genuinely cared about the economic well-being of the colony, and he lived in grand style. He also enjoyed good food and purchased a castle for his residence.[6] In time he began to view as correct his first opinion that there were two classes of people on Vancouver Island: "those who are convicts and those who ought to be convicts."[7]

Frederick Seymour was the new governor for British Columbia, an experienced colonial administrator who had been lieutenant-governor of British Honduras. The New Westminster capital finally had a governor entirely its own. The city toasted his arrival. Seymour, full of enthusiasm and good cheer, appeared just the man for the job.

CHAPTER ELEVEN

New Mine Management and Colonial Politics in Nanaimo

The last HBC officer-in-charge at Nanaimo, Captain Charles Edward Stuart, was discharged for drunkenness in 1859. George Robinson was not available for the post, since he had already concluded his contract with the HBC and had decided to return to England. So at the instigation of HBC officer Alexander Dallas, Charles S. Nicol became the resident general manager.

The Demise of Captain Stuart

After his dismissal from the Hudson's Bay Company, Captain Charles Stuart personally financed an expedition to the Alberni Canal where he began his own trading post. He landed in the area of Ucluelet where he requested permission to purchase 200 acres of land.[1]

When the brigantine *Florencia* was wrecked in December 1860, he purchased the wreck and the cargo from the crew (the captain had drowned) for $100. Authorities in Victoria later rejected this transaction.[2]

In 1863, while doing some exploratory work on Sangster Island, south of Lasqueti Island, Stuart became ill with acute bronchitis aboard his own ship, the *Red Rover*. He died before a doctor could reach him. He was buried in the Old Cemetery in Nanaimo. For a number of years, every December 25, his friends held a memorial service for the old master. Stuart Channel, west of Thetis and Kuper islands, is named in his honour.

Although Nicol had no mining experience, he was an educated man—an engineer trained as a land surveyor, and he had served in the Royal Navy. He moved to Nanaimo with his wife, and became immersed in the affairs of the community. Nicol tried to improve mine productivity, but it was a difficult task considering the scale on which the mine operations were conducted. However, to his credit he did upgrade equipment, introduce better mining techniques, and improve coal exports.

The Hudson's Bay Company sells to Vancouver Coal Mining and Land Company

The HBC had given coal mining its best effort but its expertise lay in fur trading, not coal mining. In 1861, the company began dismantling its holdings on Vancouver Island and negotiated the sale of its Nanaimo operation. At Nicol's suggestion, a British-owned joint stock company was formed specifically to purchase the "underlying coal, together with a hundred dwelling-houses, stores, workshops, machinery, powerful steam engines, wharfs, barges, sawmill etc."[3]

The Vancouver Coal Mining and Land Company (VCML), known locally as the Vancouver Coal Company, with head office in London, managed to raise capital of 100,000 pounds sterling, of which 40,000 was used to purchase the HBC property. The deal "conveyed to the VCML, 6,193 acres in Nanaimo District facing the sea and running from near Chase River on the south to the middle of Departure Bay and including Newcastle, Protection and Cameron Islands."[4] Nicol was clearly in a conflict of interest position, but he successfully conducted the sale and at the same time kept his job as manager.

The new company prospectus gave a glowing report of the future of the coal industry in Nanaimo and the resources of Vancouver Island. "Vancouver Island must become the great centre of the commerce of the North Pacific, and a chief coaling depot for all the steamers engaged in that commerce. Steam navigation is rapidly increasing."[5] The British Navy in the Pacific needed Nanaimo coal, and the prospectus noted another market potential south of the border, "San Francisco alone consumes 14,000 tons [of coal] a month." Coal had previously been shipped from England to the United States. Nicol was confident that by reducing prices, the sale of Nanaimo coal to the U.S. could be greatly increased.

There were other facts and figures given by various resource people voicing the credits of Nanaimo coal and its location. Favourable reports came from Joseph Pemberton, a man familiar with the area and now the surveyor-general, Captain Richards, RN, and MP Edward Ellice, an HBC director. MP Charles W. Wentworth-Fitzwilliam (Viscount Milton), from Peterborough, Ontario, obviously knew the town. Fitzwilliam noted,

> A 500-ton ship can come within ten yards of the shore, within forty yards of the mouth of the pit. Within a quarter of a mile of the coal mine there is anchorage for any number of ships. It is an excellent coal, very like the West Riding of Yorkshire coal, and in a vein very near the surface.[6]

The new company had a distinguished board of directors. The first chairman MP Justice Thomas Chandler Haliburton, was a Nova Scotia lawyer who had moved to England, and is better known as a literary figure and satirist—creator of the famous comic character Sam Slick. Joining him were HBC officer Dallas and lawyer John R. Galsworthy (grandfather of Nobel Prize winner John Galsworthy) and English historian Agnes Strickland, author of *Lives of the Queens of England*. This cast of distinguished directors, who probably knew little about coal mining, formed the basis of what became the biggest mining concern anywhere in Canada during the last part of the nineteenth century.[7]

The Fraser River gold rush had generated interest from investors in Great Britain, and they looked favourably on the new company and the coal-mining operation in Nanaimo. But the honeymoon did not last long for the gold rush was small when compared to the Californian one. Adding to this were fears of hostilities between Great Britain and the United States during the Civil War. These concerns translated into discouraged British investors.

From the beginning, the Vancouver Coal Company was underfinanced and had to borrow 14,000 pounds sterling on a mortgage from the HBC. After paying a dividend of 5 percent during the first eight months, it began losing money in the mines and store. Questions were asked of management. Unlike today, shareholders were a vocal lot and soon learned that the merchandise in the Nanaimo HBC store had cost four times more than anticipated. When financial statements were made available, they recognized poor management.

The company was also criticized for purchasing a steamer to carry coal to California. The steamer was wrecked and another vessel chartered from one of the directors, no doubt from Dallas. Shareholders pointed out that under the company charter a director who entered into any contract must vacate his seat. Dissatisfaction with the board of directors reached a peak in 1864

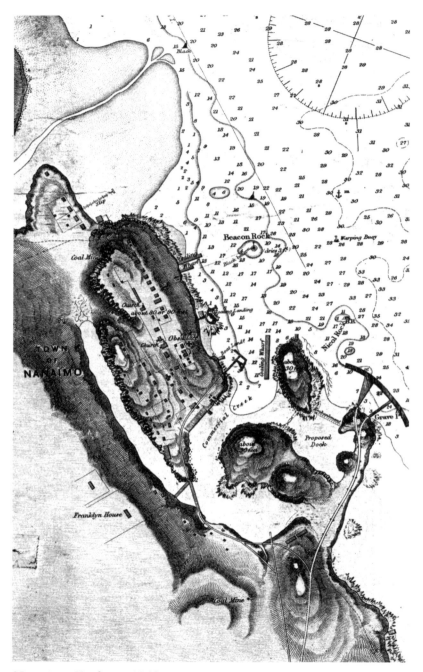

Nanaimo Harbour 1862.

when "the company sold town lots by auction in Victoria,"[8] followed by another auction in Nanaimo. Shareholders forced the directors to declare a dividend of 5 percent from the proceeds of the sale. The directors argued this money should go towards reducing the debt.

The VCML took steps to improve the coal operation by importing the first locomotive named the *Pioneer*, from England in 1863. It was immediately placed in service hauling coal to the wharves. She was the first locomotive to operate in Canada, west of Ontario.

The *Pioneer* proved her worth and substantially decreased the cost of handling the coal. At the company's first annual general meeting held in 1864, directors were so impressed they decided to add new rails and more equipment. In 1866 a second locomotive arrived from England, similar to the *Pioneer*. She was named the *Euclawtaw* after a Native group from the Campbell River area. Two more locomotives were added to the Vancouver Coal Company inventory, the first was the *Nanaimo*, almost identical to the *Pioneer*. The second was the *London*, which began work in 1884.[10]

The Tug of War

The *Pioneer* was a typical 10-ton English locomotive with an open cab, 8 x 10-inch cylinders and a boiler pressure of 115 pounds.[9]

The *Pioneer* was a curious and fearful sight to the Snuneymuxw. Wishing to stress the danger and the strength of the new locomotive, a meeting was called with the Snuneymuxw chiefs. The decision was made to make a game of the learning experience. Tracks were already laid and a length of rope attached to the engine. There would be a tug-of-war between the young Natives and the *Pioneer*. It was a battle the young men could not win. As the engine gained speed the young men valiantly dug in their heels but to no avail. Manpower could not hold back engine-power.

Sale of the Newcastle Townsite lots

The sale of lots on Newcastle Townsite was of concern to Nicol. In a letter to acting Colonial Secretary H. Wakefield dated July 25, 1864, he asked if any of the land north of Millstream River, near Nanaimo, was for sale. Nicol stated that the land in question "where Comox Road passes close by the Millstream" had been put up for sale by public auction about three years ago and there were no bidders. Now he had men interested in buying it.[11] Wakefield advised that in 1860, 47 lots in Newcastle Townsite were sold. The remaining lots of one-half to three acres were not offered at the auction "as the public did not appear disposed to bid anymore." He saw no problem

> ## Edmund Verney and the H.M.S. *Grappler*
>
> At this time Nanaimo took on new importance in the mind of one young British sea captain, Edmund Hope Verney, whose Royal Navy gunboat, the *Grappler*, visited Nanaimo on a regular basis to take on coal. In June 1864, Verney noted how the town had changed and finally had the port-of-entry status:
>
> > Nanaimo is a place that is rapidly springing into importance: a month or two ago it was declared a port of entry, and since then it has already made a start: the Vancouver Coal Company are working the mines on a large and increasing scale: they have a railroad and a locomotive engine, and the value of land is rapidly increasing.[12]
>
> The H.M.S. *Grappler* belonged to a period of transition between sail and steam, between wooden and iron ships. The ship normally proceeded under steam power, thus the visits to Nanaimo for coal, but it also handled well under sail.

with now offering the lots for sale so that "the men at Nanaimo would be able to get a lot for gardening purposes."

Coal company management investigated

In 1865, a committee was established to investigate the management of the coal company. Captain Edward Stamp was appointed to investigate the coal operation in Nanaimo. He forwarded a series of recommendations to London, which the directors expected would "reduce the expenditure for the coming year" though they chose not to divulge precisely how this would be achieved.[13]

John Galsworthy sat on the committee that produced a report criticizing the board. Thomas Haliburton claimed the report contained only partial information and urged the shareholders to hold their opinions of it. Galsworthy carried the day and was elected to the board with two of his associates from the investigation committee. Haliburton died in December, and Charles Wentworth-Fitzwilliam became chairman of the board, with Galsworthy, as his right-hand man. Other directors included George Campbell of Dickson, Campbell & Co., the Victoria agent for the coal company, and Joseph Fry and Prideaux Selby who were both directors of the Canada Agency Association.

Charles Nicol discharged

With a new board there came new policy. Instead of lavish expenditures there was fiscal responsibility. The insurance claim on the wrecked steamer was settled and the Nanaimo store sold to Thomas Cunningham & Company. Six thousand pounds were written off for what the Vancouver Coal Company considered "rubbish taken over from the HBC." A report on the "present condition and management" of the property resulted in directors' fees being reduced by one-half and Charles S. Nicol discharged. The Royal Navy veteran had been accused of making an unreasonable profit in arranging the sale between the HBC and the Vancouver Coal Company. There was little doubt he held conflicting loyalties.

Galsworthy noted Nicol owed his position to a former director

> who had a good deal to do with the affairs of the company and not to its advantage. That man's nominee had remained as financial agent [of the VCML] at a salary of one thousand pounds a year. Financial agent being another term for getting rid of money, that gentleman's services were dispensed with.

However, Fitzwilliam stated Nicol had retired from the HBC with 300 pounds as compensation for loss of salary, and that "the directors wished it to be distinctly understood that Nicol's service had been dispensed with solely with the view to economy."[14]

Charles Nicol left for Russia where he worked as a mining engineer. Later he moved to Spain as a mine general manager. Following several moves to other locations around the world, he finally retired to San Francisco.[15]

John Bryden hired

In the management shuffle that followed, Scottish miner John Bryden was hired as manager to provide expert advice in developing the coal beds. And Mark Bate was promoted to business manager.[16]

Bryden had served an apprenticeship in the Ayrshire mines before being recruited by the HBC to work in Fort Rupert. He was twenty when he sailed in 1850 for Fort Rupert aboard the *Pekin* with the Gilmour, Dunsmuir, and Dick families. There is little information about him from the time

John Bryden, mine manager.

of his sailing to his being hired again in Scotland by the Vancouver Coal Company. It is assumed he completed his contract with the HBC and returned to Scotland.

Bryden was a handsome man, over six feet tall and "straight as an arrow."[17] He married Robert Dunsmuir's eldest daughter Elizabeth in 1867. Dunsmuir both respected and admired his son-in-law and regarded him as a friend. Having him as part of the management team must have been a good mix. With Robert Dunsmuir becoming superintendent of mining operations, the local management team was firmly in place.

The coal company repaid the mortgage. Debt was reduced, and the company pushed forward to find additional coal reserves by use of a powerful diamond drilling machine brought to Nanaimo by E. B. McKay, an engineer from England. The company was the first to use this technique in North America.

Edward Gawler Prior—Solid Citizen

Edward Gawler Prior was hired to assist in the underground management and mine surveying. Prior was from Yorkshire, England, the son of an Anglican clergyman. He served an apprenticeship with an engineering firm and qualified as a mining engineer before he was hired for the Nanaimo position in 1873. He was also interested in the militia and participated in its development in Nanaimo, receiving his commission in 1876. For four years he worked with the coal company, and following the passage of the Coal Mines Regulations Act in 1877, he was appointed inspector of mines. This meant that he had to leave Nanaimo and move to Victoria.

His stay in Victoria was short, for he soon returned to settle in Nanaimo. But it was long enough to meet and marry Suzette Work, the youngest daughter of John Work of Hillside Farm who became his wife on January 31, 1878. They had four children.[18]

Like other coal company management, Prior filled many Nanaimo positions of authority. The *British Columbia Gazette* dated August 24, 1878, noted he was sheriff; assistant commissioner of lands; registrar of births, marriage and deaths; and assessor and collector under the Land Registry Act.

Prior has been described as a genial, tolerant, energetic, capable, and industrious man, an excellent businessman, and a careful administrator. And he liked the trappings that surrounded men of wealth in early British Columbia. He resigned as inspector of mines on May 12, 1880, choosing to give up government service and go into business with partner Alfred Fellows in a hardware business in Victoria. He later bought out Fellows and continued the business

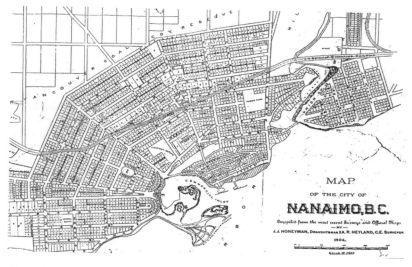

Nanaimo town plan by architect George Deverill.

by himself. E. G. Prior and Company became a major hardware and machinery business in the province and made Prior wealthy. Archibald Dick became the new inspector of mines.

Nanaimo—still a company town

The days of HBC ownership and indentured labour were over. Still, residents continued to look to their employer rather than the government for improvements to the city. The Bastion—rather than the government gunboat—symbolized community security. Even after the HBC left Nanaimo in 1862, it was the Vancouver Coal Company that owned the town and controlled the payroll.

The Colonial Government of Vancouver Island in Victoria did little to decrease this feeling of dependency. It showed no interest in funding the infrastructure of the town. Residents looked to the Vancouver Coal Company to build roads and bridges, and provide low cost housing. And for the first two decades, no one resented this coal company economic dominance. But as the population grew, some left the mines and opened new businesses on their own; others took up farming or tried other occupations.

Under the new mine management a town was laid out, subdivided and lots sold to private individuals. Those miners with property could now influence the future development of Nanaimo.

The geographic configuration of Nanaimo was a difficult one. A ravine divided the town, and the commercial area was already fully congested.[19] The town had developed along the waterfront with the early dock facilities constructed to enable the coal to be shipped out with ease. The new town plan was designed in England by architect George Deverill,[20] with the streets radiating out from the shoreline and up the hillsides, quite unlike any other town on Vancouver Island. Streets were named after HBC and Vancouver Coal Company officials, shareholders in the HBC, and royalty.[21] Not much had changed—this was still a company town.

Colonial politics— Nanaimo representatives in Victoria

Politics did not seem of particular importance to Nanaimo residents during the early colonial period. And there is little evidence anyone cared what happened in the House of Assembly of Vancouver Island in Victoria. Perhaps the miners felt they had no voice, and those who did represent the town did little to distinguish themselves to their constituency.

Dr. John F. Kennedy 1856–1859

Dr. Kennedy, who served the area from 1856 to 1859,[22] was a retired HBC employee who lived in Victoria and knew little of Nanaimo or its needs. But he had a long history with the HBC. He was first stationed at Fort Simpson on the Nass River in 1832. He was a Métis, the eldest son of Chief Factor Alexander Kennedy. Following his medical degree from Edinburgh University, he signed on with the HBC as a surgeon for a yearly salary of 60 pounds. Described as "careful and attentive" in his duties as surgeon, he was appointed chief trader in 1847 and served at Fort Nisqually and Fort Rupert, before his appointment to the first House of Assembly of Vancouver Island.

Dr. Kennedy married Fanny, the daughter of a Tsimshian chief. Kennedy knew the local customs and language and was called on as interpreter for making treaties and when gold was discovered in the Queen Charlotte Islands. He was a man of varied experience and would have been a valuable legislator. Dr. Kennedy died in 1859.

The controversy—Barnston, Swanson, or Green? 1860–1861

The next member elected was Augustus Rupert Green, and his election did not come without controversy. The man first nominated and elected was John George Barnston, a lawyer from Victoria. That election was annulled ... a campaign to draft the unwilling but elected Captain John Swanson did not succeed ... a request by Governor James Douglas allowed House of Assembly member Green to

Electoral Follies of 1859

The election of John George Barnston to represent Nanaimo has been termed "the one vote election" by historians, that one vote being from Captain Charles Edward Stuart, the only man registered or eligible to vote in Nanaimo.

The returning officer was Dr. Alfred Benson. When he posted the nomination notice he failed to note the place, time, or day the nominations would close. Since Captain Stuart was the only man present when the nominations closed, he nominated John Barnston. Dr. Benson declared him elected. The citizens of Nanaimo protested.

The writ was received in Victoria on June 2, 1859 announcing the new member from Nanaimo.[23] When the other members of the assembly learned the circumstance of how he was elected, they refused to sit with him and demanded another representative. On June 6, 1859, E.B. McKay and Joseph Pemberton introduced John Barnston. The Speaker asked if Barnston was prepared to qualify; he said he was not, and so a new writ was issued for Nanaimo.

Governor James Douglas became impatient and called the assembly to order and asked for a volunteer. Augustus Rupert Green stepped forward saying he would be pleased to represent Nanaimo. Green was sworn in by Chief Justice Cameron and served from April 16, 1860 to February 6, 1861.

But back in Nanaimo, there was no awareness of the proceedings in Victoria and the new member for their riding. Another election had been held, and this time Captain John Swanson was nominated. The Captain was well known in town; his vessel, the HBC steamer *Labouchere*, often called in for coal and freight. There were speeches for and against Swanson. Once again Captain Stuart cast the deciding vote that elected the sea captain. But Captain Swanson was not present, and the popular seafarer was not at all happy when he heard of his elevation to the assembly. And he refused to take his seat.

The people of Nanaimo thought there would be another election until they discovered they already had had a representative in Augustus Green for several weeks.

volunteer to represent Nanaimo. However Green did not last long, and within a year Nanaimo had another election and another candidate.

David Babington Ring 1861–1863

In this election Dr. Benson nominated lawyer David Babington Ring. The election in 1861 was a little livelier with 21 registered voters. Many of the miners had fulfilled their contract with the HBC and now owned property and could vote. Ring made campaign promises; he encouraged education and immigration and advocated a "restrictive economy."[24]

He even pledged himself to work towards an island highway to Victoria. If the road had been built at this time it would have cost approximately 4,200 pounds, or 60 pounds per mile.[25] One could speculate that perhaps Robert Dunsmuir would not have received the E & N Land Grant in the 1880s had the road been built. The road would have been a boon for both Nanaimo and Cowichan and would have facilitated trade between the three southern island communities.

David Babington Ring.

Campaign for an island road

David Babington Ring had an ally in newspaperman Amor De Cosmos who joined in the battle for the road. Despite De Cosmos and his power in the press, neither Ring, nor the Nanaimo constituents, were able to secure the construction of the road.

A wagon road of sorts wound its way up the east coast as far as Comox and another similar trail led to Victoria, but this trail was at the mercy of the weather; often it would be blocked by fallen trees. Legislation was passed hoping to improve the situation: "An Act to provide for the Repair, Improvement, and Regulations of roads in Vancouver Island and its Dependencies." It stated "that every male person over the age of ten years and every male and female entitled to any interest in any real estate in any of the road districts, shall perform six days labour upon the public highway, with extra days if property be extensive."[26]

A landowner or farmer could earn six shillings and three pence a day, and extra, if he had large acreage. A cart, or wagon, with a horse or oxen, was equal to two day's labour, or twelve shillings and six pence. The days of the automobile were far off in the future, but it was essential to have a road suitable for a horse and wagon. Some indication of the condition of the trail comes from a government report of 1864:

> I should say it would be advisable to complete the road as far as Nanaimo, in order that Farmers may drive their stock to and from Victoria, and in case of accident to the Steamer that letters may be transmitted rapidly. Cattle can be driven from Victoria to Cowichan in 2 days & from thence by giving them a rest at Cowichan, to Nanaimo in 2 days more. Two men only would be required to take charge of a large herd.

The road thus far, would pass through a great deal of available Agricultural and grazing Land, whereas there would, beyond Nanaimo be very little, and great risk to Cattle from wild beasts. With the exception of a little grazing at the Qualicum to Comox, and as no one would attempt to drive stock through a wild Country like this, without having some pen or enclosure to enclose them in a night.[27]

The battle to have Nanaimo declared a port of entry was equally unsuccessful. Nanaimo would have liked the same status as Victoria, but the House of Assembly thought the suggestion was premature. Ring sat in the Second House of Assembly for Vancouver Island from November 4, 1861 to February 27, 1863, and again from 1869 to 1870.

Amor de Cosmos promotes the Island road

Amor de Cosmos thought Nanaimo citizens should be outraged at the treatment the town received from government. He noted Nanaimo was practically lethargic:

> The people of Nanaimo have always been very submissive and have never dabbled in political affairs. It would be well if they would endeavour to accelerate the reforms they need.[28]

Still De Cosmos continued to wage war in print on behalf of Nanaimo and when he decided to enter politics in October 1863, the town lost a valuable voice.

In 1865, De Cosmos made an overland trip from Victoria to Nanaimo—he still had an Island highway in mind—and he wanted to see how Vancouver Island prospered. A public dinner was given in the Literary Institute attended by about 40 residents.[29] The former editor turned politician delivered his usual colourful speech attacking the policies of the House of Assembly and supporting more representation from outlying districts. The meeting was duly reported in the *Colonist* August 9, 1865, including those who made speeches, the replies, and the toasts. The people of Nanaimo liked this man.

Charles Bayley 1863–1865.

The next man to represent Nanaimo was Charles Bayley, the town's first schoolteacher, who now lived in Victoria and operated a store selling supplies to gold miners. The town probably thought they had a good man on their side, one who knew the area well and would speak for them.

Bayley served in the Third House of Assembly from September 3, 1863 to June 21 1865. Even though he knew the area well he was ineffective as a politician, choosing to devote more time to his business enterprise rather than to his constituency.[30] Nanaimo's dissatisfaction, either with Bayley or with politics, showed when a public meeting was held in October 1864 to review his political career. Only 13 people showed up at the meeting. Chairman Robert Dunsmuir dismissed the small group. It was not the barnstorming political meeting that Dunsmuir had hoped for.

Bayley's bad health caused him to sell his Victoria business and move his family to Dallas, Oregon. They made another move to San Francisco to seek further medical treatment. Charles Bayley died in 1899.[31]

Thomas Cunningham 1866

Nanaimo businessman Thomas Cunningham, succeeded Bayley on January 5, 1866 but he only served until July 25, 1866, when the two colonies united. One month into office, Cunningham, Mark Bate, and Samuel Hood tested the waters of municipal government by holding a political meeting. They condemned wasteful expenditures and set the wheels in motion towards Nanaimo's incorporation.

Joseph J. Southgate 1867

The union of the two colonies in 1866 did not create any controversy in Nanaimo, but people did seem to take a greater interest in politics at that time. Public meetings and election campaigns conducted give evidence of this interest. Joseph J. Southgate, the legislative member for Nanaimo in the Fourth House of Assembly in 1867, was the first member from Nanaimo to sit in the united parliament after the union of the two colonies.

William Hales Franklyn 1868

Before the House of Assembly reconvened in 1868, William Hales Franklyn had been appointed as Nanaimo's second representative. Franklyn, from Kent, England, had served Nanaimo and Cowichan as magistrate from 1860 until 1867,[32] so he knew the area well.

Nicknamed "The British Lion,"[33] Franklyn, a former captain of a Pacific & Orient ship, came to the colony after being discharged from the merchant navy for throwing one of his passengers into irons.[34]

His political appointment came at a time when there were conflicting loyalties over which city—Victoria or New Westminster—should be the capital of the new Colony of British Columbia.

Franklyn had already stated he favoured New Westminster being the capital city. His new constituency of Nanaimo considered Victoria its "cruel step-mother."

Franklyn was 44-years old when he was appointed magistrate at a salary of 150 pounds a year. He chose not to live in Nanaimo because he did not like any of the coal company homes offered. Instead he lived at Cob Tree Farm in the Cedar District, south of the town. When he found the daily canoe journey back and forth from Cedar up the Nanaimo River very time consuming, he reluctantly moved into town.

He built a beautiful two-storey brick mansion on five acres on the west side of the ravine. The red cedar panelling used in the interior was imported from California; and the red brick on the exterior came from England. Red cedar had never been seen before in Nanaimo. Franklyn House, at Franklyn and Dunsmuir Streets, now the site of the present day city hall, became a fashionable home where the magistrate entertained visiting government and naval personnel.[35]

For six years Franklyn conducted business for the Revenue Department of the Colony of Vancouver Island; he issued liquor licences to hotels and fined those who broke the law. But he never did win the hearts and minds of the Nanaimo residents who thought he had a salary far beyond his duties as magistrate.

William Hales Franklyn and sons.

When his term in office expired as magistrate in Nanaimo, he held a farewell banquet for his friends before returning to Victoria. He then went into private business in an auction house, but was not happy with his new career.

Captain Warner Reeve Spalding 1868

The fifth session of the House of Assembly had only one representative in Nanaimo: Captain Warner R. Spalding replaced Franklyn as magistrate. Experienced in working with the British colonies, Spalding had also served in the Crimean War. In Nanaimo he was expected to fulfill various government portfolios as well as county court judge and coroner.

Return of David Babington Ring 1869–1870

David Babington Ring returned for the sixth and seventh sessions of the House of Assembly in 1869 and 1870.

Arthur Bunster 1871

Arthur Bunster sat as Nanaimo's representative in the House of Assembly in the final session before British Columbia joined confederation.[36] He was a brewer and lived in Victoria and was a friend of Amor de Cosmos.

His opponent in the last election before Confederation was John Robson, the editor of the *Daily British Colonist.* Bunster was of the opinion he could buy his way into power by supplying Bunster Beer to the working men of Nanaimo. The vote was a narrow one; Bunster won by only 12 votes. No doubt Amor de Cosmos was delighted with the outcome.

CHAPTER TWELVE

Explorers, Missionaries, and Natives

U ntil this time much of the island lay unexplored, unlike the mainland, where mineral exploration had been successful. Governor Arthur Kennedy recognized the need for a geological survey but how to finance such a venture was a problem. He had experienced exploration expeditions in Western Australia and thought a similar expedition might be worth while on Vancouver Island. In 1863 an amount of $6,000 had been set aside "for the purpose of enabling a geological survey."[1] The following year another $5,000 was added to the project. With the government paying two-thirds of the cost and private contributors one-third, the Vancouver Island Exploring Expedition was established under Dr. Robert Brown, an eccentric young man, curious and talented. He was born in Caithness, Scotland in 1842 and arrived in Victoria in 1863.

The Vancouver Island Exploring Expedition

Brown led a team of like-minded individuals. They included astronomer, Lieutenant Peter John Leech, an ex-Royal Engineer and second in command of the expedition and a fellow Royal Engineer, John Meade. Artist Frederick Whymper, whose work on the expedition depicted the beautiful landscape of the day, had arrived in Victoria in 1862. He spent the next year in the Cariboo and in the spring of 1864 had worked building the road inland from Bute Inlet. Also included were botanist John Buttle, two university graduates Henry Thomas Lewis (Cambridge University) and Alexander Barnston (McGill University) and Ranald Macdonald whose father was a HBC chief trader and John Foley. Leech was paid a salary of $100. All other members were paid $60.[2]

119

The expedition left Victoria on June 7, 1864 aboard the gunboat H.M.S.*Grappler* for Cowichan. Here Toma Antoine or "One-armed Toma" [a.k.a. Thomas Quamtony, Thomas Anthony] joined them. He was the Iroquois who assisted Adam Grant Horne on his trip across the island to Alberni in 1856. At Cowichan Lake the group divided. Leech and his party travelled south, while Dr. Brown followed the Nitinat River. Leech's party discovered gold on what became known as Leech River, prompting a mini-gold rush.

Losing momentum at Nanaimo

The expedition party, buoyed by the gold find and anxious to make more discoveries, left on August 1 for Nanaimo. On August 6, they camped at Millstone River, then reported to the chairman of the branch committee in Nanaimo, Captain William Franklyn, who offered "every kindness and assistance." The expedition received $150 and agreed to meet the sub-committee the following day to report on their findings. Brown noted that Nanaimo was a different community from his earlier visit, and there was great "excitement about the gold discoveries."[3] The committee met the evening of August 8 at Captain Franklyn's home where Brown outlined plans for the next part of the expedition.

Captain Franklyn ordered provisions for the group, but Brown had difficulty in hiring Snuneymuxw as packers for the journey because all were working the mines. The expedition had arrived during a miner's strike that lasted from August 1864 to February 1865 because runners demanded three dollars a day. Nanaimo author Lynn Bowen wrote:

> The demand was a popular one and all the employees of the mine walked out, the miners demanding twelve and a half cents per ton increase and thirty-seven and a half cents per day on shift work. It was said that some men could not make more than two dollars per day no matter how hard they tried.[4]

The 1864 Leech River Gold Rush

In 1864, A tent city called Leechtown sprang up overnight, after the discovery of gold by the Vancouver Island Exploring Expedition. Hundreds of gold-seekers boarded steamers plying the waters between Victoria and Sooke. Even Governor Arthur Kennedy hiked in to visit the site. However, it was soon evident that reaching the gold-bearing gravel beneath the giant boulders would be a monumental task. Disappointed miners left for other strikes. During the first hectic year it is believed that $100,000 was taken out.

Each day the Snuneymuxw village was canvassed for workers but only old men and women remained there. Brown was afraid his own men would desert the expedition. His frustration shows in the journal of the Nanaimo visit:

> Friday, August 12, 1864: Tomo of course drunk. I was compelled to keep the men quiet to advance a little money of their pay which pretty much used up all the cash I had remaining over, and of course we had to return our hospitality slightly but this is essential especially in a community like Nanaimo where it is important that the good will of the people should go with the Expedition.

In hiring Snuneymuxw helpers, Brown asked for help from Mine Manager Charles Nicol. He sent for one of the chiefs who promised to try and help "but these Chiefs have little influence and do not like to interfere in making bargains with white men," Brown noted in his journal.

On this day a steamer arrived in Nanaimo from Burrard Inlet and the crew reported that "nobody was there and no lumber—all had gone to Sooke." The gold find at Leech River had even sparked interest in the Colony of British Columbia. Finally Captain Franklyn succeeded in hiring a few Snuneymuxw and "obtaining their marks to a paper with the Government Seal to it. Pay $1 per diem, a pair of boots and a premium of 12 1/2 cents for every deer killed with the proviso that at least one week's notice is to be given before leaving."

The next morning the expedition prepared to leave but only three Snuneymuxw showed up, the other two would not come because someone had told them they would not be back until the snow was on the ground and this frightened them. Captain Franklyn sent a policeman around and succeeded in obtaining one more. There is little doubt Brown was completely frustrated with the turn of events in Nanaimo. He noted on Saturday August 13, 1864:

> The labour and vexation I have had during the week cannot scarcely be conceived & all the brunt had to be born by myself alone as none could help. With cultus men they would not strike bargains and those who ought to have assisted me preferred to give me all the labour and take the honour if all went well and who never were amiss to lay the blame and responsibility on my back. It was not too late to start. Concert in Nanaimo in the evening. I am now fretting to be off—not only to go on with our work but to keep the men out of the way of excitement and desertion.[5]

The next day was a Sunday and the Snuneymuxw refused to work on the Sabbath. "Thanks to Brother Crosby, the Indians would not travel on Sunday, so we were detained another day."[6] Another day was lost. Brown visited the Harewood Coal Company claim. Finally on Monday the Snuneymuxw showed up for the trip, and Captain Leech's party was able to leave "each Indian with 100 lb. On his back!"

Once again the expedition party broke up; Leech was to travel up the Nanaimo River and then via Cowichan Lake head for Barkley Sound while Brown continued on to Comox. Brown appeared to have difficulty with Leech. He noted the gold find seemed to have turned the Captain's head:

> Vanity, &c &c. I trust that he will perform his duty as he has every advantage. He had the pick of the men and the part of the country he wished to explore.

On to Nanoose Harbour and Comox

Robert Brown withdrew $250 of committee funds from the Bank of British Columbia—no relation to its namesake today—with the help of Charles Nicol who was also branch manager. The bank had just opened in Nanaimo. Another Native couple was hired to take Brown and his party to Comox. "I found it was impossible to haggle about engaging Indians here though several Comoucs applied to me—but I knew that the prices asked were exorbitant." The Reverend John Booth Good requested and was granted passage to Comox. The expedition received a rousing farewell from Nanaimo:

> Embarked at 10 a.m. Messrs. Franklyn, Turner & c [Co.] saw us off and we cheered, and [were] re-cheered by them and the crew of H.M.S. Forward which was lying in the harbour. Passed the old works of Hudson's Bay Company & the Town of Newcastle the voters on the town lots of which can turn the tide of an election at Nanaimo. On getting outside found the wind ahead. Camped at Blunden Point.

The following day Brown and his party put into Nanoose harbour to shelter from gale-force winds. The Nanoose tribe that frequented the area was almost extinct. Many had died of disease or intertribal war, and those remaining had since moved in with the Snuneymuxw. The HBC Nanaimo daybook noted on October 9, 1855, that a northern tribe had massacred all the Nanoose tribe.[7] Brown observed there were only twelve still alive, and all their chiefs were dead.

Brown's expedition continued on to Comox where coal was discovered. Then they journeyed south into the Alberni Valley where they met up with Leech and his group.

Return to Victoria

The expedition arrived back in Victoria on October 21 after four and one-half months. Brown immediately reported to Governor Arthur Kennedy: "Had a most flattering reception and long talk of a couple of hours."[8] A month later an exhibition of 32 of Whymper's drawings was mounted.

Among the Snuneymuxw
—missionaries Demers, Crosby & Good

Dr. Robert Brown's journal clearly showed the influence of Methodist missionary Thomas Crosby in the lives of the Snuneymuxw. Crosby had only been with them a year when the Vancouver Island Exploring Expedition passed through Nanaimo. But within that short time he had established the Sabbath as a day of rest.

Brown was not, however, the first to preach to the Nanaimo Natives. Catholic Bishop Modeste Demers preached in Nanaimo for a short time in 1855. He was the consecrated Bishop of Vancouver Island, with responsibility also for the British territories on the mainland. Reverend John Booth Good arrived to strengthen the Anglican mission in Nanaimo in 1861.

Nanaimo—Crosby's mission calling

Thomas Crosby's mission began in March 1863 when he was asked to go to Nanaimo to teach the Snuney-muxw children. Cornelius Bryant welcomed the new member of the church. Soon Crosby was firmly established in the village, in a schoolhouse-cum-church building built in 1861 by the Reverend Ebenezer Robson, brother of newspaper publisher John Robson. The arrival of Crosby allowed Reverend Robson to spend time with other duties. Crosby spent the next six years teaching and administering the gospel.

Nanoose Bob
—Native Tracker

Nanoose Bob, a noted hunter, would have been living at the time of the Nanoose massacre in 1855. He could stay in the woods for days when tracking bear or deer using only a bow and arrow. Mark Bate received gifts of skins and elk antlers from him. Bate wrote that Bob was a "very determined person and would never accept defeat when in the quest for game."[9] Nanoose Bob married eight times; his last wife Mary lived to be 97.

Crosby wrote a book about his experience, entitled *Among the An-ko-me-nums of the Pacific Coast*. Published in 1907, it detailed his experience as an early missionary in Nanaimo. He was born in Yorkshire, England in 1840 and at age sixteen came with his parents to Woodstock, Upper Canada. Two years later, in 1858, the Methodist Church sent out the first band of missionaries to work in Victoria, Nanaimo, New Westminister, and Hope.

The young man had always held deep religious views so it was no surprise that he decided to listen to his heart. He left Woodstock on February 25, 1862 and crossed the Niagara River. In New York he boarded the S.S.*Champion*, crowded with 500 men, mostly headed for the Fraser River or the Cariboo gold mines. At Panama he boarded another vessel, the steamer *Golden Age*, sailing for San Francisco with 1,500 aboard. There he changed ships to the barque *W.B.Scranton* for the ten-day trip to Victoria, arriving on April 11. Crosby spent the next year working on road construction in Victoria before his calling to Nanaimo.[10]

Crosby and the Snuneymuxw

Among Crosby's first tasks was finding clothing for the Snuneymuxw children. Crosby described the Snuneymuxw children as:

> wild-looking little people with painted and dirt-begrimed faces and long, uncombed hair. Some were clothed in little print shirts, others had a small piece of blanket pinned around them, while some had no clothing at all.

Friends in Victoria sent used clothing, but unfortunately the garments were too large and had to be "fixed up." A group of women from the community under the direction of Mrs. Phoebe Raybould of Raybould's Millinery shop, sewed and altered the clothing until all the children were dressed.

Another of Crosby's tasks, mastering the Snuneymuxw language, was not so easy. He began by making a small dictionary with English words and their Native equivalent. He sat for hours at great feasts listening to the elders, who were great orators, tell of earlier days and battles. The children also helped by repeating words in their own language. Slowly he learned, and eventually he could teach and preach to the Snuneymuxw in their own language.

Crosby held regular religious services and taught the children and sometimes their parents as well. Amos Cushan, or Kook-shin, was Crosby's first convert and served as his assistant for many years. Crosby seemed particularly pleased with the 1864 conversion of the eleven-year-old boy Sa-ta-na, baptized as David Sallosalton, who later became a missionary. Unfortunately, he died at age nineteen from "lung trouble," after falling through the ice while crossing the Fraser River on his way to preach to his fellow Natives.

Crosby alternated visits to other island communities with the Reverend Edward White. In many ways Crosby taught by example. By cultivating a small garden in front of his mission house, the Snuneymuxw were inspired to plant fruit trees and grow vegetables.

Crosby left Nanaimo in the spring of 1869 to take up a new mission at Chilliwack. There is little doubt he influenced the lives of the Snuneymuxw. As to how many actually embraced the new religion, he recorded in 1872–3 that there were: 108 Native members in British Columbia. Victoria had 18; Nanaimo 36; New Westminster 4; and Chilliwack 50.

Unhappy tales of alcohol consumption

Alcohol was the scourge of many in those early years. Taverns were like social centres in the community, a place where the miners could congregate and socialize after a day in the mines. However, it was against the law to sell liquor to Natives. Joseph McKay noted in his journal August 11, 1854: "Received an Act from Governor Douglas prohibiting no gift or sale of intoxicating liquor to Indians." Still many local establishments continued the practice, some ending up in court.

A notorious resort at Departure Bay, named "The Synagogue" became a source of consternation in Crosby's fight against alcohol. He suspected it was here the local tribe and other visiting Natives got their supply of liquor. At the time of the proprietor's licence renewal, Crosby circulated a petition against it. Many prominent men in town signed the petition. The magistrate took note of the petition and said he could not renew the licence on that day. However, only a few days later, the licence was granted. The proprietor took the petitioners to court but did not include Crosby whom he figured was not worth "the powder and shot; he has no money." A lawyer hired to defend the case advised the petitioners to get evidence that whiskey was being sold to the Natives.

With the help of two Native friends Crosby lay in wait near "The Synagogue," and watched as his two friends each purchased a bottle of whiskey. Crosby had all the evidence needed. When the proprietor discovered what had happened he did not proceed with his case. The following spring the lawyer brought the matter to court, the proprietor lost his liquor licence, and was fined several hundred dollars.

Natives Decimated—Smallpox & Other Epidemics

It was not only alcohol that destroyed many in the villages. In the spring of 1862 the Native population in the colonies was hard hit by a smallpox epidemic. It was speculated the disease reached Victoria from San Francisco where several cases had been detected. Every spring large numbers of Haidas camped near Victoria having made their way down the coast in their big canoes. The *Colonist* newspaper raised the alarm first and suggested citizens should be vaccinated; and it warned the disease could reek havoc on the Native population unless sanitary measures were adopted.

In Victoria, Dr. J.S. Helmcken vaccinated hundreds but it was a little too late. Many deaths occurred in the Native village. The situation grew into a crisis. So many were infected that the Indian Hospital in Victoria could not accommodate them. Many were evicted from the city, and their homes burned. In mid-June, about 300 Haidas left Victoria in 26 canoes for the Queen Charlotte Islands. A gunboat accompanied them as far as Nanaimo, to prevent their enemies ambushing them along the way.

> Each group of Natives returning to its village brought with it the plague until even the remotest inlets and bays along the coast were filled with the dead and dying.[11]

Despite the efforts of Nanaimo and Cowichan missionaries vaccinating many, the grim armada worked its way up the coast carrying the dreaded smallpox disease. They were forbidden to land in Nanaimo. At every camp some died. Wooden pyres consumed

Tragedy of Quee-lawt and Native Females

On one occasion Reverend Thomas Crosby found three women hopelessly drunk by the roadside near the sawmill. He noted it was not uncommon to see women drunk. They had with them a little girl named Quee-lawt, the brightest and most attractive of his pupils. She had not had her forehead flattened as some of the other children had, and she learned quickly and sang sweetly. He had great hopes for her future.

Sadly Quee-lawt was drunk and had been molested by white men. The rough treatment she had received overcame the little girl. She was carried to the chief's house where she died that night.

Many young girls were sold to white men as slaves. Crosby noted in 1906, several girls were sold from $300 to $1,200, while others were sold for as little as a blanket, or a piece of gold. The mission house became a refuge for those trying to escape their masters.

the dead as the funeral armada proceeded up the coast. One canoe found floating in the Strait of Georgia contained only dead bodies. At Cape Mudge the Euclataws ambushed a party of Haidas heading home, and they caught the disease as part of their spoils.

The death toll was a heavy one. At the beginning of the nineteenth century, there were about 80,000 Natives in what is now known as British Columbia. It has been estimated that about 20,000 perished between 1862 and 1864, and their numbers continued to decline for years to come.[12]

It was not only smallpox that cut deeply into the Native population: epidemics of measles, influenza, tuberculosis, and others also took their heavy toll. Venereal disease, a result of prevalent prostitution, killed many and rendered many more infertile.

Alcohol, introduced as an item of trade, was also the direct or indirect cause of many deaths. Intertribal warfare also took its toll. The introduction of firearms made these skirmishes more lethal, and death rates were high resulting in many tribes being exterminated.

Snuneymuxw burial customs

The Snuneymuxw feared death, and bodies were quickly placed in a box and placed out of sight. The old custom was to place the boxes in trees or on scaffolds to keep them away from animals. Later they were placed in the ground.

One poor man in particular neared death. When Reverend Crosby visited the man's son, and inquired about the elderly man, he was informed the old man was in a cedar box. When the missionary checked, he found him crowded in and doubled up, his head between his knees, but still alive. Although the man was removed at once, he died the following day.

Crosby wrote about an incident at a Snuneymuxw burial ground on Cameron Island (confirmed by Mark Bate). Because the mining company planned to build a wharf to allow ships to berth and take on coal, they arranged with the chiefs to vacate their villages on the shoreline of Commercial Inlet, including Cameron Island. The payment was two large bales of HBC blankets. A 40-acre piece of land had been set aside as a reserve near the estuary of the Nanaimo River. The Snuneymuxw were then hired to remove the bodies from Cameron Island burial ground to a new cemetery on the reserve. Coffins were brought to each grave to intern the remains. Because of the presence of hardpan or rock, the graves were quite shallow. Unable to complete the task before nightfall, the coffins were left beside the graves. Crosby wrote:

Next day a great outcry was made in the camp, and intense excitement prevailed, for most of the boxes had risen up and had come out of the graves. We went down to discover the cause of the disturbance, and what had seemed to the poor people so strange and uncanny had been caused by the heavy rain of the night before filling the shallow graves and floating out what they contained. It took some time to quiet the fears of the people.

Several of the coffins floated out into the harbour. Mine manager Charles Nicol hired white labourers to finish the job. The Snuneymuxw believed disturbing the dead was a bad omen.

Cameron Island became the site of a small jetty in 1858, and the new wharf was built in 1864. Mark Bate noted that it took years to complete the transformation of Cameron Island from a burial ground into a first-class shipping centre, "second only to Cardiff, Wales."

Reverend John Booth Good

Another man who influenced religious life in Nanaimo was the Reverend John Booth Good, an Anglican. It was he who wished to accompany Robert Brown and the Vancouver Island Exploring Expedition to Comox. He arrived in 1861 only 10 days after his wife Sarah had given birth. Son John Roland was the first of 12 children born to the couple.

Reverend Good's appointment fulfilled an obligation to the Society for the Propagation of the Gospel in Foreign Parts (S.P.G.) who paid his salary. His stated mission, other than to convert Natives, was to build a church and minister to the coal miners. His superior, Bishop George Hills had determined he must strengthen the church in Nanaimo.and noted:

> This Community must be reformed ... unblushing vice which now lifts itself on high and stalks abroad must be made to cower and hide its hideous head from the gaze of the public eye and eventually be crushed out of our midst.[13]

Reverend Good soon discovered most of the Snuneymuxw knew the basics of Christian religion but he found their living conditions were less than desirable. He noted they were "living in very dirty and wretched condition on a tongue of land adjoining the Dunsmere mine."

Moving the Snuneymuxw

The Snuneymuxw no longer were regarded as essential to the coal-mining operation, even though it was their hard labour and knowledge of the area that led to the development of the mines. By 1862 their presence in the town and their longhouses' proximity to the white population, were thought to be a nuisance by mine management. Charles Nicol initiated their move to the reserve to the south by the Nanaimo River. A move which Reverend Good wholeheartedly supported, hoping that by isolating the Snuneymuxw they would be away from white temptations. With the assistance of Nicol, who was a friend of Bishop Hills and was active in the church, the band moved to the new location "complete with new whitewashed houses." This was the year of the smallpox epidemic, and Reverend Good, like Crosby, assisted in the vaccination program.

Reverend Good thought the move benefited the Snuneymuxw and that the only losers were Crosby and his Methodists who had built a school near the old Native village. Crosby never mentioned this in his Nanaimo narrative other than to comment on the burial ground at Cameron Island. However, Reverend Good suggested the Methodists should retire from the field and transfer the school to the Church of England.

The churches disagree

The disagreement between the two churches brought the Reverend Ebenezer Robson and Bishop George Hills to a meeting in Victoria on November 25, 1862. Robson said the Methodists were first in the field and the Anglican Church was intruding, and the undue competition could harm Christian work. Bishop Hills left no doubt where he stood on the issue. He firmly supported Reverend Good and told Robson that Nanaimo was big enough for both, that when the S.P.G. missionary was appointed the Methodists had no regular school, and that a one-hour Sunday visit did not constitute a Methodist mission, and it was not reasonable that the Anglicans should retire. The Methodists first established residency in Nanaimo with the appointment of Reverend Arthur Browning on February 17, 1859. The fight for the souls of the Snuneymuxw continued.

The Anglican parish stretched from Cowichan in the south and to the west and north. Reverend Good directed attention to the north where contact had been made through the Comox Natives who visited Nanaimo. He pre-empted land in Comox for a church, using his own name to take advantage of a loophole in the system. On the receipt of the Crown grant he transferred title to the church. This was only one of several parcels of land he acquired for the church.

The Snuneymuxw appeal to Queen Victoria

Governor Arthur Edward Kennedy visited Nanaimo in November 1864 to lay the cornerstone for the Literary Institute Hall. The town extended a warm welcome to the governor and his family. In his honour, buildings were decorated with flags and evergreens and stores lit with coal oil and candles. The governor led a procession to the site of the new building where he was met by a guard of honour composed of four uniformed Snuneymuxw constables.[14]

During his visit he met with the Snuneymuxw who saw their land and resources being exploited without benefit to their people. They asked Kennedy to send their words to the great Queen Victoria:

> We, the Nanaimo Indians, have long wanted to see you and speak our hearts to you; and we want Mr. Crosby to translate our words. This day our hearts are made very glad because we see you. You, Mr. Kennedy, have come from our great Queen, and we hope you have some good words to speak to us from her. We are poor dark Indians. You white people know more than we do. If all white people who come here were good, it would be better for us; but many teach our people to swear and get drunk. We hope you, our Governor, will speak strong words to them. Our hearts are very glad that good white people have sent ministers of the Gospel to us, who tell us good things about God and teach our children to read. We want them to know more than we do. We want to keep our land here and up the river. Some white men tell us we shall soon have to remove again; but we don't want to lose these reserves. All our other land is gone, and we have been paid very little for it. God gave it to us a long time ago, and now we are very poor, and do not know where our homes will be if we leave this.
>
> We want our land up the river to plant for food. Mr. Douglas said it should be ours, and our children's after we are gone. We hope you, our new chief, will say the same. We have over 300 people in our tribe, though a number are away fishing now. Many are old and not able to work, and some of our children, who have neither father nor mother, have no clothes. We hope you will be kind to them. Our hearts are good to all white people, and to you, our great white chief. We hope you will send our words to the great Queen. We pray that the Great Spirit may bless her and you. This is all our hearts to-day.[15]

Like many other tribes in British Columbia, the Snuneymuxw population had declined. They were no longer the vibrant community of families that had welcomed the HBC to Nanaimo. The smallpox epidemic had taken some, and whites seemed to think the "Indian problem" would eventually disappear. The treaty signed by James Douglas had left the hope among Natives that the land given would be theirs forever. Now as the population of Nanaimo grew, the elders could only sit and watch as their people became poorer and poorer, and as the coal resources were exploited.

Douglas had treated Natives as British subjects with equal rights and had favoured the mixing of the races. Under his successor Joseph Trutch, "segregation and inequality would now be the hallmarks of provincial policy."[16]

CHAPTER THIRTEEN

Coal Mining Expands and Nanaimo Attempts Incorporation

Most of the mining activity in Nanaimo now centered on the Douglas pit, at the head of Commercial Inlet, the largest mine in the area. There were a number of smaller mines such as the Park Head, the Dunsmuir, and another smaller mine on Newcastle Island. Robert Dunsmuir, as an independent collier, was not a popular employer; miners objected to working for a contract miner, especially one with such hard-line work ethics. There was also a new ethnic mix added to the mining community in 1867 when the Vancouver Coal Company hired the first Chinese labourers.[1] Within a few years they were employed in a variety of jobs both underground and in surface work.

Robert Dunsmuir finds coal at Wellington

In 1869, Robert Dunsmuir began prospecting for coal with Jimmy Hamilton, and they discovered a seam at Diver's Lake in the Wellington District, a few miles north of Nanaimo. The discovery resulted in a major expansion in the coal mining industry in the area. In a letter to the federal Minister of Public Works, the Honourable Hector-Louis Langevin, Dunsmuir wrote about the discovery:

> When I was in the bush about three miles from the sea, in the month of October 1869, not exactly for the purpose of prospecting for coal, but being thoroughly acquainted from past experience with all the coal formation in this country, I came across a ridge of rock, which I knew to be the strata over-lying the lowest seam that had as yet been discovered here. A short time afterwards, I sent two men to prospect,

and in three days discovered a seam of coal 3 1/2 feet in thickness, 30 feet below the tops of the ridge, dipping S.E. one foot in six.

After procuring from government a right to further prospect, I sunk slope 97 and two thirds yards in the seam, and mined therefrom about 500 tons, twenty-five tons of which were taken on board of H.M.S. *Boxer*, for trial.

As I was again strolling through the bush about ten weeks ago, about 200 yards from the place I had determined to work, I chanced to come upon the root of a fallen tree, which I thought had a peculiar appearance. On examination I found coal sticking on the upturned root, and digging a little under it, I saw that coal had been there, but was not removed by the action of fire. I then sent for two of the workmen, who brought picks and shovels, and in half-an-hour, we discovered a seam of coal left 3 feet thick, the top of course having been consumed. I set the men to work about 80 yards further to the dip and 9 feet below the surface found the seam of 9 feet in thickness. [2]

Dunsmuir needed capital to operate the mine so with his sons Alex and James took on a partner, Lieutenant Waldham N. Diggle of the H.M.S.*Grappler*. Diggle signed on for $12,000 just enough to get his name on the HBC papers, Dunsmuir, Diggle & Company. All of the decision-making was left in the hands of the twenty-year veteran miner Robert Dunsmuir.

There were two major markets for Nanaimo coal: San Francisco and the Royal Naval vessels stationed at Esquimalt. The former was the more lucrative, but in order to get coal to that market Dunsmuir needed a fleet of coal carriers. He formed a partnership with San Francisco businessman Henry Berryman to distribute Wellington coal from Berryman's sales office in San Francisco, and to charter ships to run between the Golden Gate and Departure Bay.[3] The first major contract was with Pacific Mail Steamship Company who signed a five-year deal to buy Wellington coal. This was the same company that had a contract with the HBC for Fort Rupert coal. A loading wharf was then built at Departure Bay, large enough to accommodate the Pacific Mail steamers.

Wellington townsite

Before long the countryside to the north of Nanaimo was cleared to make way for what became the vibrant community of Wellington. Dunsmuir's company land now encompassed 5,000 acres. In the

Author's interpretation of the old Wellington Mine engine house 1875.

beginning he offered his employees 500 town lots at $5 and $10 each, but most preferred the cheaper company-owned houses rented for $6 a month.[4] These small two-roomed cottages were clustered around the pithead. His decision to subdivide land was soon reversed; perhaps Dunsmuir realized it would be more advantageous to have his men in company-owned houses. Single men found accommodation in the company's boarding house managed by Walter Akenhead; visitors could room at Thomas Wall's Wellington Hotel at Diver Lake, or the Bay saloon operated by Joseph Harper.

The community also boasted of having a Methodist church under Reverend William Sexsmith, plus a school for 100 pupils and a general store. The colliery doctor was Dr. William McNaughton Jones. Dunsmuir also had 100 acres in farmland to raise feed for the animals used in the mine operation. A narrow gauge railway was built to carry coal to the loading wharf where a small fleet of steamers, the *Barnard Castle,* the *Hilton Castle,* plus a powerful tug, the *Alexander,* waited to move the coal. The steamers made two trips to San Francisco every month.[5]

The competition—the East Wellington Colliery

The Wellington coal seam appeared unlimited. When a coal seam was discovered on the Westwood Estate, three miles east of Wellington, Dunsmuir tried unsuccessfully to obtain the coal rights.

William Westwood had operated a farm there since 1864. When he died, he left his widow and their ten children the estate. The Westwood family sold 600 acres, with the coal rights, to San

Franciscan Richard Chandler, for $150,000. This became the East Wellington Colliery.

Another small railway named the East Wellington Colliery Railway, was constructed to run from new wharves on the south side of Departure Bay, five miles out to the Westwood property, almost at the back door of Dunsmuir's property. This too was a narrow gauge railway, and had two engines named the *Premier* and the *Columbia*. Now Dunsmuir had more competition.

The canny Scot watched as the new mine enterprise developed at his back door for seven more years until one day Dunsmuir discovered Chandler had trespassed and mined Dunsmuir coal over his boundary. A lawsuit ensued; Dunsmuir won and took over the railway connecting it to his own.

The *Duke* and *Duchess*

Dunsmuir improved the movement of coal in 1878 by importing two locomotives named the *Duke* and *Duchess* to replace the teams of horses and mules that were used at the start of the operation. Dunsmuir had seen the *Duke* at the 1876 American Centennial Exhibition. The *Duchess* was assigned to the Departure Bay wharves while the *Duke* worked the yards at Wellington. Later the small Wellington Colliery Railway was incorporated by an act of the legislature.[6] This was the first railway to be built on Vancouver Island. It had a 3-foot narrow gauge with 42-pound rail and carried coal from Wellington to Departure Bay. The Duchess pictured below is now on display in Carcross, Yukon.

The Robert Dunsmuir family

Robert Dunsmuir has been described as "diminutive, and fine-boned, a quick-to-anger bantam cock of a man" who possessed a relentless capacity for hard work.[7] Others called him a robber baron because of the low wages he paid employees. However, in Nanaimo, he was and still is regarded with pride. There were few civic committees that sat without his input; he was a power to be reckoned with. As the success of his coal mining enterprise increased, so did his influence.

Robert Dunsmuir.

Son Alex was 25 when his father sent him to San Francisco in 1878 to set up a sales office there. Then Dunsmuir ended his association with Henry Berryman. Dunsmuir always considered Alex more capable than his eldest son James, and over the years he had made it clear he thought his younger son would be his true successor. It was Alex he called when there was a crisis. Unfortunately, like his father, Alex enjoyed a good whiskey, and his fondness for liquor would ruin his life. He also became enamoured with Josephine, a married woman who divorced her husband and moved in with him. His parents never acknowledged their son's love interest and always referred to her as "that woman from San Francisco."

Meanwhile Dunsmuir thought enough of James to make him manager of the mine at Wellington. James had been trained as a coalminer at his father's hand from 1869 to 1872. After attending a military academy in Virginia where he gained engineering experience, he rejoined the mines becoming superintendent in 1876. This same year he married Laura Surles, from North Carolina. They met while attending college in Virginia. The couple had 12 children. Laura's southern charm made her a welcome addition to the social scene in Wellington and Nanaimo.

Dunsmuir now controlled the entire coal operation, from the mine in Wellington to its sale in California. He did not like having partners and was reluctant to share power and authority, even with Alex and James. He said in 1871, "I know I can bring the undertaking out more successfully by not having too many voices in the matter."[8]

Alex and James were never given shares in the company nor did they receive regular salaries. Their only compensation was living expenses as needed. "Take what you want, just don't want too much," their father told them.[9] Dunsmuir ended another partnership, this time with Diggle. The latter received a nice profit on his investment namely $600,000. The company was renamed R. Dunsmuir and Sons.

Dunsmuir and wife Joan had other children, but only the two boys played a role in the business. All the other children were daughters. The couple arrived here with daughters, Elizabeth (1847) and Agnes (1849); Marion was born in 1855, Mary Jean in 1862, Emily Ellen in 1864, Jessie in 1866, Annie in 1868, and Henriette Maude in 1872.[10] Joan was preoccupied with raising children at a time when Dunsmuir could little afford a housekeeper or nanny. Those who knew her say she was a good mother and the backbone of the family. Robert valued her advice and often consulted her on business affairs. To convince her to come to Vancouver Island he promised her a castle, but that was in the future.

Daughter Elizabeth married John Bryden, a man Dunsmuir admired and respected. The two men had signed their HBC contract about the same time in Scotland.

Newcastle Island coal

While Robert Dunsmuir furthered his coal empire, Newcastle Island, the small island adjacent to Nanaimo, showed promise in another endeavour. Joseph Emery paid a visit in 1869 and confirmed what everyone in the Nanaimo coal industry had known for years, that there was sandstone on Newcastle Island of unusually high quality.

But initially Newcastle Island was an early coal producer. Captain John Palliser commanded the British North American Exploring Expedition (1857-1860). Dr. James Hector, the expedition geologist, was asked by the Royal Geographical Society to examine the coal strata of Vancouver Island. His report appeared in the quarterly journal of the society in November 1861.

At Nanaimo, as on Newcastle Island, there are two seams, the "Newcastle" and the "Douglas. The first of which is everywhere about six feet in thickness, with sometimes a floor of fire clay, but more generally of sandstone. The roof consisting of a fine conglomerate bed, about sixty feet thick, on which rests the Douglas seam, with an average thickness of from three and a-half to four feet ... The coal from Nanaimo is as yet admitted to be the best in the market.[11]

There were attempts to mine coal on Newcastle Island, first by the HBC, then by independent contractors. When the HBC sold its

Newcastle Island Sandstone and the San Francisco Mint

It was not coal, however, that would identify Newcastle Island, but the stone with the "salt and pepper" appearance. At first small amounts were removed to build fireplaces. No one thought of the importance of the product until Joseph Emery paid a visit in the summer of 1869. Emery had been contracted to build the new United States Mint in San Francisco and had heard reports on the quality of the sandstone at Newcastle Island. Accompanied by Mark Bate, he inspected the stone and found it superior to anything he had seen before and signed a five-year lease agreement with the Vancouver Coal Company to cut the stone.[12]

The Newcastle Island Quarry sandstone would be the subject of much envy by American competitors, and it had to prove superior to anything available south of the border. The stone passed the test, and soon it was being loaded onto schooners bound for San Francisco. A small village called Perriman developed around the quarry at Newcastle Island Passage where about 50 men worked preparing the site and constructing buildings.

Six large sandstone columns from the quarry at Newcastle Island characterize the United States Mint at San Francisco (seen above). Construction lasted from 1869 to 1874. The building received rave reviews because of its solid construction of brick and sandstone. A test of its endurance happened in 1906 when the San Francisco mint withstood the earthquake. No doubt the 8,000 tons of Newcastle Island sandstone added to the impressive building that still stands today.

The Newcastle sandstone also contributed to the longevity of the British Columbia Penitentiary, at New Westminster. When Emery's lease expired, Kinsman and Styles, of Victoria, leased the quarry and removed 2,000 tons of stone for the construction of the penitentiary. Over the years the sandstone was shipped to locations around the world by a variety of lessees. The last stone was cut in 1955 and used at Christ Church Cathedral in Victoria.

holdings in Nanaimo, ownership of Newcastle Island was transferred to the Vancouver Coal Company. The coal company immediately contracted out the coal operation. There were two operating mines on Newcastle Island, the Fitzwilliam and the Newcastle, neither produced coal like those to the south and both had ceased operating in the early 1880s.

The Newcastle Mine closed in 1856 shortly after a rockfall accident in April, which injured Thomas Hawkes and Dick Richardson. Until this time, the mine employed almost all the miners in town. Hawkes wife Mary was a nurse and was often called upon to administer aid to sick or injured miners. When she was taken by canoe to the island to attend the injured men, she was surprised to find out that her husband Thomas was one of the casualties. Neither of the men suffered serious injury in the accident. Hawkes was one of the miners who that same year petitioned Douglas to allow miners to do more contract work.[13] After the mine closed, the miners were moved to the mine on Commercial Inlet.

Miners like Jesse Sage, a *Princess Royal* pioneer, worked the Newcastle Mine in 1868 with his son-in-law Edward Walker. The two men built wharves and a steam winch to wind the coal to the adit.[14] A premature explosion resulted in Jesse breaking his leg in three places. Edward rushed him to Nanaimo in a canoe to have the leg set by Dr. Alfred Benson. When the leg healed, Jesse was left with a noticeable limp that stopped him going into the mines again.[15] Joseph Bevilockway, another *Princess Royal* pioneer, also did contract work on the island.

Nanaimo's first incorporation attempts

Nanaimo had not been pleased with the treatment it had received from the Colonial Government for some time, therefore an editorial in the *Daily British Colonist* only served to highlight the grievances. The editorial suggested:

> There was no reason that every community on the Island, populated by a few hundred people, should not govern itself. Nanaimo would be none the worse with municipal privileges and a town council head to replace the local magistrate.[16]

One Nanaimo resident responded with support for the editorial, expressing discontent with conditions and incompetence of the government's representative Magistrate William Hales Franklyn. He reasoned, why should one break one's neck on a dark night stumbling over obstacles on the so-called streets? There was also the ravine that divided the town and was impassable at high tide.

> We want our taxes appropriated to better advantage than paying large salaries to useless officials and their satellites, which are only dead weight on the prosperity of the town.[17]

Nanaimo bitterly complained that Victoria had done little to improve roads, build bridges, or correct other conditions in the community. Some thought it was time to take action and incorporate. Governor Arthur Kennedy sympathized with those feelings. The town now had a population of 800 and was regarded as the future Newcastle of the Pacific, but it had suffered from inadequate representation in the House of Assembly and from the refusal of legislative members to give a fair share of money appropriated for public works.

The first attempt to incorporate failed. Thomas Cunningham introduced the Nanaimo incorporation bill to the House of Assembly. On March 29, 1866, "An Act to incorporate the Town of Nanaimo," passed first reading.[18] Only two weeks before, the executive council of the colony commented in a memorandum about the "state of affairs at Nanaimo."[19] No salaries had been paid to officials such as Magistrate Franklyn. The House of Assembly of Vancouver Island had refused to include the officials' salaries on the civil list. In January 1866, Franklyn had been informed his services were no longer required, and he had returned to Victoria.

Governor Arthur Kennedy spoke to the House pleading the case for Nanaimo receiving funding. He argued that in 1865 the community had received no less than $5,896, and now the House of Assembly of Vancouver Island proposed carrying on the public business of the district with the

> very inadequate sum of $800 for postmaster, harbormaster and collector of dues. No provision whatever being made for the expenses of the administration of justice or for the protection of life and property.[20]

The consequences of no funding for the town, second only in importance to Victoria, Kennedy argued, "have been highly detrimental." Without police supervision the sale of alcohol to Natives had gone unchecked, and there had been "crimes of violence and unrestrained rioting."[21] The executive council found it necessary to appoint an officer to collect harbour dues, hoping to defray costs from the dues collected. Constable William Stewart maintained law and order, and unpaid justices of the peace acted in Franklyn's absence.

By April 10, 1866 the Colonial Secretary received another petition from Nanaimo "praying the Council not pass" the incorporation bill.[22] The document claimed there had been fraud, misrepresentation, and undue influence applied to the previous petition. Yet another communication requested an investigation into the genuineness of the signatures to the previous petition.[23] No doubt members of the House of Assembly were totally confused over the Nanaimo incorporation issue and ordered all petitions referred to a select committee to investigate allegations.

Nanaimo citizens opposed to incorporation decided to express their displeasure on the subject. A "Charter" was placed in a tin box and sealed tight. Protesters marched behind some musicians playing appropriate music to Long Bridge that crossed the ravine at Commercial Street. The tide was out, leaving thick oozy mud. The tin box was gently lowered into the ravine. In an instant the box disappeared from sight.[24] The mock funeral was creative but lost much of its credibility. Most of the audience was Snuneymuxw. One observer was appalled by this "diabolical mummery" which he called prudently:

> the most impious desecration of the funeral ritual of the Church of England, rehearsing the solemn service with wanton buffoonery.[25]

The select committee concluded no case had been made for incorporation, and that the central government could best deal with the town's requirements. On May 28, the executive council indefinitely postponed the bill's second reading, thus ending the incorporation issue for the time being.[26]

The town remained divided on the issue. An editorial in the *Nanaimo Gazette* alleged the Vancouver Coal Company opposed incorporation, and that municipal institutions "could not be granted until the value of the property owned by the petitioners was greater than that owned by the company" If the legislative council wanted to throw out the incorporation bill, it would find a way to do so.[27]

Joseph McClure published the *Gazette* every Monday from his Front Street office. His was a well-written little paper that hammered away at the Colonial Government for not spending funds on public improvements in Nanaimo. The paper had a liberal tone to it much like Amor De Cosmos but also reflected the views held by the Vancouver Coal Company. The first editorial promised to conduct the newspaper on "independent principles."[28] While the paper started vigorously with about 18 local businesses buying advertising, it did not prove successful and had ceased publication by 1867 when it emerged as the *Tribune*. It too ceased publication within the year.

Mark Bate was part owner of the *Tribune* and supervised the editorial department. He had opposed incorporation from the beginning as had Mine Manager Charles Nicol. Only John Bryden remained in favor. The forces attempting to incorporate Nanaimo appeared to have been dealt a fatal blow.

A second incorporation bid failed in 1870 when David Babington Ring introduced a Nanaimo incorporation bill to the Legislative Council. While this bid also failed, the groundwork had been laid for another try at another time.

The miner's strike of 1870–71

There had been several miner's strikes in the past but the one in the fall and winter of 1870–71 perhaps heralded the unrest to come. When the Vancouver Coal Company cut the price per ton paid to the miners by "one bit," or 12 1/2 cents, the miners went on strike and were joined by those loading coal on the dock. For several months the strike dragged on with the warship H.M.S. *Sparrowhawk* stationed in the harbour to curb any violence.

The situation reached a crisis stage after stores cut off credit. Some people nearly starved. Others organized a "begging party" to solicit food such as potatoes, vegetables, and an occasional sack of flour from settlers on the Gulf Islands.[29]

The coal company could afford to wait out the strike; there was enough coal stored at the docks. It was business as usual at the docks as ships arrived and departed loaded with coal. Meanwhile, the miners and their families suffered.

Six months later an agreement was reached with the coal company. By this time the stockpile of coal had been reduced considerably. The miners accepted the reduction in wages, while the company agreed to screen the coal above ground, a practice that had previously been done by the miners below ground.

Somehow the mining pioneers of Nanaimo pushed through trails that eventually became roads. They constructed wooden sidewalks, eliminated barriers such as rock formations, built bridges, filled in ravines, and surmounted major obstacles to make movement around the town more accommodating. But it did not happen overnight. Obstacles such as these require leadership and political weight before money would be forthcoming. There was also the Vancouver Coal Company to deal with and the Colonial Government in Victoria. Soon there would be another level of government that would impact on Nanaimo.

CHAPTER FOURTEEN

The Colonies Unite and the Confederation Train Heads West

While the incorporation issue faded and Nanaimo continued to mine and export coal, forces were at work that changed the face of the country. The colonies of Vancouver Island and British Columbia each had their own capitals, governors, and even their own postage stamps, and they differed over the issue of union. Meanwhile, they drifted deeper into an economic recession. The Colonial Office in London decided there would be union whether the two colonies liked it or not. At noon, November 19, 1866, Queen Victoria gave Royal assent to "The British Columbia Act" that united the two colonies as the Colony of British Columbia.

Sir James Douglas did not celebrate the occasion. In his daughter's diary he wrote: "The Ships of war fired a salute on the occasion. A funeral procession, with minute guns would have been more appropriate to the sad melancholy event."[1] It had been eight years since Douglas had been installed as governor of the original mainland colony.

The union of Ontario, Quebec, Nova Scotia, and New Brunswick into the Dominion of Canada soon followed. The British North America Act was signed by Queen Victoria on March 29, 1867, proclaimed on July 1, and the first Prime Minister of the Dominion of Canada, John A. Macdonald, was sworn in.

Meanwhile, the fractious united western Colony of British Columbia entered another debate over which city would become the capital, New Westminster or Victoria? On May 25, 1868 to the horror of New Westminster, Victoria became the seat of government and capital of British Columbia.

Great Britain took action to join its West Coast colony to the Dominion of Canada by assisting the new Canadian government in buying out the rights of the Hudson's Bay Company to the land between Ontario and British Columbia. This was the largest real-estate deal in Canadian history. For $1.5 million the HBC sold all of Rupert's Land.

The legislative assembly tackled another important resolution: "to secure the admission of British Columbia into the Confederation on fair and equitable terms."[2] In Nanaimo, the *Tribune* saw the British connection as a "fast sinking ship," whereas the United States was a "gallant new craft, good and strong, close alongside, inviting us to safety and success."[3] Nanaimo had a close relationship with the United States as a trading partner.

The three delegates from Victoria who negotiated the deal with Ottawa were Dr. Robert William Weir Carrall, Dr. John Sebastian Helmcken, and Joseph Trutch—the man who had made a fortune from the tolls over his suspension bridge on the Cariboo Trail. Canada would assume British Columbia's debt; the new province would be represented in the Dominion government by three senators and six Members of Parliament; and the Dominion would begin to build a transcontinental railway within two years and complete it within ten.[4] The terms of union were passed unanimously by the British Columbia legislature. Ottawa and London gave official approval.

At midnight, between July 19 and 20, 1871, British Columbia became part of Canada. The next day *The British Colonist* declared:

> Today British Columbia passes peacefully and let us add gracefully into the confederated empire of British North America. It will draw together all the peoples of British North America into a common brotherhood, and beget a national sentiment, a sentiment more truly British than would be compatible with isolation and discontent.

Not everyone was so enchanted with being a new Canadian. "Dear old Victoria will be sadly different in many respects," one official commented. "We are a conquered country & the Canucks take possession tomorrow."[5]

With Confederation, the two colonies were now united as the Province of British Columbia. Everyone was expected to put aside personal and geographic differences. Even though, the old battle cry, the Island versus the Mainland, still survived, there was a feeling of renewal and recovery after the depression of the previous few years.

In 1871 the population of the province was 37,247, 5,627 on the mainland and 5,959 on Vancouver Island. The Native population was estimated at 25,661.[6]

PART THREE

NANAIMO FACES CHANGE AND ECONOMIC GROWTH

The first 25 years of incorporation mayor and councillors of Nanaimo were not paid for their services. Yet all took pains, took the fullest interest in the work serving their fellow citizens, each as an "Here in the strife." I know I gave my best service when in office, always endeavoured to do my duty effectively. The whole of us strived to deserve well of the ratepayers. The feeling that you are doing all that is expected of you in a public capacity is very gratifying, a pleasure is given to the individual in such a circumstance, which cannot be paid for in gold.

—Mark Bate, Nanaimo mayor,
1875–1879, 1881–1886, 1888–1889, 1898–1900

CHAPTER FIFTEEN

The City of Nanaimo Is Born

*U*ntil incorporation, Nanaimo was still a frontier town, with coal its main resource. It was unlike similar coal towns in Great Britain, which were typically sooty and grimy with heaps of slag visible. Perhaps the West Coast climate had everything to do with the picturesque coastal town that either sparkled in the rain or glowed in the sunshine. Residents had only to look across the Strait of Georgia to view the snow-capped mountains of the mainland, or look to the natural sheltered harbour in their midst, to be thankful to live at such a beautiful location. Here coal was king and jobs were secure. The potential of the city was not lost on the residents who were willing to put up with the wooden sidewalks, wooden houses, and sometimes, muddy roads. The huge cedar and Douglas fir trees that once reached to the sky and presented such an impenetrable wall to early settlement were now just a memory.

The original townsite was confined to the rocky peninsula where the chief business of the town was conducted. Two wooden bridges spanned the deep ravine that led to the newer portion of the city, where private residences were built. Miners' cottages were usually located near the mine on narrow lots along Fry and Strickland streets and in the south end of town. These were modest company-owned homes. The mine managers, businessmen, and trades people were located in the upper part of the downtown along Selby, Milton, and Kennedy streets. The upper class homes were along Esplanade, Nob Hill, and Newcastle. The large estates of the mine owners and wealthier members of the community were located on large parcels of land to the north and west of town.[1]

Nanaimo incorporates

In 1874, the third incorporation attempt proved successful. Alex Dunsmuir and Police Constable William Stewart circulated a petition advocating the incorporation of Nanaimo and Newcastle townsites. They successfully obtained 221 signatures of the approximate 260 signatures entitled to vote at municipal elections. The petitioners requested self-government—they wanted town revenue to be put towards improving roads. Roads, or lack of them, continued to be a major issue.

The *Nanaimo Free Press* endorsed the movement stating that "one thing is certain, we want some change to lift us out of the muddy condition in which we are at present."[2] The Nanaimo *Gazette* once the vehicle of the Vancouver Coal Company opinion championed by Mark Bate, and the *Tribune* had long since disappeared into the history books. A new press, the *Free Press* signaled a "fresh germ of hopefulness."[3]

Alex Dunsmuir presented the petition on December 21, 1874. His "strenuous efforts" to obtain a bonus for the city were unsuccessful. He was later criticized for having acted as the community's self-appointed "ambassador."[4] The circulation of the petition for incorporation without any conditions caused some to oppose the scheme. Unless the government granted a bonus or subsidy for needed public works, there would be no general support. The government for years had gathered taxes, while "roads, streets and bridges" had been built by, and at the expense of the Vancouver Coal Company, with the government looking on. The opposition was strong. According to Mark Bate,

> The government by "private treaty" undertook to place a first class bridge across the ravine, known as Bastion Street Bridge and build a new Commercial Street Bridge.[5]

A counterpetition was circulated opposing incorporation unless a bonus of $40,000 was granted as reimbursement for the years of neglect the town had suffered. The petition stressed the government had neglected Nanaimo and used its tax money for other purposes. New Westminster and Victoria had benefited from incorporation, and petitioners believed that all public buildings and bridges needed in the community should be constructed out of general revenue and not local government funds. The counterpetition, received on January 2, 1875, had collected only 134 signatures; a number of petitioners had also signed the incorporation petition. One of the signatories to the counterpetition was Mark Bate.

On December 24, 1874, the City of Nanaimo was incorporated by proclamation of the lieutenant-governor in council. The document describes the area:

> All that piece of land (and the inhabitants thereof) known as the Townsite of Nanaimo and the Townsite of Newcastle and bounded as follows; Commencing at the North-East corner of the Indian Reserve at Nanaimo Harbour, thence in a northerly direction following the sinuousities of the shore line to the South-East corner of Millstone River Bridge, to the point of commencement, including all wharves, jetties and buildings abutting on the shore line and all bridges crossing and connecting the boundaries above described.[6]

The new city became the eighth municipal corporation and third city municipality. The population of Nanaimo and Newcastle Townsite was approximately 1,500 residents. Nanaimo city council had the main streets graded and named only to discover several years later the Newcastle Townsite was controlled by the Esquimalt & Nanaimo Railway Company, and it had already registered street names with the Land Registry Office. In 1875, the provincial government finally voted a $3,000 appropriation to defray the costs of construction of the first bridge across the ravine at Bastion and Fitzwilliam streets.

First municipal election

The first municipal election was held on January 18, 1875. Fourteen candidates ran for council and two for mayor. Despite the cold January weather 219 voters cast their ballots. Mark Bate was elected the mayor by a slim majority of seventeen votes over businessman James Harvey. Friends of the new mayor carried him on their shoulders through the town in celebration. Bate rewarded everyone with a champagne supper at Peck's Hotel.

Magistrate Warner R. Spalding swore in the mayor and council at the first meeting held January 22 in the old Courthouse on Front Street.[7] The first council included Mayor Bate and councillors John Bryden, Richard Nightingale, Richard Brinn, John Pawson, William Raybould, John Hirst, and John Dick. In his inaugural address, Bate asked that in all their deliberations they would treat each other with courtesy and forbearance. He advocated "economy in the expenditure of the City Revenue and urged the desirability of being mild with taxation."

Nanaimo's first aldermen with Mayor Mark Bate centre. From top clockwise: John Bryden, John Pawson, John Dick, Richard Brinn, City Clerk Charles Newton Young, John Hirst, Richard Nightingale, William Raybould.

The first official business was procuring a city seal, taking a census in the city, and establishing an assessment roll. Victoria engraver James Benjamin Launders designed the seal in March 1875. It depicted a locomotive pulling a train of cars that overflowed with coal. The train was crossing a track laid over trestlework, and in the background a steamship was anchored in the harbour. Launders died in Nanaimo only three years later, in March 1878.

City of Nanaimo official seal. Designed by James Benjamin Launders.

City divided into wards

In 1879 the city was divided into three wards. The North Ward, the portion of the city north of Bastion and Fitzwilliam Streets, was represented by two councillors; the Middle Ward between Victoria Road and Bastion and Fitzwilliam streets had three councillors; and the South Ward, south of Victoria Road was represented by two councillors. Each candidate could only spend $100 on election expenses.

Until 1890, each council consisted of a mayor and seven councillors. The term "councillor" was changed to "alderman" in April 1888. The city had grown so much that in 1891 the number of aldermen was increased to nine.

The Stone House becomes City Hall

The Stone House, built in 1852 by William Isbister was purchased and renovated and became the second City Hall. Nicknamed the "Tyee House" by the Snuneymuxw, over the years, it served various functions for the HBC and colliery officials, and was used as a court house and even a school room. Now it was renovated to become the second city hall. On May 19, 1875, the first regular meeting was held. And the Stone House continued to be used until 1886 when the city purchased the old Literary Institute Hall for $2,300. The upper floor was renovated into a new city hall chamber and the lower floor remained for social events. The Bank of British Columbia then occupied the Stone House 1887 until 1889.[8]

Mayors and councillors

Seven men served as mayor during the period 1875 to 1900. Mark Bate was a steadying force within the community and gave a total of sixteen terms to the administrative duties of the city. Andrew Haslam, Edward Quennel, John Hilbert, and Joseph Davison served two terms; and John Pawson and Richard Gibson each filled a one-year term. Richard Nightingale was the longest-serving alderman with fourteen years to his credit, followed by George Baker who served ten years. Two aldermen had sons who followed in their footsteps: Joseph P. Planta and his son Albert; and Joseph Bevilockway and son George.

Nightingale, employed as manager at the Newcastle Quarry, met an unfortunate end. On August 17, 1898, the Union Railway Bridge over the Trent River, north of Union Bay, collapsed taking a twenty-car train over an embankment 120 feet into the water below. Several Nanaimo people were killed in the wreck including Nightingale; Alexander Mellado, grandson of the *Princess Royal* Thompson family; and Walter Work, another grandson of the 1852 miners. Against the coal company regulations, two young women were aboard; one was 17-year-old Frances D. Horne, granddaughter of Adam Grant Horne. She was badly injured and died later from burns received in the accident.[9]

City clerks: Young, Manson & Gough

The first City Clerk Charles Newton Young was appointed February 1, 1875. He arrived in the colony in 1862 and was a teacher in Victoria before coming to Nanaimo to teach in 1868. During his tenure as clerk (1875–1880), council reduced his salary believing he was overpaid for the little he did. He was hired at $87.50 per month then two weeks later his salary was reduced to $60. The *Free Press* reported that Young recommended that the city advertise for a new clerk in both Chinese and English.[10] When council decided to reduce his salary further, Young returned to teaching. He taught for a number of years before working for the Wellington Colliery at Departure Bay.[11]

Michael (Mike) Manson was the next city clerk, hired on June 14, 1880.[12] Manson was born on the Shetland Islands, in Scotland, in 1858 and had come to British Columbia at age 16 to work on his aunt and uncle's farm. After a few years he moved to Nanaimo. When he first arrived he found it difficult to find a place to board. One night he slept in a hayloft of Wilson's barn across Millstream Bridge.

He went to Wellington to ask Robert Dunsmuir for a job, and when he saw him, Dunsmuir asked where he came from. When he learned Manson was from the Shetland Islands, Dunsmuir commented, "Ay man ye will ken gay weal how to handle they mules." He was told to come on Monday, and Dunsmuir would give him a job.

> At that time Dunsmuir was hauling coal from the Wellington Mine to Departure Bay with mules in cars which held about three tons. These cars were running on wooden rails.[13]

Manson did not like the job prospect with Dunsmuir so checked out opportunities with the Vancouver Coal Company, and became a brakeman on a coal train. Harry Cooper, the outside boss, said he was glad to see him work there so that "he did not [have to] go to Dunsmuir to drive 'they mules.'" He found room and board with Mr. and Mrs. Leask and stayed with them for over two years until he built a house for himself on Haliburton Street.

The story is told of Mike Manson's courtship and subsequent marriage to Jane (Jenny) Renwick whose father was very religious and did not approve of his daughter's suitor. Mike gave Jenny an engagement ring, and the father not wanting to lose such a good worker as his daughter, beat her over the hands and broke the ring. This action only made the young couple more determined.

In August 1873, as Jenny's father came home from work, he passed his daughter and assumed she was on her way to a prayer meeting. In fact she was on her way to meet Mike, who had hired a canoe and six Natives for their elopement. They paddled all night and arrived at Sidney the next morning where a team and wagon were waiting to take them to Victoria to be married.[14]

Mike and Jenny Manson started a family, and although the first child died in infancy, they had five more children. In the fall of 1890 all the children caught diphtheria. One after another, the four youngest died. Jenny got the disease too and was so sick that twice preparations were made to take her out of the house—dead. Then one evening she told Mike that she was sure she would be dead before midnight. She fell asleep, and Mike turned the clock ahead, so when she awoke the clock would show 12:30 a.m. She was still alive and slowly recovered. Later Jenny gave birth to two sets of twin girls plus three other children.

Mike was interested in public life and became city clerk in 1880, then secretary to the Nanaimo School Board.

In 1887, he pre-empted land at Flint Lake on Cortez Island where he built a home as well as the store at Manson's Landing. He also bought a couple of steamers, the first being the *Rustler,* which

Samuel Gough, city clerk, with his mother Elizabeth.

was wrecked off Nelson Island. His other vessel was the *Thistle,* that had a crew of 10 and could sleep 32. It carried copper ore from Texada Island, fish from the Queen Charlotte Islands, seals from the Bering Sea, and furs from the Columbia River.

In 1896, James Dunsmuir persuaded Manson to leave the sea and take the position as Harbour Master at Union Bay. Manson first leased the *Thistle,* then finally sold it to Dunsmuir who used it as his private yacht. Mike continued his interest in public life and became MLA for Comox in 1909 and again in 1924, this time representing the new district of MacKenzie.

A man, who had spent seventeen years in the mines, became the next city clerk on July 19, 1880. Samuel Gough was also expected to fulfill the duties as the city assessor, city collector, and clerk for the mayor. For these services Gough received a salary of $400 a year plus 10 percent on all collectable taxes. He also received another $5 a month for lighting and cleaning the council chambers. Each year Gough had to be reappointed because council did not recognize its employees as being permanent. This practice changed in 1898 when Gough became a permanent employee.

Gough was only 5-years old when his father Edwin signed on with the HBC and together with his mother Elizabeth and his sister Amanda

Theresa, he sailed on the eventful voyage of the *Princess Royal*, arriving in Nanaimo in 1854. His Nanaimo schoolteachers were Charles Bayley, Christopher Finlay, and Cornelius Bryant. At the age of 13 he started work in the Douglas mine. On November 11, 1877 his former teacher Cornelius Bryant married Samuel to Emily Elizabeth Woodward. The couple had eight children, but only one, Hiram Edwin, lived to maturity.[15] Like his father, Hiram became city clerk, in 1911.

Population growth and mining

Nanaimo grew rapidly after incorporation into the largest settlement on Vancouver Island north of Victoria. By 1877 there were 1,150 while adults and 300 Chinese living in Nanaimo, while nearby Wellington had a population of 1,000. The British Columbia Directory noted there were 50 retail outlets and 24 service establishments, plus 1 store and a hotel at Wellington. The census of 1881 showed the total population of the area had grown to 2803; this would have included the town of Wellington.

The Nanaimo coal operation encompassed the Douglas Pit, No. 1 shaft, and Esplanade, in Nanaimo; the New Douglas Mine near Chase River; the South Field Mine south of Chase River; and the Fitzwilliam Mine on Newcastle Island. There were 325 people employed in the coal mining industry 1881, this figure included 60 Chinese and Natives. The average wage for whites was between $2.00 and $3.75 per day; Chinese $1.00 to $1.25 per day and Natives $1.00 to $1.50 per day. Miners earned between $2.50 and $5.00 per day. The men were charged $5 a week for board at the local hotels, and $25 per month for both board and lodging.

By 1882, large coal wharves dominated the downtown waterfront. Freight and passengers were unloaded at either the Gordon Wharf or Hirst Wharf. At Departure Bay, the harbour accommodated a large number of vessels, some loading coal and others waiting for cargoes. Both the Wellington and South Wellington Mine wharves were on the west shore of the bay, and the Vancouver Coal Company wharves were on the opposite side at Midden Bay, on Newcastle Island.

City streets and roads

The town had been physically transformed. Massive rock formations that were barriers to traffic were cut through. The construction of the downtown streets was the work of pioneer councils: from Dallas Square along Commercial Street and Victoria Crescent right up to Haliburton Street, and from The Crescent up Victoria Road. Selby Street from Albert to Fitzwilliam streets had been cleared of giant trees. The yawning gap was filled between Victoria and Winfield crescents, as was the ravine on Albert Street in front of the businesses from Cavan Street down to the inlet. Also Wharf Street was raised from the beach up to the level of Commercial Street.[16]

Burnt coal cinders scattered over the streets resulted in a hard, dry surface. Later when George Baker became councillor and chairman of the street committee, he successfully obtained a road roller and a rock crusher. This equipment greatly improved the muddy road situation in the wet season.

When the E & N Railway was completed, trap rock was delivered from Chemainus, then broken in Nanaimo and used to dress the streets.

Cattle trails & stagecoaches

The road promised back in 1862 finally showed some promise when in 1875 a cattle trail opened between Cowichan and Nanaimo, but this was mainly to provide an alternative market to Victoria for Cowichan farmers.[17] Jesse Sage was named the first road foreman.

However, travel between Nanaimo and Wellington became easier in 1878 when Joseph Ganner inaugurated a passenger stagecoach service twice a day, a service that continued until the arrival of the railway. The Ganner's Daily Mail Stage got the government contract to carry mail to the newly established post office at Wellington.[18]

Joseph, the son of Elijah and Frances Ganner, became a successful businessman. He mined until 1870, then began a transfer business, starting with a horse and dump cart hauling coal. By 1878, Ganner's sons had joined him in the business. The small company had the first covered moving van on Vancouver Island. Their wagons were often volunteered for community services such as hauling picnic baskets for special outings. Joseph also raised horses for sale, charging $40 each, or $70 a pair.[19]

Over the years the family acquired property in the Cranberry District, in Newcastle Townsite, and a large lot on Vancouver Avenue. In 1883, when Joseph's health began to fail, he sold his sixteeen-seat passenger stagecoach and some of his property. He died on December 26, 1903, and his wife Dorathy died two days later. They were buried together on December 31. They left a large family of 10 children.

Joseph Harper also operated a stagecoach daily, between Departure Bay and Nanaimo, charging 25 cents return. Or if one wanted to take a Sunday drive, one could rent a horse and buggy from Fred Wilson's livery stable at Departure Bay for $2.50 per day.

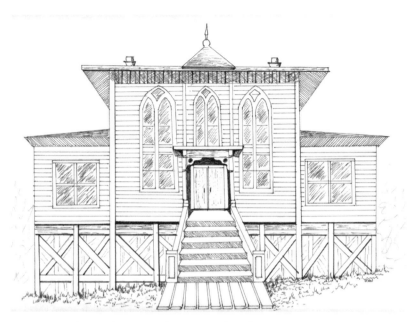

Drawing of wooden courthouse and jail on Front Street.

Courthouse and jail

The wooden courthouse and jail looked temporary, as if waiting for the city to erect a more permanent structure. County court was held monthly by a judge from the Supreme Court. The first resident judge to be appointed was Eli Harrison, on August 13, 1889.

Post office

In 1878, a small portion of a second-hand store operated by William Earl served as a post office. Mail arrived by boat weekly from Victoria to Gordon's Wharf. Earl collected the mailbags and brought them up to his store. Outside a crowd waited by an open wicket for Earl to begin reading out the addresses "like a schoolmaster calling the roll," and each addressee would shout "Here!" Then the letter or article would be passed out to him. Should Earl stop for a minute to untie the bundles of letters, someone would remark, "Now he's reading a postcard."[20]

The Dominion Government eventually showed faith in the community by constructing a new post office. By 1884, Nanaimo had a beautiful new Dominion Post Office building on Front Street. This event perhaps demonstrated the city had come of age.

Dominion Post Office, Front Street.

The nuisance bylaws

The Municipal Act of 1872 gave Nanaimo council authority to regulate slaughterhouses and to prevent nuisances. After Nanaimo's incorporation, the first sanitary committee was appointed in April 1875 to deal with a nuisance caused by the carcass of a dead pig. It was the sanitary officer's responsibility to investigate and enforce the bylaws, but sometimes police were given that responsibility.

Among the nuisance bylaws were some that in light of today's attitudes seem a little wacky, but Nanaimo was still a frontier town without paved streets, sanitation, water, or electricity so it was important to maintain public order.

The first sanitary bylaw was passed in 1876 to regulate the killing and butchering of animals. This became a contentious issue, because sometimes council amended the bylaw to allow butchering in certain areas at various times of the year. If you were charged with having a nuisance on your property, you had 48 hours to rectify the situation before council took action against you. Eventually the sanitary bylaws were incorporated into public health provisions.

There were other perceived nuisances such as street gutters, drains, privy pits, laundries, Chinatown, and the Snuneymuxw dwelling areas. The city's drainage system was rudimentary, and the clearing of culverts was a constant problem. The Snuneymuxw and their lifestyle also irritated authorities. Between 1875 and 1889 attempts were made to have a village on Newcastle Townsite and another on the north bank of the Millstone River removed from within the city limits; Council's will eventually prevailed.

Animal round-up

City workers spent a good deal of time rounding up cattle and other animals roaming at large. Bylaw No. 6 ruled there could be no horses, mules, oxen, bulls, cattle, goats, sheep, or swine running at large within the city. The large number of dogs running at large resulted in a dog tax being introduced. Horses at large were similarly taxed. Eventually it was ruled against the law to keep farm animals within the city.

Public morals

The Public Morals Bylaw No. 18, of 1895 ruled on such items as bathing, indecency, swearing, drunkenness, gambling, begging, cruelty to animals, houses of ill-fame, and sale to minors of liquor, tobacco, or cigarettes,

On the subject of bathing, no one could bathe or swim in Millstone River or in the harbour within the city limits between the hours of 6 a.m. and 10 p.m. without wearing a proper bathing suit covering the body from the neck to the knees. If you were so covered you could swim at any time.

Council felt it necessary to state that no person could indecently expose any part of his or her person in public, and the call of nature in public was considered an offence.

Anyone knowingly frequenting or connected with, or contributing to any disorderly house or house of "ill-fame," would be subject to a penalty.[21] A "no drinking on Sunday bylaw" was passed in 1896, but it was two years before it was enforced.

Public safety

The Nanaimo Curfew Bylaw of 1898 set a curfew for children of "tender" age, under 14 years, from roaming the streets after 8 p.m. or 9 p.m., depending on the season There were two warnings, and on the third the young person was arrested and fined of $5. [22]

It was also against the law to drive fast on bridges, ride horses on the Haliburton Street sidewalk, or leave building materials on the streets.

No one could fire a gun or herd cattle on Sunday mornings as local residents were on their way to church.

Even the Salvation Army was censured for its indiscriminate use of its drum when marching. The noise had apparently proved to be a great danger to those driving when the sound might startle the horses.

Council tried to enforce the filling of dangerous wells, and have residents construct fire escapes.

Sidewalks

The subject of sidewalks occupied council during 1875 when it regulated the construction, maintenance, and repair of wooden sidewalks, footpaths, and verandahs.

Under another bylaw, council could force owners of lots on graded streets to construct a sidewalk along their lots. If they failed to do so within a certain time limit, the sidewalk would be constructed by the city and the cost charged to the property owner. Eventually all the wooden sidewalks were replaced. The first concrete sidewalk was laid in 1902 on the front of City Hall on Bastion Street.

Quality of life

There were other actions taken by council that improved the quality of life in Nanaimo. To beautify the main street, 200 shade trees were planted in 1886.

By 1889 the old bridge across the ravine from Bastion to Fitzwilliam Streets, built in 1875, needed to be replaced. A bylaw was defeated that would have seen the ravine filled in and the need for a bridge alleviated. But ratepayers had a change of heart when one month later they agreed to a loan bylaw to rebuild the bridge. The new bridge was completed in 1890 but it was not until 1898 the old bridge was finally removed.

Nanaimo Cemetery

Under the Municipality Act 1872, Nanaimo was authorized to establish and regulate its cemeteries. Nanaimo Cemetery, located at the corner of Comox Road and Wallace Street, now known as the Pioneer Cemetery, was overcrowded. Council applied for a land grant to establish a new one, but its application was refused on the grounds that all government lands were reserved for railway purposes. A grant to purchase land was also refused. Mayor Mark Bate suggested that council petition the Vancouver Coal Company to grant it the land. As a result five acres on Comox Road was donated. By July 1877, the site had been surveyed and two acres cleared.

Lighting the city

In 1879 street lighting was inaugurated when coal oil lamps were installed. It was Alexander Shaw who saw the need for electric light and began gathering the capital to support the venture. In 1888, Shaw built the first Edison electric light system. On June 30, 1890 Nanaimo received its first electrical power with Shaw named manager of the Nanaimo Power Company. The city was poled and wired with heavy insulated electrical conducting wires. A few private homes also were lit by electricity. Electric lights were used on Nanaimo streets for the first time in November 1891. However, the city still had a number of gas lamps with Nanaimo Gas Company supplying the power.

Shaw's under-financed enterprise failed. One day when he was out of the office, the sheriff arrived to claim the business. Shaw, now a grandfather, was over 60-years old and bankrupt. But he didn't let this little setback deter him—he could always teach.

Black Diamond Fire Company

The town may have had a cemetery but it did not have a fire department. This fact was brought home vividly to residents in 1878 when fire destroyed a good portion of the lower side of Commercial Street. On April 20, strong winds fanned sparks from a chimney fire setting adjacent buildings ablaze.

There was no ready water supply, although the Nanaimo Water Works, established in 1866, took water from a spring in the ravine and distributed it by bucket. There were also several wells in the area.

Until this time Snuneymuxw women had served with distinction in the bucket brigade. Now all residents could do was watch helplessly as flames licked away buildings one by one. Eric Duncan and his fellow workers at the Nanaimo sawmill were given time off work to watch the blaze. The following is his eye witness description of events:

> At that time the leading merchants were Alexander Mayer, a German Jew, and John Hirst, and Englishman. As the fire spread there was a call for blankets, to be soaked in water and spread over the buildings to quench sparks, and Mayer, though aloof from the fire, turned out rolls of them, but Hirst would not furnish one. There were loud comments on the generous Jew and the skinflint Englishman, whose storefront was charred black by the blaze across the street. Mayer afterwards sold the damaged blankets for $3 each. Bottles of liquor were thrown from the burning buildings,

Black Diamond Fire Company, Fire Hall No. 2.

and many of the mill-hands got drunk that night, and pursued each other with axes over and around the great lumber piles. But Carpenter was highly elated, saying that now he would have a call for some of it.[23]

Duncan's initial view of the "skinflint Englishman" was soon dispelled when a month later John Hirst and Josiah Walter Stirtan donated a central lot on Commercial Street for the newly organized Black Diamond Fire Company.[24] In the fall, enough money had been raised from the public to purchase a Burton and Blake fire engine from the fire department of Portland, Oregon. The cost was $700—plus 500 feet of hose for another $250.

A fire hall was built and opened on January 21, 1879. This became Fire Hall #1. Another fire station was constructed in August 1890 on a narrow strip of land between Nicol Street and Victoria Road and became

Fire Hall #2. After the first station was destroyed by fire in 1894, Fire Hall #2 became the main station. The tower was added in 1914.[25]

In 1901, the Black Diamond Fire Company ceased to exist when the city took over fire protection services, becoming the Nanaimo Fire Department.

Nanaimo Water Works Company

In 1881, council authorized Josiah Stirtan to lay a system of wooden water mains.[26] In return, Stirtan supplied the fire company with free water.

In 1884, the Nanaimo Trades Association conducted a water survey, and the following year the Nanaimo Water Works Company Limited incorporated and took over Stirtan's system. Nanaimo City Council attempted to purchase the Nanaimo Water Works Company plant as early as 1889. In order to bring the waterworks under municipal control, council had the Legislative Assembly pass the "Corporation of the City of Nanaimo Water-Works Act, 1895." The act specifically authorized the city to provide an adequate supply of water through the purchase of the existing waterworks plant, or the construction of a new one. The company rejected the city's offer, and a board of arbitration fixed the purchase price at $104,000. The Nanaimo Water Works Company did not formally transfer its plant to the city until June 19, 1901.[27]

The Nanaimo Telephone Company

The Nanaimo Telephone Company began operation in 1889. The telephone exchange was in George Cavalsky's store with Mrs. Cavalsky as the first operator. Twelve poles were erected and twelve telephones ordered at a cost to each customer of $31.80. The telephone exchange relocated to the third floor of the *Nanaimo Free Press* building in 1892 and remained there until 1908. The first telephone communication with Victoria was established December 12, 1901.

However, the telephone company did not have the first telephone in the Nanaimo area. In 1877, William Wall connected two telephones between Wellington and the loading docks at Departure Bay for the convenience of Dunsmuir, Diggle & Company.[28] This was the first private telephone system in British Columbia.

CHAPTER SIXTEEN

Nanaimo Builds for the Future— Schools, Hospitals and Churches

Governor James Douglas recognized the value of education when in 1853 he transferred Charles Alfred Bayley to Nanaimo to teach the miners' children. Humble beginnings also marked the arrival of the first hospital in the small community—a combination of two miner's cabins—Bigg's cabins, named for their owner, *Princess Royal* pioneer John Biggs. The missionaries too, came to save souls—it took years to build congregations and places of worship.

School days—difficult beginnings

Cornelius Bryant succeeded the early teachers and stayed on through successive colonial governments until 1870. It had not been an easy position for anyone to fill, considering the limitations of resources and funding.

A number of Scottish parents refused to send their children to school rather than pay the small amount of money required. Even the establishment of the School Act in 1865 that provided free education for the first time did not diminish the financial problems associated with the Act. Still parents contributed funds to support their school.

When the colonies united, more difficulties arose. Bryant complained about the slow payment of his salary until the day he resigned in June 1870. His salary was then in arrears by $450. His journal entry recorded his disappointment at the small number of students. "I re-opened the school this morning with less than thirty pupils." He knew there were a number of school-age children in the community who did not attend. Some of the mining families thought it better that their boys work in the mines than spend their day in school. The extra income would have been welcomed.

First Nanaimo School Board

In 1869, a new Education Act passed, abolishing free common schools and adding some structure to the process. School districts were established and school boards elected. Robert Dunsmuir, Pat Faith, and Thomas James were named to the first Nanaimo School Board. Charles Newton Young, a young schoolteacher from Victoria, replaced Bryant. Young's government salary was $900 per year. But when the city incorporated in 1874, Young became the first city clerk.

Crace Street School

Schools had operated continuously in Nanaimo from 1853 in various buildings. Then in 1873, the first Nanaimo Public School was constructed on Crace Street at a cost of $2,500. Bruno Mellado, a young man from Chile whose family lived in Esquimalt, designed the school, which still stands today as one of the city's oldest surviving buildings. Mark Bate noted the new schoolhouse was erected after years of waiting and pleading.

> The transition from a low stuffy, dingy room, to lofty light, airy, commodious quarters, was very agreeable alike to trustees, teachers and scholars. A new spirit of buoyant youth seemed to be awakened on the playground.[1]

Joseph Phrys Planta, who had been vice-principal of Victoria College, was appointed first principal of the new school on Crace Street. The Planta family was prominent in the early life of Nanaimo.

First Marriage Licence in B.C.

Aside from designing and building the first school, the young architect had another historic distinction. Bruno Mellado's marriage to fifteen-year-old Mary Ann Thompson on August 14, 1871 was the first marriage licence issued in the new province of British Columbia. (The document is now in the care of the British Columbia Archives in Victoria.) The young couple returned to live in Nanaimo where Mellado continued to design and build into the 1880s.

Of their twelve children, only eight reached maturity. Those who died may have succumbed during a diphtheria epidemic when the family was quarantined. "Mary Ann used to tell her grandchildren that she had to pass her dead babies through the window for her husband to take them for burial."[2]

Joseph and Margaret Planta and their eleven-year-old son Albert Edward came from Adelaide, Australia to British Columbia in 1870, where Joseph took a teaching position in New Westminster.[3] His next teaching job was at Victoria College. Within a few years, the family moved to Nanaimo and to his new position. Elizabeth Young, the wife of the former teacher, and Katie MacGregor assisted him. John Mundell and Miss M.E. Mason joined the school the next year. Mundell succeeded Planta as principal at the school when Planta left teaching to become a justice of the peace.

As the population in the area grew, the school system expanded. By the time the city incorporated in 1874, schools had opened in Wellington, Gabriola Island, and North Cedar.

> ## Emily Stark—First Afro-American Teacher
>
> Emily Stark was the first Afro-American to teach in the Nanaimo District at North Cedar and the first teacher of colour in British Columbia schools. Her parents were freed slaves who moved to California and took up farming. Although they were successful, California enacted legislation that made it difficult for Afro-Americans to own businesses there. Governor James Douglas invited those families to come to Vancouver Island. The Stark family accepted the invitation and arrived in 1858. Emily studied to become a teacher and was hired to teach in the new Cedar school in 1874.[4]

Increased enrollment in Nanaimo resulted in the building of a new three-room girl's school at the corner of Selby and Franklyn Streets. It opened in 1878 with Margaret Planta as principal, the first such appointment for a female teacher in Nanaimo. Her husband's school then became Crace Street Boy's School.[5] Husband and wife now taught at two separate schools. Katie MacGregor moved with Margaret to the new girl's school where over 100 girls were enrolled.

South Cedar got its new school in 1880.

The city had moved to a ward system of municipal government when the Middle Ward School opened in 1885 between Nicol Street and Victoria Road with John Shaw as principal. Enrollment at this school consisted of 137 boys.

Sisters of St. Ann's day school

In addition to the public schools, the Roman Catholic order, Sisters of St. Ann, operated a day school starting in 1877. A school was not what the Sisters had in mind when the possibility of establishing a mission in Nanaimo was discussed. The Mother General, in 1867,

Middle Ward School opened in 1885 with John Shaw as principal. It was located between Nicol Street and Victoria Road.

had envisioned a hospital here, but there were not enough nursing Sisters at the time to proceed, and she decided instead to open a school.[6] The school first opened in the home of Father John Nicholas Lemmens and was non-denominational. Sister Mary de la Croix Perreault and Sister Mary Eleanor Dignen taught with assistant Susan Suckley. The first school operated only from May to July with 29 pupils registered; 15 were non-Catholics.[7]

The teachers' report noted that they were happy with their pupils. The first pupil to register was Laura Gordon, who later became Mrs. Albert E. Planta. Students learned music, drawing, needlework, as well as French, English, and arithmetic.

A two-storey wooden convent was completed in 1879 on Wallace Street, and for the next several years enrollment remained at 35 students with still only a small percentage being Catholic children. Community support for the school came from Mark Bate and Robert Dunsmuir.

Alexander Shaw—the Power of Self-edcation

John Shaw had a long career teaching in Nanaimo schools; it was a vocation started by his father Alexander Shaw who moved to Gabriola Island to raise pigs and beef cattle in the late 1850s. As there was no school on the island, Shaw began teaching his nine children what he knew. With a limited education, he realized he would be able to teach his children better if he learned more himself. Thus began a period of self-education, sending to Victoria for books, settling down after a hard day on the farm to study. Soon he felt capable of taking the teacher's examination.[8]

In the spring of 1881 Alexander built a rowboat. When the time came to write the examination, he rowed all the way to Victoria, returning the same way armed with a three-year teaching certificate. He continued to teach his children and others to read and write. Twenty-seven students attended school under Shaw's tutelage; five of them were his own.

Older Gabriola Island students attended school in Nanaimo and boarded with families during the week, returning to the island on weekends. In 1884, his two sons Alex and John, and another boy, James Gray, plus three others, were so far along in learning that when it came time for Shaw to renew his certificate, four of them rowed to Victoria, each returned as full-fledged teachers. John Shaw became one of the foremost educators in British Columbia. He served as principal of the Boys' School, then later principal of the co-educational school in Nanaimo.

Alexander Shaw remained on Gabriola Island for another six years, teaching, farming, and operating the telegraph system. His older children grew up and left home for Nanaimo. The family eventually all moved to Nanaimo when Shaw became the first station agent for the E & N Railway. He was a man of varied interests and enjoyed prospecting for gold around the hills of Nanaimo. His home was cluttered with samples of rock and little jars of flakes of gold washed from the creeks.

After a failed business venture Alexander once again successfully wrote the teacher's examination. His first assignment was to Five Acres School just outside Nanaimo.

Before long he was posted to Alberni to teach at Beaver Creek School. As he had done so many times in the past, he again built a house for his family. The small cottage was less than half a mile from the school and stood for many years afterward—with several additions made to the school. At the time of his arrival at Beaver Creek, there were hardly enough pupils to keep it operating. Eight was the required number of pupils needed. Some of the students were beginners; others had some education, which had been interrupted by periodic closure of the school. In order to keep enrollment up, Shaw sent to Nanaimo for some of his grandchildren to come live with him and attend school.[9]

Alexander Shaw was aged 74 when he retired from teaching and returned to Nanaimo to again build yet another house, only this time his son John helped with some of the work. During the

Central School, at Selby and Franklyn Streets, opened in 1896.

early years of the First World War, he joined the Home Guard, seldom missing a drill. He marched side by side with his young grandson. His Sunday school class and his knitting, at which he was an expert, occupied his spare time. In 1916, at age 83, he died of pneumonia following a cold contracted while drilling with the Home Guard. His wife, nine children and thirteen grandchildren survived him. Alexander Shaw influenced education in three communities: Gabriola Island, Alberni, and Nanaimo. His son John Shaw accumulated 24 years teaching in Nanaimo schools.

Nanaimo's high schools

A one-room addition to the Middle Ward school in 1886 became the first Nanaimo High School with E. B. Paul as principal. Only twelve pupils were registered, six boys and six girls. New schools were opened in 1893 in the North and South wards.

Crowded conditions continued to be a source of concern for the school board as the town population grew and prospered. The middle school and high school were overcrowded. As a temporary measure the old Presbyterian Church (across from today's church on Fitzwilliam Street) and the old Methodist Church on Chapel Street were utilized for the younger students.

A new school was planned on the site of the Girls' School on Selby and Franklyn. In April 1896, Central School opened with eight classrooms on the first and second floor and an enrollment of 594. Boys and girls now shared the same classroom, and while they may have been educated together, they were not permitted to play together. A high board fence divided their playground.[10]

Caroline M. Edwards was the 1892–93 Nanaimo High School bronze medallist, and Arthur D. Morgan was the medallist in 1894.[11] (Arthur Morgan's father, Thomas, was a Welsh miner who eventually became government mine inspector in Nanaimo.) Arthur graduated in medicine with honours from McGill University in 1901, returning to B.C. to practise first at Quesnel, then Alberni in 1906 when he was appointed the Indian Medical Officer. He was one of Alberni's pioneer doctors.[12]

Nanaimo schools had improved considerably from the old log house first offered free by the HBC.

Health care and the first Nanaimo hospitals

The first hospital in the small community was not an imposing structure, just a combination of two miner's cabins—Bigg's cabins, named for their owner *Princess Royal* pioneer John Biggs.

The one-room cabins were originally occupied by one or two bachelors, or by family members brought over from Great Britain until a home could be provided for them. The occupants usually kept a cat as a companion, and for the animals' convenience a square hole was cut in the bottom of the door. In one case the kind-hearted owner cut a hole of regulation size plus a much smaller one beside it. When asked why he did this, he replied, "Faith and would I be after littin the mother in, an leaving the kitten out in the cowld."[13]

Because of fear of the Natives camped at Millstone River, only a mile away, the back of the cabin was left intact, except for a small porthole fitted with a heavy wooden shutter that could be pushed up from the inside. Early tenants recall it was not unusual to hear knocks on the shutter over the porthole—by Natives demanding "fire-water."

Chapel Street Hospital

Martha A. Kenny, a Nanaimo historian, described the Chapel Street Hospital as consisting of two low, long buildings forming an "L." The two buildings were not connected, so as to allow an opening for the occupants to reach the steep rocky trail leading down into the ravine. Here a spring provided a ready water supply. Each building had ten beds and was divided off into four rooms by partitions running from front to back. These buildings were periodically painted inside and out with a coat of whitewash. A small window in the front of each room lit the interior.

It was to these modest cabins that the sick and injured were brought for treatment by the colliery doctor. Unfortunately the hospital only catered to male patients and was totally inadequate for the growing community. When there was a mine accident, a hotel room had to be rented in which to treat the patient.

Everyone agreed a new hospital was needed. The Reverend George Mason, the rector of St. Paul's Anglican Church, called a public meeting for January 31, 1878 to discuss the subject. Government Agent Thomas Lea Fawcett acted as chairman, with former teacher Charles Newton Young as secretary. A committee was established with Captain Thomas A. Bulkley as president, James Harvey as vice-president, John Pawson as treasurer and Young as secretary. The directors included David W. Gordon, Thomas Wall, John Dick, Richard Nightingale, Charles W. Chantrell, George Norris, and J. Gillespie. This committee looked for ways to finance and maintain a new public facility and arranged for the continued use of the Chapel Street Hospital. They appointed Dr. Loftus R. McInnes as medical officer in charge.[14]

Sometime between 1878 and 1881 another hospital came into use on the southeast corner of Fitzwilliam and Prideaux Streets. Not much is known about this facility, but it may have been an answer to overcrowding at the Chapel Street Hospital. Judging from an advertisement placed in the *Nanaimo Free Press* on April 19, 1879, the committee must have been thinking of vacating the Chapel Street Hospital. The advertisement gave notice:

"Raffle! A Raffle for the Town Lot and Buildings thereon (now used as the Nanaimo Hospital) will take place at Wall's Britannia Hotel. Notice will be given of time of raffle. The title to property is undisputable. 160 chances at $2.50 per chance." Signed John Biggs.

Franklyn Street Hospital
The Nanaimo Hospital Association formed in 1881 with Robert Dunsmuir as president, Alex Mayer, vice-president, and directors John Hilbert, Donald Smith, John Pawson, William Earl, and W.E. Webb. The secretary was M.B. McKay and James Harvey was treasurer. Government appointees were Mark Bate and William Raybould.

The Vancouver Coal Company donated a parcel of land on Franklyn Street, and with Government help and private subscription the hospital was constructed for $3,000. A debt of $900 remained on the books.[15] Dr. Daniel Cluness, a graduate of McGill University, was the colliery surgeon in attendance. His practice was on Commercial Street.[16]

The city was growing at such a rate, even with the new hospital, there was still not enough space for the services required, and the Chapel Street Hospital continued to operate. An extension was added to the Franklyn Street Hospital that began accepting patients in 1883 and enabling the Chapel Street facility to be finally closed.

Above: Author's sketch of Nanaimo Hospital, located at Franklyn and Kennedy Streets. Below: Nurses on the porch of the hospital.

Women of the community waited until the early 1890s for a women's ward to be established. The Mary Ward came under the management of Matron Mrs. Natrass.

A nurse's residence and two more wards were added: a maternity ward and the John Pawson Ward. By the turn of the century, thoughts were given to establishing a training school for nurses. This opened in 1906.

Public health

Of all the feared infectious diseases, smallpox ranked the highest. There were several outbreaks in Nanaimo before the turn of the century. After the calamities of the 1860s, the most serious outbreak was in 1892 when city council considered cutting off all communication with the outside world. Preventive measures such as the inspection of boats and trains arriving at Nanaimo and the vaccination of residents helped the city escape unscathed. An isolation hospital was built, quarantine guards were posted, and contaminated property was destroyed.

But there was another more deadly disease, and that was leprosy. Nanaimo had its first case in 1894. A Chinese man was transferred to D'Arcy Island near Victoria, a site that had been reserved for the care and isolation of lepers. The City of Nanaimo paid for his care until June 1901. When the Dominion Government passed a bill in 1902 granting an increase in the Chinese head tax paid to the provinces, the city eventually received a refund for the entire amount paid for the man's upkeep.[17]

Congregations & churches

Ebenezer Wesley Robson, Cornelius Bryant, Thomas Crosby, Modest Demers, John Booth Good, and others gave religion a firm foundation in the early days of the town. Four congregations were established in the 1860s: the First Methodist Church, St. Paul's Anglican, St. Peter's Roman Catholic, and St. Andrew's Presbyterian. Among later congregations were the Salvation Army, the First Baptist Church, and St. Alban's—a congregation that broke away from St. Paul's Anglican, but later returned.

Methodist churches

On a site deeded by Alexander Grant Dallas, volunteers built the First Methodist Church facing the harbour on Front Street in 1860 (near the present-day Globe Hotel). It had a finished interior of California redwood, and even at this early date, beautiful stained-glass windows and four ornate bronze chandeliers.[18] It was named the Ebenezer Wesleyan Methodist Church for Reverend Ebenezer Robson an early missionary, and brother of John Robson.

Reverend Cornelius Bryant performed an unusual wedding in 1877 when he united in marriage a Chinese couple, Mah Lee and Si Sing.[19]

To accommodate a growing congregation, another church was built. The Wallace Street Methodist Church was dedicated on January 12, 1890, at the present site of City Hall Annex. The Methodists also had a church in North Wellington that was built by John Hilbert.[20]

Anglican church & Reverend John Booth Good

The Reverend John Booth Good had made it his mission to build a church when he arrived in Nanaimo in 1861. He initially held services in the Hudson's Bay Company's schoolroom with the support of Mine Manager Charles Nicol. Authority figures did support the Anglican Church, for the HBC assigned land for a church and rectory just off Dallas Square. The transfer of the land for the church became complicated by the HBC sale of the mining operation. The land deed was not transferred to the Bishop until after the church was completed in 1862. The opening service was held June 8, 1862, the deed conveyed in July 1864, and the consecration service was held August 27, 1865.

The Reverend Good left Nanaimo to serve the church in various communities around the colonies. His first request to return to Nanaimo was rejected, but his old friend Bishop George Hills intervened on his behalf. Good arrived back in his old parish on a temporary basis in November 1882. Since he had left the congregation, several ministers came and went. The Reverends Roberts, Malachi, and Clarke preceded him, and now the church was ready for some stability. By Easter of 1883, Good's family joined him.[21] And Good stayed until retirement in 1899.

Good had been particularly looking forward to renewing an acquaintance with one of his first Snuneymuxw parishioners—Louis Augustine Good—whom, as a young man, he had almost adopted twenty years before. Louis was now a Chief of the Snuneymuxw and was in a position of power and influence.

Good was dismayed to find that no religious services had been held for ten years in the Snuneymuxw community, and many had rejected Christian doctrine.[22] Those who still believed had transferred to Good's old competitor, the Methodist Church. Good persevered and within ten years had Louis back in the Anglican

St. Paul's Anglican Church and bandstand in Dallas Square.

fold again, working as an interpreter for East Coast Indian Agent William Henry Lomas.

St. Paul's schoolroom

Once again, Good became immersed in Nanaimo community life, holding fund-raising events for the church, such as dances, whist tournaments, and the Christmas Tree Festival. He opened two private schools held in the rectory, a Boys' School held in St. Paul's Schoolroom, and a Girls' School taught by his daughter Amy. Each school had an average of ten students. St. Paul's schoolroom was well used by the community during the 1860s and 1970s for concerts, lectures, and other entertainment. Mark Bate described it as a "tastefully designed structure."

Roman Catholic churches & priests

The Roman Catholic Father Modeste Demers was consecrated in 1847 as the first Bishop of Vancouver Island, "with responsibility also for the British territories on the mainland."[23] He was the first Catholic priest to visit Nanaimo. In 1855 he preached to the

Snuneymuxw for a short time. Another ten years passed before a small wooden chapel was dedicated on August 6, 1865 and named St. Peter's.

In 1876, the first permanent priest was assigned. Father John Nicholas Lemmens soon discovered the old church was not large enough to accommodate the growing population, and a new St. Peter's Church was built a short distance from the old one. The Sisters of St. Ann taught school in the old church until the Convent was built in 1879. The old church was converted into a rectory until a new residence was built for *St. Peter's Roman Catholic Church.* the priest, then it was used as a Parish Hall. The Young Men's Institute held meetings there, and the hall became known as the C.M.I. Hall.[24]

Father Lemmens was elevated to the position of Bishop of the Diocese in 1882 and six years later was transferred to the West Coast Mission in Alberni where he built that city's first Roman Catholic church.[25]

The next priests to serve St. Peter's in Nanaimo stayed for only a short time: they were Father John Althoff, Father J.A. Durant, Father Emile Sobry and Father F. Verbeke. In 1898 Father W. Haynen arrived and provided continuity to the church, serving until 1937.

Presbyterian churches & ministers

Presbyterians first worshipped in the old courthouse until 1866 when Peter Sabiston built the first St. Andrew's Presbyterian Church. Peter was one of the three Sabiston brothers from the Orkney Island brought by the HBC to work at Fort Rupert.[26] It was a common practice in the early days of the colonies to hold church services in courthouses. The first church, at Fitzwilliam and Wesley Streets, was a wooden building, described as "neat and commodious" and was home to the congregation for the next 22 years.

Reverend Robert Jamieson, was the first Presbyterian itinerant missionary to come to Nanaimo. He divided his time between Nanaimo and New Westminster. There were familiar names on the list of the 19 members taking the first Communion in 1866. Included were the Dunsmuir, Dick, and Bryden families. Jamieson was described as a man "with indomitable courage." Initially he built the first St. Andrew's Presbyterian Church, in New Westminster, then St. Andrew's in Nanaimo. Before the church was completed, the *Nanaimo Gazette* reported a wedding of note: Reverend Jamieson married Eliza Malpass and William Parkin.[27] Eliza's parents were Lavina and John Malpass *Princess Royal* pioneers. The Parkins settled in the Comox Valley.

Another prominent Presbyterian, John Dick, married Esther Ann Richardson in 1872, but their wedding was held in the Wesleyan Methodist Church because St. Andrew's was without a minister. The Dick family were staunch supporters of St. Andrew's Presbyterian Church.[28]

Reverend Jamieson served the Nanaimo congregation until 1869 and was succeeded for a short time by Reverend William Aitken.

St. Andrew's Presbyterian Church 1893, corner of Fitzwilliam and Wesley Streets.

176

The church remained without a resident minister for a number of years until the Church of Scotland sent out Reverend William Clyde, 1875-82.

It was the practice until 1891 for the Church of Scotland to appoint ministers. Then the Presbyterian Church of Canada united with the Church of Scotland, giving more independence to the Canadian Presbyterian churches. This union brought Canadian-born Reverend D.A. McRae to Nanaimo in 1891, and under his leadership a new church was built. The cost of construction was $30,000, and it had seating for up to 1200 people.[29] The cornerstone for the present day St. Andrew's (United) Church was laid on July 18, 1893. Adjacent to the old one, it was completed on February 11, 1894.[30] The old church was converted into a classroom for Sunday School and social events.

Reverend McRae stayed for five years and was replaced by Reverend W.B. Cumming who served the congregation until 1903.[31]

Later Congregations

At Confederation in 1871, it was said Nanaimo "was a hardy little town of 1,000 people with about as many religious congregations as there were liquor outlets."[32] This source claimed there were twelve congregations in existence at that time.

The Salvation Army

The Salvation Army arrived in June 1888 under Officer-in-charge Captain McDowell, and Lieutenants Richardson and Greatrex. Meetings were held in the City Hall. Musical instruments came the following year, and a band was formed under bandmaster Joe Williamson. One old soldier recalled:

> It was no unusual sight to see the Hall packed to capacity with devoutly attentive worshippers, the windows of the Hall down, so that the crowds outside might also hear the message of salvation.[33]

There were a few converts from the Methodist Church. George Sage and his family joined when there were only a few other families. George, the son of Mary Ann and Jesse Sage, was born at sea on the voyage of the *Princess Royal* and was often referred to as the "man without a country."

The founding Booth family made three visits to Nanaimo in the 1890s. Eva Booth, daughter of the founder of the Salvation Army visited in 1894; her brother and their father General W.

Booth visited in 1895.[34] For these occasions the Sage family put on new uniforms of bright yellow, red, and green, instead of the usual navy blue.[35]

Only once did a hostile crowd confront the Salvation Army. One Sunday afternoon, as the band marched along Commercial Street, it was pelted by a barrage of potatoes. Not everyone liked the music! City council received complaints about the noise when the group met to sing and preach. In 1892 a lot was dedicated at the corner of Winfield Crescent, the present site of the Salvation Army Citadel.

First Baptist churches

The First Baptist Church was organized in 1889 under Reverend J.A. Banton. The congregation of 32 members met first in the Good Templar's Hall, until a church was built next to the hall on Crace Street. This church opened in 1891 and served the congregation well until 1911. Then a new church opened on Albert and Prideaux Street under the Reverend D.G. McDonald.[36]

St. Alban the Martyr church

In 1891, a number of members of the Anglican congregation seceded from St. Paul's and started another church, St. Alban the Martyr located on Victoria Road.

Bishop George Hills faced a difficult dilemma; he did not want to see the parish split, but had no alternative except to appoint Reverend Gavin Tovey from New Westminster to the new church. Within a period of two years St. Alban's accumulated a debt of $9,000. Reverend Tovey had struggled as Rector of St. Alban's for two years, then gave up and returned to England. Reverend George William Taylor, of St. Barnabas in Victoria, succeeded him. He resigned in 1896, and Reverend Bosanquet was appointed.[37]

St. Paul's also suffered financially as a result of the separation. At the time of John Booth Good's retirement on October 15, 1899, there were two parishes without rectors. Good's successor was the Reverend Charles Edward Cooper.

In February 1900, St. Paul's Church was repaired, cleaned, and painted. While these renovations proceeded, church services were held in the institute behind the church. This same year, the old rectory was pulled down and replaced with a stone and brick building.[38]

In 1903, St. Alban's closed, and its congregation returned to the fold of the larger St. Paul's. And then there were plans to build a new church.

CHAPTER SEVENTEEN

The Making of a City —Business and Social Life

T he *British Columbia Directory*, published yearly, outlined the growing commercial aspect of Nanaimo, noting that what had originally been a simple mining village and trading post had grown to have a thriving business center. The 1882–83 directory positively glowed in describing the community: the shipbuilding opportunities, the brewery, and the newspaper. As well, there were the numerous hotels, saloons, and restaurants that filled the need to accommodate the hundreds of young single men. Also, the directory noted that the residents took advantage of the sheltered harbour:

> It is indeed a pretty sight to see upon a summer evening the numerous boating and yachting parties which take their recreation upon the placid waters of the harbour.

Local businesses

As the Nanaimo community grew, so too did the number of businesses. At first there was only the Hudson's Bay Company store, but by 1862 three non-company stores had opened: those of Copperman, Horne, and Mayer. William Copperman, a Polish man, operated a drug store and a general trading store. For the benefit of the Snuneymuxw, he advertized his goods in Chinook, since his best customers could not read. The Chinook posters caused some amusement with his customers, but the shrewd businesman knew that someone would tell the Natives what was printed and therefore draw their attention to his shop.

After the HBC divested itself of its Nanaimo holdings, Adam Grant Horne, their storekeeper, went into business for himself, until he signed up again with the company to go to Fort Simpson. An American from Portland, Oregon, Alexander Mayer operated the third business. His "Red House" Pioneer Store became a landmark because of its visual impact on the small community.

Hotels

Scattered throughout the town were ten hotels. These included The Old Flag Inn and the Temperance on Bastion Street; the Royal, the Miners' Exchange, the Hotel Wilson, and the Nanaimo Hotel on Commercial Street; the Provincial and the Identical on Victoria Crescent; the Newcastle on Wellington Road; and the Dew Drop Inn (now the Patricia) on Haliburton Street.[1] The Dew Drop Inn, built by George Baker, had the distinction of having the first bowling alley.[2]

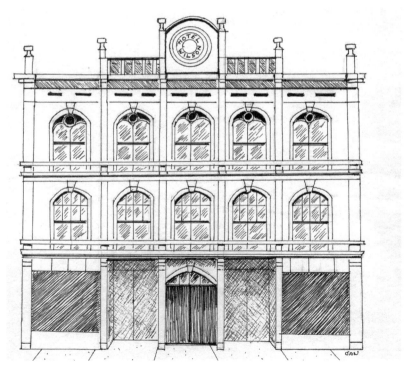

Hotel Wilson, Commercial Street, was built in 1892 for tinsmith Walter Richard Wilson. Drawing by author.

Other hotels had come and gone, their frail wooden structures unable to stand the test of time. The hotels had no trouble securing liquor licences that were often obtained over the protests of residents. The government needed the revenue.

The Nanaimo Brewery & the Union Brewery

Beer could be obtained locally from the Nanaimo Brewery operated by John Mahrer. The brewery, first established in 1879 on Mill Street, could produce 30,000 gallons per year.[3] A new building was built in 1890 on Commercial Street on the site of the former Nanaimo Hotel.

His father, a distiller in Austria, taught Mahrer the brewery business. John Mahrer came to Nanaimo for a year in 1870, and then for a time operated a bakery and a restaurant in the Cariboo. He returned to Nanaimo in 1876 and started a bakery, then a soda water factory, a soap factory, and eventually opened the Nanaimo Brewery. He married Sarah Jane Woods of Nanaimo in 1879.

On March 10, 1893, the Union Brewing Company purchased the Nanaimo Brewery for $10,000 with the promise inserted in the deed that the brewery would not be used for the manufacture of beer for a period of ten years. (A Port Angeles company expressed interest in purchasing the effects of the Nanaimo Brewery.)

The principals involved in the Union Brewing Company Limited in 1900 were John Pawson, president, Fred S. Whiteside, secretary, Marshall E. Bray, treasurer, Henry Reifel, manager, Conrad Reifel, labourer, and Hy Reifel, brewer.[4] John Mahrer was appointed vice-president. President John Pawson built the Old Flag Inn near the Bastion Street Bridge. He was an alderman on the first city council and mayor of Nanaimo in 1880.

The Reifel family lived in the Franklyn House and operated the brewery on the site next door. Brewer Hy Reifel's salary was increased to $150 a month, and he was given management of the brewery. The minutes of the company show the cost of production for the month of June 1900: malt $1,740, hops $201, labour $889, coal $155, sundries $100, and horse feed $100. Total cost: $3,185, leaving a profit of $520.[5]

On August 11, 1893, Henry and Hy Reifel told the board of directors that a committee of saloonkeepers had asked them for a reduction in the price of beer owing to the five-cent movement. The Victoria Brewing Company had tried to sell its beer in Nanaimo and Comox at reduced rates. Business must have been good because the Union Brewing Company managed to give its shareholders a dividend of 5 percent in January 1895. The Union Brewing Company operated until 1918 and was one of the most successful breweries in the province.

Horse and wagon of the Union Brewery

Two other breweries turned out quantities of beer in bulk and in family kegs and bottles; they were the Empire Brewery and the Lansdown Brewery.[6] Their product was mainly for home consumption but some was shipped down to Victoria. However, they offered little competition for the larger Union Brewery.

Mahrer & Company was the wholesale liquor distributor in town with an office on Front and Wharf streets.

John Hirst—Entrepreneur

On the harbour side of Front Street, John Hirst, an early community-minded entrepreneur, built a large stone warehouse in 1875. The thick stone walls still serve the present-day Nanaimo Port Authority offices at this site. Stone for the warehouse came from the Newcastle Island quarry.

Hirst also built a general shipping wharf along the south side of the HBC coal jetty, known as Hirst's Wharf. The *Beaver* was the first steamer to dock at the wharf in 1878.[7]

Hirst operated a grocery store on Commercial Street with a staff of ten, and a delivery service of three wagons. Early advertising noted the store was the sole agent for the popular Monsoon Tea. The store dated back to 1863.[8] Hirst also served on the first city council of 1875, continuing into 1878, and again in 1881 and 1882.

John Mahrer later used the upper floor of Hirst's warehouse for liquor distribution: Mahrer & Co.'s Liquor House. Frank Stannard used the lower floor facing the water for a flour, seed, and produce business. Later Stannard took over the entire building, "F.J. Stannard" as agent for Ogilvie Flour Mills and the only feed store in the area.

Interior of Hirst Brother's Store on Commercial Street.

John Hirst died in 1882 leaving a large estate including farms at Englishman River and Gabriola Island, as well as his warehouse and wharf. It took over ten years to settle the estate. Son James took over the business.

The town of Parksville has its beginning with John Hirst, who first bought land there in 1870. Three years later in order to control the flooding from Englishman's River, he built a system of canals and dikes. The area was then known as Englishman's River. The family built a house on their property that became the first school. It was not until 1890 that the area became known as Parksville after the first postmaster, Nelson Parks.

A.G.Horne & Son

Adam Grant Horne returned to Nanaimo from Comox in 1878, and opened a dry goods and grocery store: A.G. Horne & Son, on Victoria Crescent. His wife Elizabeth wanted better educational opportunities for their children and also wanted to be closer to her sister and brother, and their eldest son, Adam Henry Horne, who was married and living in Nanaimo.

Horne's store advertisements in the *Nanaimo Free Press* make interesting reading:

> There are many grave doubts about the Settlement Act becoming law, but it is a settled fact that Horne & Son of

Victoria Crescent have the finest and cheapest display of FASHIONABLE HATS direct from the manufactory.

Another ad noted:

During the boisterous month of March people cannot be too careful of their persons, and the best place in town to purchase the finest and cheapest UNDERCLOTHING— direct from the manufactory—is at Horne & Son's store, Victoria Crescent.[9]

Audacious Burglary

The Horne store made the headlines in January 1881 when it was robbed. The *Free Press* headlined the crime "Audacious Burglary." Horne discovered the burglary when he opened for business. Thieves had taken a large quantity of the most expensive goods in the store. The intruders entered through a rear window; they tried to open the safe but the article noted "the safe being one of J. & J. Taylor's did not budge worth a cent."[10]

Later some of the merchandise was found on Cavan Street. Police Constables Stewart, Drake, and Pargeter searched Snuneymuxw and Chinese houses. When police entered a small house occupied by a Chinese family, Ah Jake and his wife Ah Dok Leet, they found blankets identified as part of the stolen goods from Horne's store. Ah Jake, Ah Dok Leet, and Ah Kling were jailed.

A total of five Chinese were tried for the robbery: Young Dok Leet, Lee Hung, Ah Jake, Ah Klung, and Fook Loye. Mark Bate was the only person to testify on behalf of the accused. He said he had known Ah Jake for eight years and always looked upon him as a very good man indeed.

Young Dok Leet and Lee Hung were convicted of breaking into the store, and Ah Jake for receiving stolen property. The three received a three-year sentence at the prison in New Westminster. At that time there were only three prisons in the province at: New Westminster, Kamloops, and Victoria.[11]

Hilbert's Home Furnishings and Undertaking Parlour

John Hilbert also operated successful businesses. A patternmaker by trade, he turned his hand to making furniture. Hilbert and wife Mary Jane immigrated from England in 1873. He rented a vacant building on Bastion Street and opened his business under the name of Hilbert's Home Furnishings. He built cupboards, tables, and chairs, and other household furnishings.

Hilbert also built the Methodist Church in North Wellington, the schoolhouse on Crace Street, and several homes in town.

Later Hilbert expanded his business into manufacturing caskets and started a new business, Hilbert's Undertaking Parlour. This was probably a lucrative business considering the number of deaths in the mines. Eventually the furniture business closed to enable him to concentrate on the undertaking business. Son Albert apprenticed under his father and when old enough joined the family business.[12]

John Hilbert and wife Mary Jane in 1890.

Raybould Millinery Shop and the Nanaimo Emporium

Raybould Millinery shop was situated on Front Street then later moved to the Odd Fellows building on Commercial Street. The large shop windows revealed the latest fashion in millinery imported from England.[13] These were always of interest to the women in the community. While Phoebe Raybould was busy with the clothing business and charity work, her husband William partnered with Mr. Shakespeare in 1866 and opened the Nanaimo Emporium that supplied apparel for men.

The Raybboulds from Staffordshire, England came to Vancouver Island on the clipper *Napoleon III* in January 1864.[14] Phoebe's sister-in-law, Mrs. Noah Shakespeare also came to join her husband in Nanaimo.

The Raybboulds took a keen interest in community affairs and politics.

"The Red House"–Pioneer Store

Another shop of interest was the Pioneer Store, or "Red House," operated by Alexander Mayer and situated on the northeast corner of Bastion and Commercial Street. It operated from 1863 to 1890.

Historian Martha Kenny wrote how she loved the old shop, painted red,

> ... quite violently, so-real honest to goodness wagon red, and gloried in the fact. I loved that old store chiefly because of a wonderful bargain sale of real silk ribbons at ten cents a yard. Daddy Mayer's, as he was known, eyes twinkled behind his steel rimmed glasses. Mayer's stock was most comprehensive, and any reasonably minded customer could be satisfied whether he sighed for a darning needle, a barrel of molasses, or a bale of hay."[15]

Mayer, from Portland, arrived in Nanaimo in 1861 with two large trunks of goods to establish his clothing shop. He began by opening his trunks at the street corner and quickly sold out. Returning with another selection of dry goods, he opened a shop in the lobby of the Miners' Hotel and again sold out.

In 1863 he bought a lot with a log building on it for $600. Thinking the structure a bit drab, he mixed up a can of paint, adding what he thought was a touch of red. Thereafter it became known as the "Red House–the Pioneer Store." The general store was a success from the beginning. His two sons-in-law Sam Levi and Marcus Wolfe joined in the business that thrived for many years.[16]

George Bevilockway eventually purchased the Red House store and carried on the business. George had spent thirteen years mining before going into business and opening meat markets in Nanaimo and Wellington.[17]

Hamilton Powder Company

In July 1890, the Hamilton Powder Company built a plant at Northfield on 165 acres of land purchased from the Vancouver Coal Company. The machinery was shipped out from Scotland, and the plant went into operation in November with the first shipment made November 22, 1890.[18] Twenty-five people were employed making blasting powder.

A few years later, another plant was built at Departure Bay with the first shipment being made on December 15, 1896. A one-horse wagon transported the nitroglycerine from the new plant to Northfield for mixing.

> The product was known as Dualin Stumping Powder and consisted of three parts black powder and one part nitroglycerine. This was carried on safely for about four

years, but after an accident the Dualin was made at Departure Bay.[19]

George Norris—the *Nanaimo Free Press*

From the time George Norris established the *Nanaimo Free Press* in 1874, he made it his business to chronicle the day-to-day happenings of city council and early Nanaimo. The first edition was printed on Wednesday, April 15, 1874, as a four-page semi-weekly. In the early years, it averaged three columns of advertisements to two of news items.

The first newspaper office was at the present location of the Globe Hotel.[20] A few months later the paper moved to a more permanent location on Commercial Street. From here Norris kept the community informed, or entertained, for a subscription cost of $4 per year, or 50 cents a month.[21]

Mark Bate noted the arrival of the newspaper:

> The *Free Press* came somewhat suddenly upon us bringing a fresh germ of hopefulness, and by the energy and push of the editor and proprieter, George Norris, a splendid work was begun in disseminating intelligence of doing and happenings hereabout. Mr. Norris, as a publisher, did not dally with his duty.[22]

Norris was born in London, England, and came with his parents to Toronto, where he spent his formative years. At eighteen years of age in 1863, he came to Vancouver Island and began working in Victoria on the *Chronicle* newspaper. While in Victoria he met Amanda Theresa Gough, the eldest daughter of Edwin and Elizabeth Gough of Nanaimo. The family often made trips to Victoria, and in 1867 they had family photographs taken at George Robinson's Photographic Studio.[23] On one of these trips Amanda met George Norris and a romance blossomed. They were married in 1869. When

Blasting Shakes Victoria Road Neighbourhood

On March 30, 1891 the *Nanaimo Free Press* reported a giant powder explosion had taken place on Victoria Road causing extensive damage. Fortunately there were no fatalities. A city work crew had been thawing out some powder used in blasting rock—when it exploded. Many of the windows in the neighbourhood were blown.

The dangerous nature of the product resulted in the city passing the Explosive Bylaw mandating that no more than 50 pounds of blasting powder could be carried on any vehicle within the city, and no more than 50 pounds could be stored in any building within the city limits.

Interior of Nanaimo Free Press *Print Shop*

the *Chronicle* merged with the *Colonist,* Norris joined the new enterprise.

He saw an opportunity for a newspaper in Nanaimo and moved Amanda and their three small children, Mary Elizabeth, George Edwin and William Frederick, and started the *Nanaimo Free Press*. Amanda helped her husband in the print shop but eventually George and William took her place.

The introduction of the newspaper fit perfectly with the city's incorporation, for it gave a clear picture of the growing community. On the front page you could find the city directory listing all of the councillors, the provincial inspector of mines, the justice of the peace, the collector of customs, harbour master, and country court judge, plus the Nanaimo Literary Institute's president and treasurer.

Editorials were of general interest, about education, roads, and communication, and critical comment about the actions of the provincial government. Norris considered all were fair game and worthy of space. He never missed a council meeting and declined municipal office as he considered it conflicted with his newspaper business. And the *Free Press* played a large part in preserving Nanaimo's history through special editions of the newspaper.

It was not unusual to see an entire column taken up with jokes or unusual stories. This humorous tale from the April 19, 1879 edition is entitled "Pat on the Road."

An Irishman, driven to desperation by the money market and the high prices of provisions, procured a pistol and took to the road. Meeting a traveller he stopped him with: "Your money or your life!" Seeing Pat was green at the business, the traveller said: "I'll tell you what I'll do, I'll give you all my money for that pistol." "Agreed." Pat received the money and handed over the pistol. "Now, " said the traveller, "Hand back that money or I'll blow your brains out!" "Blaze away, my harty," said Pat, "never a drop of powder is there in it!"

There were also the more serious notices:

Strangers visiting Departure Day or Wellington are strictly prohibited from riding on the cars on the Wellington Colliery railway. DUNSMUIR, DIGGLE & CO.

The Vancouver Coal Mining and Land Co. Limited, hereby gives notice that after this date, any person found cutting or removing timber from their land, outside the city limits, without obtaining permission at the Company's Office will be prosecuted. March 13, 1877.

Advertisements also made for interesting reading. Fletcher & Thomas, made boats, skiffs, and coffins on the shortest notice, and advertised, "Funerals carefully conducted."

George Bevilockway gave notice he had purchased the Wellington Market from John Thompson. The butcher shop was now prepared to supply all kinds of meats and vegetables.[24]

With Bill Hopkins as his assistant, Norris and his *Free Press* continued for eleven years as the undisputed newspaper in the Nanaimo area. Then in 1885, a number of competitors entered the field. Some lasted months, others several years. Mechanical presses were installed at the *Free Press*. And in December 1888 the *Free Press* became a daily and blew away all the competition until 1899 when the *Nanaimo Herald* entered the field. These two newspapers survived side by side until 1938 when the *Free Press* bought out its rival.

Norris had a fully equipped commercial printing plant that also did show printing, ledger printing, and bookbinding. The plant was considered one of the best on Vancouver Island. Orders received from as far away as San Francisco were brought to the city by the colliery boats and returned the same way. The business employed 43 men.

The newspaper publisher also was interested in law and had a good library of legal books. On occasion Norris' knowledge of law was of great assistance to the city council. In some instances he not only advised his neighbours on legal matters but on one occasion also successfully argued his own case in a libel suit brought by Robert Dunsmuir.

During a strike in 1877, Norris had covered a union meeting and reported on comments made by two men, George Vipond and Uriah Hockyard; these were given good coverage. It was duly reported Vipond had called Dunsmuir a liar. Dunsmuir did not take the comment lightly and sued the two men and the newspaper for libel. Charges against the two men were dismissed a few days later. Norris successfully defended himself against the libel charge that went all the way to the Supreme Court before Dunsmuir decided to withdraw the charges. This particular precedent-setting case is still cited when a lawsuit involves freedom of the press.

On another occasion two men came to Norris seeking a legal judgment over an argument about a fence. Norris took a law book off the shelf, handed it to the men and said, "Look it up for yourselves." They sat down together, read the arguments and came to an agreement. When they were about to leave, they asked Norris what they owed him. He waved them aside then added "If you really want to give some token of appreciation, you might pay a year's subscription in advance to the *Free Press!*"

Most residents of Nanaimo remember George Norris as a good citizen and a good neighbour. One man recalled his first Christmas Day in the city. He was walking along down the street when a bearded middle-aged gentleman met up with him. Was he a stranger? Yes, he was. "Then come home and have dinner with us," said the man. The bearded gentleman was Norris, the stranger a very young and lonely William McGirr, who later ran the old Nanaimo Hospital.

Norris served his community in more ways than as a publisher. In 1889, he was sworn in as the first charter member of the Nanaimo Board of Trade. He was a member of the Pilot Board, the Nanaimo Hospital; he was also a School Board trustee, treasurer of the fire department and on the board of the Agricultural Society. When he died in January 6, 1902 at the age of 57, his two sons George and William took over management of the newspaper. They continued the business until 1912 when George became the scle owner. Amanda remained active in the community and is reported to have been an astute businesswoman. She died in 1928.

In 1897 George Norris married Clara Emma Brown, or Bernie as her friends nicknamed her. Bernie was a trained milliner. They had three sons, Ronald, Oswald "Ossie," and Eugene "Dude." The family connection with the newspaper ended when it was sold in 1954.

Nanaimo Board of Trade

On May 6, 1889 the merchants in town formed the first Nanaimo Board of Trade with Andrew Haslam as Chairman. The Act of Incorporation and bylaws document is dated May 21, 1889. The act was revised on February 24, 1903. Marcus Wolfe was appointed secretary, and Notary Public Edmund Montague Yarwood took the oath of office from the membership. City Clerk Samuel Gough swore that the City of Nanaimo had a population of "not less than two thousand five hundred at the present time." Membership was $6.00 payable in quarterly installments of $1.50.[25]

The board was made up of influential Nanaimo businessmen: Samuel Robins, mine superintendent; Andrew Haslam, sawmill owner; George Norris, newspaper publisher; John Hilbert, furniture manufacturer; Donald Smith, real estate agent; Edwin Pimbury, dispensing chemist; George H. Blakeway, druggist; and stationer Alfred Raper. The merchants were George Bevilockway, James Abrams, James Harvey, Thomas Watson Glaholm, and Thomas and William Hirst. These men set the tone for business development and the promotion of Nanaimo.

Lodges and fraternities

There were a number of fraternal lodges in town. Masonic fraternity Ashlar Lodge No. 3 owned a building on Commercial Street, as did the Odd Fellows' Lodge, Black Diamond No. 4. Other fraternity lodges such as the Foresters' Lodge, the Ancient Order of United Workmen, the Good Templar, and Onward Lodge No. 2, held their meetings in a hall on Front Street near the Methodist Church.

Creating a social life

Nanaimo has had a rich cultural life almost from its beginning. Not much is known about the orchestra that played for the Christmas ball in 1854 that was held in a 12 x 12 foot building. It had been whitewashed in and out for the occasion. There was not enough room for everyone, so that those who could not get in crowded about the door and windows. Christmas trees had been brought in from the forest nearby, and paper decorations and odds and ends hung about the hall. Fish oil lamps and a fireplace gave the only light.[26] Many at the party were those families who arrived on the *Princess Royal* only weeks before. Edwin Gough's organ and Matthew Miller's violoncello may have provided the music.

Nanaimo's literary life

Nanaimo has a long literary history. The first literary meeting in 1859 had netted $44 to purchase books for a circulating library. But it was not until November 25, 1862 that St. Paul's Literary Society was founded and the church school used for meetings.

Reverend John Booth Good, as a founding member supported by Bishop Hills, proposed rigid control over who could join. He dictated that those men who "lived in states of fornication, habitual drunkenness or other gross immoralities," would be excluded. As superintendent, he held veto power and kept tight control of the organization. The annual membership was $5. Charles Nicol was elected first president, and Bishop Hills delivered the first lecture.

A few meetings later Mark Bate was concerned at the slow pace of the group's development. In the 1862 report he noted the group's "rather cheerless existence" and hoped there would be an attempt made to infuse new life into the group. To entice others to join the society, he suggested "no name be left untried that would render the Institution popular and secure for it official support." [27]

The membership took the report to heart and changed the constitution allowing more flexibility for membership. Reverend Good lost his veto power and position as superintendent. A little annoyed at the turn of events, he retaliated by banning the society from using St. Paul's church school building for meetings.

Two years later the Literary Society decided to build its own hall. Nicol wrote to the Colonial Secretary concerned about the piece of land the coal company had granted to the society on Bastion Street. Since the members were not considered a corporate body, they could not hold land. Nicol hoped there would be no objection to the Colonial Secretary, treasurer and chief justice having their names added to the Board of Trustees. [28]

Governor Arthur Kennedy officially opened the Literary Institute Hall, a two-storey building, in November 1864. The building had a meeting room below and a reading room above. Reverend Good was placated with the position as vice-president and played an active role in fund raising for the new building. For an annual membership fee, members could use the reading room with its newspapers and periodicals from England, or borrow books. This hall became the centre of the social life of the community since it could accommodate 250 people.

The Literary Institute was enlarged and reopened on August 18, 1877. In honour of the occasion Joseph P. Planta read a poem he had composed. These are the first few lines:

Well met are we, on this auspicious night,
To hail the opening of our town's delight!
This spacious hall with various rooms in suite,
That make Nanaimo Institute complete;
An honour to our city and this coast,
Alike the people's honest pride and boast!

The celebration of the reopening concluded with a piano overture by William John Goepel and violin solo by Mayor Mark Bate. Goepel married Bate's daughter Sarah Ann. The president of the institute at this time was William Raybould and the treasurer was Thomas Morgan.[29]

There were many other performances held at the Literary Institute, perhaps one of the most unusual was a magic show by a deaf mute. The program contained many magical tricks and closed with a grand aerial suspension. The price of admission was 50 cents for front row seats and 25 cents for back seats.

Philharmonic Orchestra Society

The first musical group expanded as more miners arrived from Great Britain in later years, enough to form a philharmonic orchestra in 1864. They included: Mark Bate and Thomas McLean on violins; Thomas Hindle on cornet; Joseph Lawlese on flute; John Holden, the local blacksmith on violincello; and pianist Thomas Parker. The small orchestra was in great demand for special events, and on occasion its size grew as some musicians came in from Victoria.

Junior Brass Band–Silver Cornet Band

In the fall of 1872, the Nanaimo Junior Brass Band was founded. During the summer of 1872 funds became available to purchase instruments from the Georgetown Military Band at a cost of $300. The purchase included reeds, brass, and snare and bass drums.

The instruments arrived in the fall and members began practising in earnest under the direction of the Reverend James Raynard, who was considered "a high class musician." He had been choirmaster of Yorkminster Cathedral in England. Raynard was the rector of St. Paul's Anglican Church. He and Mark Bate along with Dr. William MacNaughton Jones, the colliery surgeon, and John Holden, made the band a reality. The first public performance was given on the occasion of Queen Victoria's birthday, May 24, 1873.

When Raynard left to take a position in Saanich, a farewell concert was held in his honour. Miss Dunsmuir and Mr. Harvey sang a duet:

The Silver Cornet Band at May 24 celebrations.

"Gypsy Countess." "Miss Dunsmuir had a sweet and clear soprano [voice] and Harvey was a clear baritone."[30] This baritone was probably James Harvey who married Dunsmuir's second daughter Agnes, and who also ran the post office and his own store, James Harvey's General Store. The soprano became his future wife. Mark Bate replaced Raynard as president and conductor of the band.

Somehow Bate managed to keep the musical group alive with his sons Mark, Jr., and Thomas; Joseph Randle; John and Thomas Morgan; David Nebb; and numerous other players who came and went over the years. Their next big event was the launching of the barque *Nanaimo* in September 1882. When a bandstand was built in Dallas Square, designed after the one at Beacon Hill Park, Victoria, the band entertained many during warm summer evening concerts.

March 23, 1889 was the day that the Junior Brass Band officially became the Silver Coronet Band,[31] and new rules of conduct were adopted at the first meeting. Under Article III:

> no member while on duty or on parade shall in any way use any bad or vulgar language or shall conduct himself unseemly.[32]

The bylaws were adopted April 8, 1889 by president Thomas Morgan, bandleader Joseph Lawden, treasurer George Lee, and secretary Charles Wilson.

Over the years the band attended events in New Westminster, Victoria, Vancouver, and Seattle. It performed at fund-raising events, the agricultural fair, sports days, and May Day concerts and balls. It even sponsored a moonlight cruise, organized to circumvent the Sunday-closing bylaw, so patrons could enjoy a drink while they listened to the band music.

None of the musicians made money playing at the events; they did it for the love of music and often paid for their transportation from personal funds. The Silver Cornet Band continued to provide entertainment for other generations, and it is still performing today under another name, changed in 1950 to the Nanaimo Concert Band.

Performing arts

The first dance academy was established in 1867 under Signor J. Hazazer and the first ballet performance given in 1874.

Fund-raising events were held in aid of the hospital and cemetery site in 1877. The first of a series of lectures for the Hospital Fund was held in the Literary Institute on *The genius of Shakespeare*. A piano and violin overture concert performed by Mrs. Joan Dunsmuir and Mr. Scales also enriched the coffers for a new cemetery site. Mrs. Dunsmuir performed a solo entitled "The Return of Spring."[33]

There was also a Shakespearean reading group of ten men known as The Bard's Club, formed in 1878. For ten years they gave readings once a month, until the group disbanded.

There were other types of entertainment, not always musical. One of the most popular entertainers was Captain Jonas Hewett, skipper of the barge *Thames*. Captain Hewett was a magician and showman and was often joined by local blacksmith, Jim Miller, who was a talented musician and comedian.[34] The two men put on quite a show.

Theatrical performers came from San Francisco taking advantage of the time when the coal ship was docked, to entertain Nanaimo residents. In 1877, Mr. J.A. Sawtelle accompanied by a theatrical troupe arrived on the *Maude* and performed a three-act play entitled *Driven from Home*. The troupe concluded the performance with a roaring farce *Taraxicum Twitters*. Sawtelle was a regular visitor to Nanaimo, and the audience still remembered fondly his previous performance of *Rip Van Winkle*. On this recent visit he brought a new set of scenery. Another group, the Wilton Theatrical Troupe arrived on the *Cariboo Fly* to stage the play *The Tiger Girl of Cuba*. The leading actresses were well regarded in Oregon and California.[35]

If the weather was favorable, performances were held outdoors; this was especially accommodating if the show happened to involve animals. These outdoor events were held at what later became the Central Sports Ground (now Harbour Park Mall). The area came into existence when the narrow gap between Nanaimo and Cameron Island was filled in, and the island ceased to exist. Billboards advertised the main events appearing in the city. One such event was the Great Professor LeClair who appeared in Nanaimo on June 9, 1886 with his giant balloon. Few had ever seen such a balloon.

Professor LeClair's Great Balloon Act

Professor LeClair secured the use of a clearing near Skinner Street, not too far from the Institute Hall where the rest of his show would be performed. A furnace warmed the huge balloon bag that had a single trapeze suspended in place of a basket. On June 9, 1886, when the crowd gathered to witness his ascent into the sky, the professor firmly gripped the trapeze as his assistant released the balloon from its mooring Suddenly the professor shot up in the air, caught by a wind current that snapped the single mooring line.

The plight of the professor did not go unnoticed. One man who witnessed the ascent realized the professor would be in great danger once the hot air cooled off. A downdraft then sent the professor and his balloon plunging towards the water of the harbour. The man ran to the harbour, cast off with a rowboat, and was out in the water by the time the balloon came down.

Professor LeClair realizing he was in serious trouble, jumped as soon as he was over the water, and dived deep to clear the balloon. When he emerged he was surprised to find a rowboat waiting to pick him up. Several other boats also came out to rescue the professor and salvaged the balloon and trapeze. The good professor, undaunted by his near fatal accident, disappeared to change into dry clothes only to reappear on stage to the great applause of the audience.[36]

Nanaimo Opera House

The Nanaimo Opera House, opened in 1889, provided another venue for local and visiting performers. The three-storey brick building operated as a hotel on the upper two floors and as a theatre on the ground floor.[37] The latter had a beautiful mirrored rotunda, a royal box and loges, as well as upper and lower galleries and an orchestra pit.

The prime attraction in 1900 was a visit from Pauline Johnson and Company.[38] The well-known poet, daughter of a Mohawk chief and an English woman, would dress in buckskin and give popular recitals across Canada and Great Britain.

She had performed in Nanaimo several times. Perhaps the most memorable is recorded in Betty Keller's biography *Pauline* published

Nanaimo Opera House, Church Street, opened Nov. 16, 1889. Drawing by author.

in 1981, where her "escape at Nanaimo" is discussed.[39] The date was September 28, 1894, the same evening the Royal and Nanaimo hotels burned to the ground, along with Fire Hall #1 and Stephenson's store. Patrick Magee lost his life in the blaze that engulfed the entire block.[40]

Johnson performed in Nanaimo again in 1903 before her retirement to Vancouver in 1909.

Many of the musical productions in the Nanaimo Opera House were lavish affairs, as evidenced by the photographs of the cast from the various performances now in the Nanaimo Centennial Museum.

Official celebrations

City council could mandate public celebrations, days of mourning, or civic holidays. These various celebrations show the rich cultural diversity before the turn of the century.

A lavish production in the Opera House.

Queen Victoria's birthday

Queen Victoria's birthday was officially celebrated beginning May 24, 1881. It had, of course, been celebrated unofficially for many years before. After the Queen's death in 1901, the celebration became known as Victoria Day, then Empire Day.

The *Free Press* listed the sporting events planned for the Queen's birthday celebration in 1881. They included canoe and boat races starting from the new coal wharf. The foot races rounded the grandstand onto the Green. The weather, of course, was always a factor to be considered.

> If the weather proves propitious, the visitors and city residents can have a pleasant day's sports to celebrate the 62nd birthday of Queen Victoria, whose honoured name is revered, wherever her virtues and her wisdom are known. Long live our Noble Queen, Long may she live to reign over us, God Save the Queen.[41]

On this same occasion, the steamer *Wilson G. Hunt* offered an excursion cruise to Victoria, leaving Tuesday and returning Thursday.

Steamer Wilson G. Hunt *was a regular visitor to Nanaimo carrying mail, freight and passengers.*

The *Hunt* will arrive in Victoria in time for excursionist to witness the festivities, which comprise a regatta and horse racing only. Fare for the round trip: Gentlemen $3: Ladies $2: Children (under 12 years) $1 each.

The *Hunt* was a regular visitor to Nanaimo carrying mail, freight and passengers.

Nanaimo's first Labour Day

The first Labour Day to be celebrated in Nanaimo was on September 20, 1890. Irishman Tully Boyce, who came to the area in 1889 and worked in the Wellington and Nanaimo mines, is credited as the founder of Labour Day in the Dominion. Boyce was active in the Labour movement and lobbied for the first Monday in September to be established as Labour Day.[42]

Boyce took his lead from the Knights of Labour who had held the first Labour Day parade in New York on September 5, 1862. The day was chosen because it was spaced far enough ahead of other holidays to give the workers a rest, and it also meant the end to summer holidays.

Guy Fawkes Day

From the earliest days Nanaimo celebrated Guy Fawkes Day on November 5. This was the anniversary of the Gunpowder Plot of 1605 when a group of Catholics plotted to blow up the British Parliament at the very moment it was being opened by the king. The British miners did not forget this defiant act of aggression against authority. On November 5, 1856, Captain Charles Edward Stuart noted in his journal:

> 8.15 being the anniversary of "Gunpowder Treason" the inhabitants amused themselves with bon-fires, firing guns etc. The carpenter Nelson burned himself severely during a state of intoxication.

Other celebrations

The Scottish miners did not forget their heritage and celebrated Hogmanay every New Year's Eve. A Scottish Hogmanay is a festival of Old Year's Night, a celebration designed to bring good luck in the New Year.

Robbie Burns Day on January 25 was not forgotten either. Robert Burns is Scotland's bard and a world famous poet born in 1759. In 1875, Robert Dunsmuir presided over a Burn's Supper in Nanaimo. He spoke of how the poet's memory was revered, and he had seen the house where he had lived and was pleased to see so many present to honour Burns.[43]

Friends gather for a sewing bee. Amanda McGregor (Meakin), Phoebe Raybould (Shakespeare) and Sabra Thompson (Gough).

Nor did Welsh miners forget their roots; they celebrated in 1879 on St. David's day, with a supper and dance at the Royal Hotel. Mark Bate composed an arrangement of the Welsh piece, "Let the hills resound," that was played by the Nanaimo Brass Band under the leadership of Samuel Drake. At a similar celebration in Wellington, the Wellington Colliery Band under Mr. Quinn played the traditional song, "Men of Harloch."

A Welsh male voice choir formed in 1874 brought credit to the community in national competitions.

Joseph Planta arranged the first May Day celebration in the city in 1876. The pupils paraded to the Green where Miss Eliza Randle was crowned Queen of the May.[44]

Dominion Day was observed from 1889. Special events included sports, bicycle races and later horse racing on Haliburton Street.

Days of mourning were declared following the death of MP David William Gordon in 1893 and Queen Victoria in 1901.

CHAPTER EIGHTEEN

Rail Transportation—The Esquimalt and Nanaimo Railway

O ne of the conditions under the Terms of Union made in 1871 which admitted British Columbia into the Dominion of Canada was the construction of a railway connecting the Eastern provinces to the Pacific. Prime Minister John A Macdonald envisioned a Canada stritching together scattered provinces and territories thwarting any possible American expansion in the West. Construction would begin in 1873.

The question was, would the transcontinental railway end at Burrard Inlet, or would it cross Seymour Narrows and run south on Vancouver Island through Nanaimo to a terminus at Esquimalt? The Royal Navy base located at Esquimalt, just a few miles from Victoria, was an important location, and Victoria was the largest and most politically sensitive community on the West Coast at this time. But survey reports on the route showed the impracticablility of building a rail connection to Vancouver Island.

The route on the island, however, presented few problems except finding a right-of-way around the Malahat Range north of Victoria. Vancouver Island residents considered the construction of a rail line between Nanaimo and Esquimalt a necessity. As if to hasten things along, on July 19, 1873, a sod-turning ceremony was held at Esquimalt and a short section of a line cleared.[1] There had been surveys done by the Dominion Government, and bits and pieces of railways built in the East, but none further west than Winnipeg.

In the meantime, back in Ottawa, there was a political scandal brewing. Prime Minister Macdonald had accepted campaign funds from people expected to get the contract to build the railway. The Pacific Scandal became headline news and caused Macdonald and his government to resign. The new prime minister was Alexander

Mackenzie, a Liberal, whose speeches in the house denounced the railway saying it would financially cripple the Canadian economy. Mackenzie also thought little of British Columbians whom he considered lazy and eccentric.

The island railway land reserve

The frustration of Vancouver Islanders showed when in 1874 about 800 Victoria residents stormed the "Birdcages,"the legislative offices of the government, demanding the railway. In order to facilitate the best result that British Columbia could expect from the bitter discussion that followed, the B.C. government established a railway land reserve. The *British Columbia Gazette,* dated July 18, 1874, states: "A strip of land Twenty Miles in width along the Eastern Coast of Vancouver Island between Seymour Narrows and the Harbour of Esquimalt, is hereby Reserved."[2] This description was never used but it did prevent further land alienation. The legislation became known as the Esquimalt & Nanaimo Railway Act.

Western terminus decided

After more delays it was finally announced the western terminus of the transcontinental railway would be at Burrard Inlet. The Seymour Narrows crossing had been abandoned. The proximity to Vancouver Island had been a deciding factor in the choice; it also helped identify the new terminus geographically in the minds of world travellers.[3] The Dominion Government in Ottawa now firmly believed the Vancouver Island portion should be a local project. Meanwhile settlers continued to move into the Railway Reserve lands. From Confederation in 1871 to 1884 the province could not issue any land grants within the Railway Reserve, despite the large number of settlers who had been granted pre-emption records.

The "Carnarvon Terms"

When there was still no progress made towards construction of the island railway, residents of Vancouver Island threatened secession. They protested to Her Majesty Queen Victoria. Lord Carnarvon, the British Colonial Secretary, was appointed arbitrator and he ruled the section of line on Vancouver Island between Esquimalt and Nanaimo must be an integral part of the system. This became known as the "Carnarvon Terms."

It was a Dominion Government responsibility to arrange the construction of the railway, but because of the long delay British Columbia attempted to contract out with two rival companies: San Francisco businessman Lewis Clement's Vancouver Land and

Railway Company and Robert Dunsmuir's Victoria, Esquimalt & Nanaimo Railway Company. The latter presented a petition to the British Columbia Legislative Assembly entitled "The humble Petition of the Victoria and Esquimalt Railway Company." Dunsmuir's company had incorporated on February 21, 1873. The document stated that since the Dominion Government had abandoned the proposal to construct a railway from Esquimalt to Nanaimo, it asked the legislature to give the company full power and authority to construct the railway.[4]

Prime Minister Alexander Mackenzie introduced in Parliament the Esquimalt & Nanaimo Railway Bill giving private enterprise an incentive of cash and land.[5] The Senate defeated the Bill in April 1875 by a vote of 23 to 22, because it contained no provision to submit the contracts for parliamentary sanction.[6] British Columbians were incensed. Some believed that Mackenzie had rigged the vote in the Senate.

In the state of frustration, Premier of British Columbia George Anthony Walkem introduced in the legislature a resolution for secession if the Dominion Government did not start the transcontinental railway by May 1879. The vote carried and was sent to Ottawa, and to London. It seemed the dye was cast for British Columbia seceeding.

In order to placate the irate westerners, the Governor General Frederick Temple Blackwood Dufferin, otherwise known as Lord Dufferin, came to Vancouver Island in 1876 hoping to heal wounds. In Victoria, he was met with a banner proclaiming "Carnarvon Terms or Separation."

Ensuring the railway—the Governors General and diplomacy

Among the Mark Bate papers is correspondence related to the elaborate protocol for a visit from a Governor General. A letter from the Mayor of Victoria to Mayor Mark Bate, dated July 8, 1876, noted a public meeting would be held at the Mechanic's Institute in Victoria on Thursday July 13 at 8:00 p.m. to discuss the "most appropriate manner of receiving Lord Dufferin." The letter invited Mayor Bate to be present and, as a favor, asked if he would distribute invitations amongst the farmers in the district and "influence with them to carry out the object in view."

This may have been Bate's first knowledge of Dufferin's visit to Vancouver Island, and he would have been a little annoyed that Nanaimo was not being honoured by a visit from the Governor General.

Whatever happened in the interim is unknown, because another letter from Government House, Victoria, dated August 18, 1876, advised Mayor Bate of Dufferin's visit to Nanaimo on August 24. "His Excellency will arrive in H.M.S. *Amethyst* in the evening, disembarking if convenient to you about 10 on the 25th, sailing northward at 1 p.m. the same day."[7] Here is Dufferin's address given in Nanaimo:

I beg leave to thank you for your Loyal address: I am very glad to have an opportunity of paying a visit to the Harbour and the City of Nanaimo and of appreciating by personal observation the satisfactory indications of the mineral resources by which you are surrounded. As every sound economist must do, I regret with you the existence of those heavy duties along the United States Frontier, which impede, so disastrously, to every one concerned, commercial intercourse between the communities of this continent.

I shall not fail to bring to the notice of the proper authorities the absence of those conveniences as regards both your telegraphic communications and your public buildings generally of which you complain. I can assure you I fully sympathise with the anxieties to which you give utterance in respect of the accomplishment, by the Dominion, of those engagements to which you refer as the "Carnarvon Terms." More especially the performance of one of them in which I understand you consider yourselves so deeply interested, the construction of the Nanaimo and Esquimalt Railway, has, through the actions of one branch of the Canadian legislature, become extremely problematical.

I can only hope that a friendly consideration by the parties concerned of the difficulties which have arisen out of this disturbing incident, may lead to the substitution of some equivalent, which may be found acceptable by the Province. With regard, however, to the principal feature, of the original agreement, namely the construction of a Railway to the Pacific Ocean, although it is no part of my business to give you any assurance on that point, I sincerely hope that your just expectations may be realized.

And an old B.C. political ally was in the wings and ready to do battle again. Prime Minister Mackenzie's Liberals were defeated in the federal election of 1878, and Macdonald's government was returned to power even though Macdonald himself lost his seat in the Kingston riding. He was re-elected in a Victoria by-election and now became a Member of Parliament for Victoria as well as prime minister of Canada. There now seemed an added incentive to push ahead for the construction of the railway on the island. The Islanders waited.

In the fall of 1882, the Governor General, the Marquis of Lorne and his Royal Consort, Queen Victoria's daughter, Princess Louise, visited British Columbia. They arrived in Victoria to a town decked out with arches and decorations in celebration of their arrival. The Marquis knowing of the friction between the two levels of government over building the railway on the island hoped to bring about better feelings, something similar to what Lord Dufferin had accomplished a few years before.

A delegation from Nanaimo met the Marquis in Victoria and invited him to visit their city. The group included the Nanaimo MLA William Raybould, Mayor Mark Bate, Alexander Mayer, and George Thompson. The Marquis seized the opportunity and invited them to persuade Robert Dunsmuir to renew negotiations to build the railway, recognizing it was the key to solving the bitter feelings between the two governments.[8]

Premier Robert Beaven approached Robert Dunsmuir, who was at first reluctant to put his money into the construction and operation of the railway. The Marquis persisted, and Dunsmuir consented to build the railway if suitable terms could be reached.[9]

Dunsmuir's terms

Robert Dunsmuir laid down specific terms that were almost unacceptable. In addition to the coal, he wanted the Indian Reserve land at Nanaimo, Esquimalt, and Victoria, as well as a money subsidy and other concessions to include freedom from taxation for the railway lands. It needed both levels of governments to agree to the terms. For the next three months the Governor General and the Princess remained in the province attending balls, social functions, shooting, and fishing. They left December 7, 1882 for San Francisco.

Robert Dunsmuir's first effort to get the railway contract had failed, but time had a way of changing situations. However, now there was another bid made by a syndicate headed by Lewis Clements who proposed a line all the way to Seymour Narrows. Dunsmuir seemed confident his proposal would succeed, and off he went on a holiday in Europe. His timing could not have been worse for it was the eve of a provincial election, and he had let it be known he would be interested in representing Nanaimo.

Sir John A. Macdonald had decided he would let the province decide between the Clements' bid and Dunsmuir's bid. The House dissolved in April with only the Clements' bill having received government approval. Dunsmuir was astonished when he heard the news, then delighted when he further learned that Clements did not have secure financial backing. It was only a matter of time before the Clements contract collapsed.

Dunsmuir was elected MLA in the 1882 provincial election.

Railway consortium formed—E & N Land Grant

On August 28, 1883, Dunsmuir, his son James and son-in-law John Bryden, plus four noted American railway tycoons, Collis P. Huntington, Mark Hopkins, Leland Stanford, and Charles Crocker of the Southern Pacific Railway, signed a contract with the Dominion Government to build the railway. The Americans were known masters of the art of wheeling and dealing, but then Dunsmuir was no slouch.

By the Settlement Act of March 28, 1884, and the Dominion Lands Act that complemented it, the federal government transferred the Vancouver Island lands to the Dunsmuir group. The railway was to be completed by June 10, 1887. The federal government also agreed to take over the costs of the Esquimalt dry dock that had been losing money and was still incomplete.

And in the 1883 session of the legislature, B.C. Premier William Smithe had introduced and passed the Island Railway, Graving Dock and Railways Lands Act.[10] The complete settlement, The Settlement Act of 1884 (also known as the E & N Land Grant), received official sanction during the 1884 session. The consortium received a $750,000 bonus to help with construction and 1.9 million acres of land on the southeast side of Vancouver Island, from Goldstream, north of Victoria, to Crown Mountain near Campbell River. The Settlement Act of 1884 was the first land grant in the province and became known as the E & N Land Grant. It contained some of the finest timber in the world. In addition, the consortium was granted mineral rights, all free from taxation, just as Dunsmuir had requested.

Nanaimo's early settlers petitioned against the Act claiming it gave the Dunsmuir group a monopoly over almost half of Vancouver Island. There were many familiar names on the petition, such as Abrams, Bevilockway, Biggs, Bryant, Dick, Gough, Hilbert, Hirst, Hunter, Isbister, Malpass, Manson, Meakin, Morgan, Muir, Quennell, Sabiston, Sage, Tranfield, Walkem, Westwood, and York. Three hundred and seven Nanaimo residents signed the petition.[11] Those settlers who had occupied land within the E & N Railway belt prior to the Settlement Act of 1884 eventually won their claim to full title. For many, however, it was a long legal battle.

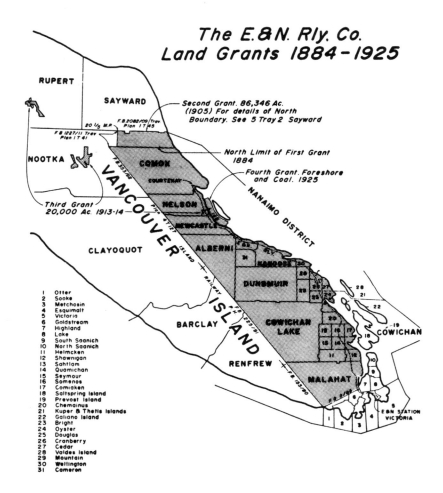

Esquimalt and Nanaimo Land Grant.

However, building a railway took a lot of money, and Dunsmuir had to raise $2.225 million The sale of timber alone from a small portion netted him $25 million.[12]

Building the E & N Railway

Building a railway from Victoria to Nanaimo seemed like a daunting task considering the mountainous terrain. Engineers had declared it impossible to find a pass over the Malahat section. But Dunsmuir knew of a young civil engineer, Joseph Hunter, who had experience finding routes on the mainland and who had also surveyed a section between Nanaimo and Mill Bay when the railway was first being discussed. In April 1884, Dunsmuir commissioned Hunter to survey and construct the railway. His instructions were characteristically terse, and written on a single piece of paper: "Build the railway." Hunter spent five months surveying and preparing for construction. The route chosen climbed the Malahat Range, wound along cliffs hundreds of feet above Finlayson Arm and crossed deep canyons until it reached the Malahat Summit where it leveled off. From there the route descended past Shawnigan Lake, across Cowichan River to Duncan and from there to Nanaimo, an easy part of the route but still heavily forested.[13]

The $200,000 contract for the Nanaimo Division of the railway was let to Graham & Bush, in September 1884. Their contract required preparing the railway bed for 22 miles between Chemainus and Nanaimo. The countryside was heavily forested and required considerable bridging and trestle construction. At Oyster Harbour, Ladysmith, a large wharf was constructed to unload rails and equipment.

Work began with a crew of "100 white men, principally wood choppers and hewers,"[14] and eventually about 800 men were employed in the project. The contractor emphasized only white men would be hired. But there were Snuneymuxw men who obtained contracts to provide railway pilings, and several others who owned their own team of horses were hired to clear stumps.[15]

The following year, A.J. McLellan was awarded the contract for the first 22 miles north of Esquimalt, extending over the Malahat to Cliffside, near Shawnigan Lake. Another contract was given to Bell, Larkin, and Paterson to lay the tracks, from Nanaimo south to the McLellan's site at Cliffside.

Advertisements for workers were placed in Victoria newspapers for "tracklayers." Pay for "good men, $2.26 per day." Bell, Larkin & Paterson, Contractors, Chemainus."[16] The farming village previously named Horse Shoe Bay now took the name Chemainus; a railway construction camp was located nearby.

In July 1885, the first locomotive (No. 1) was unloaded from the steamer *Wellington* at Oyster Harbour. The *Nanaimo Free Press* speculated about why the locomotive would be unloaded there. It noted the arrival of the, "ponderous locomotive of 40 tons weight in one piece at an out of the way 'port' like Oyster Harbour."[17] The locomotive was immediately put to work enabling construction to be stepped up. The second locomotive (No. 2) arrived at Esquimalt the following month.

In August 1885, as the E & N Railway inched towards completion, Nanaimo received a visit from the new Governor General, the Marquis of Lansdowne. He was the first Governor General to journey by rail on the new Canadian Pacific Railway's "All-Canadian route," and he was able to travel as far as 18 miles east of Revelstoke. From there he rode 47 miles on horseback to reach a train from the west, which was waiting to carry him to Port Moody. On his return, the gap had been reduced to 28 miles.[18] He visited, Victoria, Nanaimo, and New Westminster.

E & N's last spike and a Nanaimo civic reception

The first spike had been driven at Esquimalt on May 7, 1884, and rails were laid into Nanaimo by February 26, 1886. The first passenger train arrived at Nanaimo on February 28, 1886. On August 13, 1886, at 10 a.m., Prime Minister Sir John A. Macdonald drove the last spike at Cliffside Station at Shawnigan Lake, where the north and south construction crews had met.

As the prime minister hammered home a spike he declared the 75 miles of track to be an "extension of the Canadian Pacific." He turned to Robert Dunsmuir and congratulated him on the completion of the railway. And to the crowd he beamed, "Everyone must admit the pluck and energy of Mr. Dunsmuir, which has brought this important work to a successful conclusion."[19] Macdonald had missed the ceremony when the Canadian Pacific Railway's last spike was driven on November 7, 1885 at Craigellachie. The Dominion Government's contract with British Columbia was now fulfilled.

Sir John and Lady Macdonald and Robert and Joan Dunsmuir then continued by a special train to Nanaimo where a civic reception was held.[20] Macdonald and Dunsmuir enjoyed a good relationship. Beyond their political views they both shared a Scottish background and love for good whiskey, and both had wives who disapproved of alcohol. Dunsmuir had made sure there was a good stock available in his private coach, the *Maude*.

At Nanaimo, the cannons from the Bastion were hauled up to the railway station, and seventeen shots were fired in honor of the occasion.[21] The celebration had just begun. At the reception held at the Royal Hotel were Mayor Bate and council members W.H. Webb, John Hilbert, W. Wilson, James Knight, George Bevilockway, Adam Grant Horne, and Charles Wilson

Macdonald and Dunsmuir were noticed pacing back and forth on the verandah of the hotel. They had been frustrated in their attempts to toast the occasion with a little whiskey because of the presence of their wives.[22] Then Dunsmuir suggested a trip down a mine, and it was there that the two men truly toasted the construction of the E & N Railway.

Among the Mark Bate papers donated to the Nanaimo Community Archives is a copy of the speech he made as mayor at the opening ceremony of the railway:

> The Esquimalt and Nanaimo Railway, over which we anticipate you have had a delightful run, is now very nearly completed, and we feel it our duty to draw your attention to the great benefits that would accrue to us from the establishment and maintenance of ferry communication between the Mainland Terminus and Nanaimo so as to make the Island Railway a branch of the Transcontinental Line and Esquimalt the Ocean Terminus.
>
> Our coal is remarkable for its supericity over that found in the adjacent States, and our coal mines are prepared for a largely increased demand. For many years the import duty of 75 cents per ton, chargeable upon foreign coal entering California and Portland, has been a great hindrance to our prosperity, and we look forward to the time when, by mutual concessions, a Reciprocity Treaty will be adopted between the United States and Canada to the lasting advantage of both.
>
> Within a few miles of this City there exist iron ore of a high grade, and limestone in great abundance. At our doors we have quarries of first class building stone, while we are surrounded with a plentiful supply of valuable timber. The Harbours of Nanaimo and Departure Bay are capacious, easy of access, and afford, as you will observe, secure accommodation for many thousand tons of shipping.
>
> That you may long be spared to occupy the proud position of Premier of Canada, and be permitted to render to our country a continuance of your eminent services, is our most heartfelt wish. We sincerely trust that your visit to British Columbia will be beneficial to yourself and Lady Macdonald, and we hope your return to Ottawa will be pleasant and safe.[23]

Daily trains

The first train pulled in to Nanaimo from Russell's Station in West Victoria on September 24, 1886, and daily service began six days later. The Nanaimo station had a café, telegraph office, and living quarters for the station agent. The first agent was Alexander Shaw who had since moved his family from Gabriola Island to Nanaimo. It was not until March 29, 1888 that trains actually entered Victoria, after a swing bridge across the harbour was completed at Dunsmuir's expense. During the first year of operation, the E & N Railway carried 13,000 passengers.

In 1887, the rail line was extended to Wellington. A railway trestle was built to span the Millstone River and construction continued to North Wellington. "No Trespassing on Trestle" signs were posted along the right of way which at the time was one of the highest structures in the area. Those who trespassed knew the schedules of the passenger and freight trains; they ignored the signs, stepping aside to wave to the engineers in the locomotives. Train crews complained of seeing trespassers crossing in front of the engines and of close encounters with horse-drawn vehicles at road crossings.[24]

There were skeptics about the future success of the railway. Some believed it would never pay operating costs, and claimed that railways could not compete with water transportation. However, it was not long before many of the steamships were withdrawn from the Victoria to Nanaimo route, and nearly all traffic, passenger, and freight, was carried over the railway.

The cash subsidy was held up for ten years after the railway was completed, because government engineers believed there were too many curves. The subsidy was eventually paid, and the curves remained.[25]

E & N train at Nanaimo Station.

The first Governor General to arrive by the E & N Railway in Nanaimo was the Governor General Lord Stanley of Preston, accompanied by his wife Lady Stanley, on November 5, 1889. The couple had first visited Vancouver, before sailing for Victoria on the H.M.S. *Amphion.* On their return trip from Victoria on November 6, the *Amphion* struck a rock in dense fog and had to return to Esquimalt. The ship narrowly escaped sinking. Despite the misfortune, the Stanleys declared the trip "most enjoyable."[26] Stanley Park takes its name after Lord Stanley.

The next Queen's representatives to arrive by train were the Earl and Countess of Aberdeen (Lord and Lady Aberdeen), visiting the city on November 9, 1894. They took the train to Wellington where school children were given a place of honour around the reception platform. After the children sang "God Save the Queen," Mr. T. B. Hugo welcomed Lord and Lady Aberdeen on behalf of the residents of Wellington.

The couple returned to Nanaimo where Mayor Edward Quennell met them at the train station. A luncheon was held aboard the train before the entourage continued on to Dallas Square where they were entertained by the Silver Cornet Band. Miss Stannard gave an address of welcome on behalf of the school children of Nanaimo.[27] Vancouver Coal Company manager Sam Robins took them on a tour of the Nanaimo coal operation, and they visited the hospital before leaving on the steamer *Joan* for Vancouver.

Railways Change the Region—the New Port City of Vancouver

On the mainland it was now certain the railway would come to Granville. William Cornelius Van Horne, the general manager of the Canadian Pacific Railway, had earlier declared this would be a wonderful location for a seaport. These were the same sentiments expressed earlier by Gassy Jack Deighton who predicted Granville would be a port some day. For a time all the residents of the village could do was sit and watch ships sail past on their way to Port Moody.

The provincial government wanted to establish the terminus at Granville and as an inducement granted the CPR thousands of acres of land in and around what would become the province's largest city.

On April 6, 1886, the Village of Granville officially became the City of Vancouver. On May 3, the first municipal election was held. Mayor M.A. Maclean predicted the city would become second only to San Francisco. In February 1886 Granville had 100 residents; by May there were 6,000; New Westminster now had 4,000, Victoria 14,000, and Nanaimo over 1,600.

Nanaimo Looks to the Future

A decade after incorporation, Nanaimo was a well-established community with a thriving coal industry. The New Vancouver Coal Company and the Wellington Colliery maintained a steady workforce. As well as being employed in the coal industry, Mark Bate served all of those years as mayor, except one. He was also succeessful in his involvement in community life—from the Nanaimo Literary Institute, to the Hospital Board, to the Board of Education, and to memberships in various lodges. He was a tireless volunteer, offering his administrative capabilities to many fledgling organizations.

One of the early pioneers, Adam Grant Horne, the strapping Highlander with the adventurous spirit, who had managed the first HBC store and explored the central island region, settled in Nanaimo and opened his own business. Horne had bridged two cultures. He had made friends with the Natives, had dealt honestly with all, and was often the peacemaker in disputes. He was truly a personality who linked the early settlement with the present.

Robert Dunsmuir, with his sons Alex and James, was building an empire within the coal industry. The family would become a formidable force to be reckoned with politically and economically. Their influence would be felt throughout Vancouver Island.

As the number of Chinese working in the coal industry grew, the largely European population regarded their presence in the community as a nuisance. Nanaimo residents viewed the Chinese with suspicion, because they looked and dressed differently, and their language and culture were foreign. But Dunsmuir liked them— they were cheap labour and they worked hard.

The Snuneymuxw were in decline. Confederation had brought rules and regulations that allowed the federal government to interfere in all aspects of Native life. The Indian Act of 1876 assumed Native inferiority. Now all "legal" Natives became wards of the federal government and were to be treated as minors without the full privileges of citizenship. Those who had shown the HBC the coalfield in Nanaimo were now relegated to a reserve, and like the Chinese, were regarded as a nuisance.

The past quarter-century was a period of incredible change for Nanaimo and Vancouver Island. First came the fur-trading Hudson's Bay Company and the subsequent arrival of miners, farmers, and immigrants who settled island shores. Then the gold prospectors passed through by the thousands. They searched creeks and mountainsides and found only disappointment. However, many made a new lives for themselves in a new country. Industries sprang to life to supply the needs of growing communities. There were changes in transportation from sail to steam, and still ahead, train travel, and motorized vehicles.

Nanaimo miners and their families had an active social life; they had access to other communities and the wonderful sea and countryside that surrounded them. Miners were no longer indentured to a company: they were free to work and live where they pleased. They could own land, build their own homes, and there were schools and a hospital for their families.

The Hudson's Bay Company had woven its presence into the history and geography of Vancouver Island. The early forts were really company towns, and they took on a life of their own after the HBC departed. On Vancouver Island, towns like Victoria and Fort Rupert, had their beginnings with the fur-trading enterprise. But Nanaimo began with the coal discoveries. By 1870, trading furs was no longer a viable business, and the HBC began selling off its large real-estate holdings. It turned its business expertise to merchandising goods to miners and farmers, something that would have made Alexander Grant Dallas happy.

In conclusion, noted historian Dr. W. Kaye Lamb put it best when he said,

> The honoured old initials HBC have been interpreted facetiously as meaning "Here Before Christ," instead, they might more fittingly be taken as signifying "Here Before Canada." And if this had not been so, it is unlikely that Canada as we know it today would now exist.[1]

In Nanaimo, old-timers like to say "Here Before Coal."

APPENDIX

Hotels and saloons in the Nanaimo, Wellington, Cedar, and Nanoose (before 1900)

Abbotsford Hotel, Wellington.

Arlington Hotel, Nanoose, opened December 21, 1894 by J.A. Thompson.

Balmoral Hotel, Haliburton Street.

Black Diamond Hotel (1887), Victoria Crescent. Also known as Provincial.

Britannia Hotel, (1881) Commercial Street.

Commercial Hotel, corner of Bastion Street and Commercial Street, was licensed in 1875. Operated by partners J. Wilcox and Peter Sabiston. The present Commercial Hotel was built in 1913 adjacent to the original building as an addition for proprietor Angelo Balzano.

Columbus Hotel (1885) on Haliburton Street was built by Joe Cuffalo. See Italian Hotel.

Crescent Hotel (1890) on Victoria Crescent was built by Frederick Rowbottom. The hotel was demolished in 1960s.

Departure Bay House, Departure Bay. Also known as Harper's, or the Bay Saloon, operated by Joseph Harper.

Dew Drop Inn (1879) on Haliburton and Baker Streets, was built by George Baker. The two-storey hotel with veranda had the first bowling alley in Nanaimo, sixty feet long by eight feet wide. The hotel name was changed to the Patricia Hotel.

Doon Hotel (1895) on Commercial Street, (Gibson Block) was built by Richard Gibson. As well as sleeping accommodations, it had a fine dining room on the ground floor adjoining the licensed premises.

Eagle Hotel, Victoria Crescent, was designed by Toronto architect J.A. Harvey and built by contractor J.Henry Walker on the site of the Identical and Oriental Hotels for Mrs. Busby. After remodelling it became the Terminal Hotel.

Globe Hotel (1887) Front Street. Site was chosen for its unobstructed view of the harbour. Built by Alexander Henderson two years before, to house his Nanaimo Marble and Monumental works. Opened as a hotel in 1889.

Grand Hotel, Victoria Crescent, a large brick hotel with dining room was sold in 1923 to David Spencer Co., which sold to Eaton's.

Half-way Hotel (1860), East Wellington.

Identical Hotel (1871) Victoria Crescent, a small wooden saloon built by Bruno Mellado for James McKay Sabiston. Bruno, from Santiago, Chile, had studied architecture. He also designed the first government school on Crace Street.

International Hotel, Victoria Crescent. Known originally as the Davidson Block after its first owner, Joseph H. Davidson. It was first licensed as the International Hotel and renamed the Queen's in 1899. Local architect James Kelly designed the hotel with a grand dining room, lounge, dance hall and assembly room.

Italian Hotel (1885) at Haliburton & Needham Streets was built by Joe Cuffalo from money he saved working in the mines. The hotel was renamed the Columbus Hotel.

Lotus Hotel, Commercial Street. Formerly the Temperance Hotel.

Miner's Hotel (1861), Commercial Street. Alternate names: Miner's Exchange, Central, and Retreat. Joseph Webb bought a half interest in Augusta Pujol's hotel in 1861. It had the only liquor license in Nanaimo at that time other than one held by the HBC. Pujol sold his half interest to contractor Richard Nightingale. This partnership did not last long and Webb became sold owner. His wife, Naomi Webb, operated a successful dining room in the hotel. A two-storey addition was added in the 1880s. Peter Sabiston managed the hotel until his death in 1893. The present Ashlar Lodge Masonic building is on this site.

Mount View Hotel, (1886) built by John Thompson on the Newcastle Reserve. Thompson later sold it to James Bennett.

Nanaimo Hotel, (1874) was built by Edwin Gough in partnership with William Wall. After the partnership was dissolved in 1875, Edwin and wife Elizabeth ran the hotel. It was destroyed by fire in April 1878 and a new Nanaimo Hotel was built on Commercial Street. It too was destroyed by fire 1894. The Hotel was again rebuilt.

Newcastle Hotel (1876), or New Castle, Wellington Road, operated by A.P.Smith.

Northfield Hotel, owner Tom Peck.

Old Flag Inn (1874), near the Bastion Street bridge, was built by John Pawson, a city alderman and later mayor. In 1882-3, operated by J.E. Jenkins.

Occidental Hotel (1887) on Fitzwilliam Street was built by Samuel Fiddick to accommodate E & N Railway patrons. The original hotel had a billiard room, dining room and a large hall leading up to thirteen bedrooms on the second floor. Since it was close to the railway station it became known as the first and the last as it was the first stop in Nanaimo for thirsty travellers, as well as their last stop before leaving.

Opera House (1888) on Church Street was a three-storey brick building with the upper floors used for hotel purposes. The Opera House was located on the ground floor. The building was later incorporated into the Windsor Hotel.

Oriental Hotel (1874) Victoria Crescent, a small wooden saloon.

Palace Hotel (1889) on Skinner Street opened March 23, 1889. It was one of the first brick hotels in the city. First owner was R. Morella.

Patricia Hotel. See Dew Drop Hotel.

Peck's Hotel, Victoria Crescent. In 1875, Mayor Mark Bate gave a champagne supper at the hotel after becoming the city's first mayor.

Pink 'un, Stuart Avenue. Owner Tom Peck. Site of the Grotto Restaurant.

Provincial Hotel, Victoria Crescent, operated by N. Smith. See also Black Diamond Hotel.

Quarterway Hotel (Pub) built by George Mitchell was so named because it marked one quarter of the six-mile journey to Wellington.

Queen's Hotel. See International.

Royal Hotel (1878), on Wharf Street, was built by Richard Watkins. Prime Minister Sir John A. Macdonald stayed here after participating in the ceremony marking the completion of the E & N Railway in 1886. The two-storey structure was destroyed in the 1894 fire. Later owned by Beveradge and L. Lawrence.

Somerset Hotel, Wellington, (1879-80) built by John D. Dixon and Thomas Eric Peck.

Telegraph Hotel, Cavan Street. In 1878 Elijah Ganner Jr. operated the hotel. He was refused a liquor license there were too many licences within the city limits.

Temperance House, Bastion Street, operated by Mrs. J. K. Gilbert.

Terminal Hotel. See Eagle.

Vendome Hotel (1898), corner of Commercial and Bastion streets, was a two-storey building.

Wellington Hotel (1875), at Diver Lake, was built by Charles Chantrell. The next owner was Thomas Wall. The hotel was destroyed by fire and rebuilt twice.

What Cheer House, Commercial Street, was destroyed in the 1878 fire, and was replaced by the Royal Hotel.

Wheatsheaf Inn, Cedar. Andrew Mahle purchased the original Wheat Sheaf Inn in 1908. This building was destroyed by fire in 1927 and Mahle had the present building hauled to the site.

Wilson Hotel (1892) was built by tinsmith Walter Richard Wilson. The hotel was judged the leading hotel of the day. Charles J. Trawford later managed it. The walls of the hotel displayed hunting trophies; one was a fourteen pronged elk head shot by Trawford. The stagecoach called at the hotel every Tuesday and Friday. Although built of brick it was destroyed by fire in 1930.

Windsor Hotel designed by architect Thomas Hooper for owner Reverend A. Green. A new wing was added in November 1889. The hotel had twenty-eight parlours and sleeping compartments. The building was later renovated and became the Plaza Hotel in 1924. The adjoining building, the Opera House, was incorporated into the hotel facility. The name was changed several times to Shoreline and Nat Bailey's Villa, and is now the Dorchester Hotel.

ENDNOTES

Part One—Historical Homeland
1. Public Archaeological Excavations at the Departure Bay Midden Dh Rx 16, Permit 1992-29; Volume II. Nanaimo District Museum.

Chapter One
1. Public Archaeological Excavations at the Departure Bay Midden Dh Rx 16, Permit 1992-29; Volume II. Nanaimo District Museum. See also Homes G. Barnett (1955), 22.
2. Crosby, 49.
3. Ibid, 86.
4. Adam Grant Horne exploration stories. Courtesy Terry Simpson.
5. Public Archaeological Excavations, Volume II, pA11.
6. Pojar & MacKinnon, 404.
7. Littlefield, citing Fort Langley Journal 1827-1830.
8. Barnett (1955), 22.
9. Public Archaeological excavations at DepatureBay, vol. II, 25.
10. See Crosby, 107.
11. Barraclough, "Wooly White Dog," 15-17.
12. Public Archaeological excavations at Departure Bay, vol. II, 25.

Chapter Two
1. Bartroli, 51. See also new research by historian Nick Doe of Gabriola Island. He suggests the place of anchor may have been Pilot Bay not Descanso Bay. See *Shale*, 1.1 Nov. 2000, published by the Gabriola Historical & Museum Society.

Part Two—Black Diamonds Transform the Wilderness
1. Ormsby, 80.

Chapter Three
1. Newman (1987), 303.
2. Ray, 174.
3. Reksten (1986), 5.
4. Hardy, 76.
5. History Box 1, Code 5. Undated newspaper article "Nanaimo's name adopted in '53".
6. Barman, 53.
7. Nanaimo History Box 1, Code 5, document "Ownership of Gordon Street, Commercial Inlet," 2, NCA. See also British Columbia Archives A/B/14/4
8. McKelvie, 135.
9. Pethick, 79-80.

10. Johnson, 4.
11. Newman (1985), 73.
12. Gough, 40.
13. Gough, 34.
14. Mayne, cited in Paterson (1979), 44.

Chapter Four
1. Newman (1989), 187.
2. Ball, 46.
3. Brown, Jennifer S.H.
4. Underhill, 21.
5. Ibid, 21, 59, 60.
6. Clearibue, 33.
7. Hendrickson, vol 1, 377-378.
8. Helgesen, 289.
9. Andrew Muir diary. Families file, Code 22, Box 12.
10. Helgeson, 163.
11. Akrigg, 30.
12. *BCHN*, 32.1 (1998-99): 33.
13. Akrigg, 30.
14. Fort Rupert file, NCA, untitled article about Fort Rupert, dated spring 1972.
15. Reksten (1991), 8.
16. Gough, 37.
17. Joseph E.L.Muir oral interview by William Barraclough, Oral History Tape Transcript, Box 6, loc. A-0505.
18. Akrigg, 22.
19. James Douglas to John Henry Pelly, Fort Victoria, December 5, 1848, in Bowsfield, *Fort Victoria Letters*, 34.
20. Barman, 57.
21. Ray, 173, 187, 186.
22. Ibid., 192.

Chapter Five
1. Bate, box 3, 1997.
2. Joseph McKay family history file.
3. Ibid., reprint from McKay's "Recollections of a chief-traded in the HBC 1878."
4. Reksten (1986), 86.
5. Orford, also Reksten, 86, 87.
6. Lillard.
7. Douglas, 247.
8. HBC Fonds 1852-1857: File 92-038-M.
9. HBC Fonds 92 03 M. Joseph McKay Journal.
10. John Meakin family history file.
11. HBC correspondence, James Douglas to Joseph McKay, July 1853.
12. Nanaimo Memoranda 1855-1859, March 17, 1856.
13. *Nanaimo Free Press*, 17 July 1971.
14. HBC Correspondence: McKay to Douglas, 9 Sept. 1952.
15. Ibid., 18 Sept. 1852.
16. Ibid., Douglas to McKay, 27 Oct. 1852.
17. McKay Journal, 6 Dec. 1852.

18. Arnett, 110.
19. McKelvie, "Founding of Nanaimo."
20. Hardy, 70.
21. Littlefield, 104.
22. Joseph E.L.Muir interview by William Barraclough, tape transcripts, box 6, loc. A-0505.
23. McKelvie, "Founding of Nanaimo" 5. Correspondence McKay to Douglas.
24. Ralston, 42-55.
25. *Nanaimo Free Press*, 16 Feb. 1907.
26. Akrigg, 75-76.
27. McKelvie (1944).
28. McKay family history file.
29. Nicolls, vol 5.
30. Glaholm family file.
31. Forbes, 115.
32. Nicolls, vol. 4, "The Sage Descendants." References to Nicolls, with permission.
33. *Western People* 12 May 1983. See also correspondence: George Robinson to Douglas, August 20, 1855.

Chapter Six
1. Nicolls, vol. 1.
2. Ibid., vol. 2, John and Jane Biggs.
3. Log of the *Princess Royal* used with permission of the Hudson's Bay Company Archives File C.1/975. See also *British Columbia Historical Quarterly* 3 Jan. 1939, 15-24. Barrie H.E.Goult, "First and Last Days of the Princess Royal." Also Log of the *Princess Royal* 1854-55 by Charles Gale, First Mate. File NCA Families, Code 22, Box 12. Voyage of the *Princess Royal*.
4. Nicolls, vol. 1, "From Brierley Hill to Vancouver's Island."
5. British Columbia Courthouse Library Society, "An Act to amend and consolidate the Laws relating to the Carriage of Passengers by Sea," 30 June 1852, Passengers Act Amendment, 244, Cap.44, 15 & 16 Vict.
6. HBV Fonds, 92 03 M. Indentures, or Contract of Service.
7. Nicolls, vol. 2, Samuel Gough.
8. William Cartwright diary. File 96-015-A.
9. Nicolls, vol. 4, "The Sage descendants."
10. Rhoda M. Beck, "Brierly Hill by boat to New Homes in Nanaimo." Undated article. Malpass file.
11. Helgesen, 249.
12. Akrigg, 78.
13. Mark Bate Papers, "Reminiscences," NFP 4 May 1907.
14. Nicolls, vol 4, "Thomas and Anna Maria York."
15. Bate, "Reminiscences," NFP 4 May 1907.
16. Nicolls, vol. 3, "Miller Family."
17. John Cass research.
18. HBC Nanaimo Memoranda 1855-1859, Box 1992 38 M, February 20, 1857.
19. Description of the home from Mark Bate speech, "Toast of the pioneers."
20. Nicolls, vol. 4, "The Malpass Descendants."

Chapter Seven
1. Littlefield, 77.
2. Barman, 58.
3. Norcross (1979), 14.
4. Douglas advised he had settled the claims of the Nanaimo Indians upon the land as per instructions given to him by letters dated January 16 and November 18, 1853. File AC 90 H86 Extract No. 2. BCA.
5. *B.C.Historical Quarterly* 4.1 1 Jan. (1940): 55, quoting 1855 census of Vancouver Island by W.K.Lamb.
6. Pethick, 53.
7. Natives Code 16, Box 2, Nanaimo Museum Collection Industry, "Death of Che-wich-I-kan."
8. Nanaimo Museum Collection Industry—Natives, Code 16 Box 2. Royal Commission on Indian Affairs for the Province of British Columbia, Extract from proceedings of meetings with the Nanaimo tribe, Nanaimo City Reserve No. 1, May 28, 1913.
9. File AC 90 H86, BCA
10. Nanaimo Museum Collection—Families, Code 22, Box 12. Mark Bate Papers, "A Story Of Olden Days," 1907.
11. Nicolls, vol 2.
12. Charles Edward Stuart file, information from HBC archives, Winnipeg.
13. Nanaimo Memoranda 1855-1859, October 12, 1855.
14. Ibid., Feb 16, 1907.
15. History Box 1, Code 5. HBC files.
16. HBC's Journal, 1855-57, Oct 6, 1855.
17. Captain Stuart journal, Aug 22, 1855.
18. Littlefield, 107.
19. Mayne.
20. Mark Bate papers, description of arrival at Nanaimo.
21. George Heaton, BCA, GR 1372, File 748/24a, microfilm B1333.
22. *B.C.Historical News*, summer (1993).
23. Norcross (1979), 40.
24. Joseph Despard Pemberton family file, "General Report on Country around Nanaimo, July 11, 1859" to J.D.Pemberton Esquire, from B.W.Pearse.
25. Littlefield citing Charles Bayley.
26. Macfie, 143.

Chapter Eight
1. Walkem, 37, excerpts on Adam Grant Horne 1831-1901.
2. Olsen, 17. See also Brazier, 22-24.
3. Bird (1971), 35, 166.
4. Owen.
5. Horne file, Carrie Brown Doney, Alberni District Historical Society archives.
6. Minister of Mines Report 1879, 250.
7. Mark Bate papers, "Speech to Native Sons and Daughters."
8. Ibid.
9. Ibid.
10. Ibid., "A Stroll around Nanaimo in 1874."
11. *Nanaimo Free Press,* 1924 Jubilee Edition.
12. Bate, "Description of arrival at Nanaimo."

13. Bate, "Toasting the Pioneers."
14. Brown, 331.
15. John Cass Fonds Box 2, 1993, 003 A. Frances G. Claudet article "The Photographer."
16. Johnson, 34-39.
17. Norcross (1979), 41.
18. History Box 1, Code 5, misc.
19. Bowen, 88.
20. Nicolls, vol. 2, Samuel Gough.
21. *Nanaimo Free Press*, 17 Mar. 1994. Alfred Robson Benson family file. NCA.
22. Nicolls, vol. 5, Daniel and Eliza Anne Dunn.
23. *Nanaimo Free Press*, 17 Mar. 1994.
24. Bate, "A story of olden days, 1907."
25. Reksten, (1991), 18.
26. John Cass Fonds Box 2, 1993 003 A. Article "The Photographer" by Frances G. Claudet.
27. Reksten, More English than the English, p. 54.
28. Reksten, The Dunsmuir Saga, p. 21
29. McKay family history file.
30. Mark Bate Fonds, Series 1, File 4, NCA.
31. Pemberton file, ADHSA.
32. Minister of Mines Report 1876.
33. Nicolls, vol. 2. Samuel Thompson.
34. *Harewood—Land of Wakesiah*.

Chapter Nine
1. Hendrickson, Vol. II.
2. Hardy, 73.
3. Blakey Smith, 333-34.
4. Crosby, 33.
5. Bate, "Toast Of The Pioneers."
6. Hardy, 114.
7. Newman. 312.
8. Hardy, 120.
9. Bowering, 118.
10. Pethick and Baumgarten, 77.
11. Hardy. 121.
12. Karr, 70.
13. Leduc, 76.
14. Humphreys, 3.
15. Ralston, 54.
16. MacDonald, 401.
17. Leduc, 77.
18. Strickland, 7.

Chapter Ten
1. Leduc, 77.
2. Akrigg, 278.
3. Newman, (1987), 315.
4. *Daily British Colonist*, 4 Aug. 1877.
5. Ormsby, 213.

6. Bowering, 136.
7. Sproat, 49.

Chapter Eleven
1. Charles Edward Stuart file: Letter to W.G.Young from Stuart, Victoria 1860 from HBC archives.
2. B.C.Coast Names, excerpt in Stuart file.
3. MacDonald, 367, VIRL Northwest Collection 971.1.
4. Nanaimo History Box 1, Code 5, Paper, Ownership of Gordon St., Commercial Inlet, 2.
5. MacDonald, 367.
6. Ibid, 369-370.
7. Currie. All information about the financial circumstances of the VCML is from this source unless otherwise stated. With permission.
8. *Daily British Colonist*, 17 May 1864.
9. Turner, 14
10. Ibid., 24.
11. Nanaimo History Box 1, Code 5, Newcastle Townsite.
12. Pritchard, 209.
13. VCML Company Mining Journal, 2 June 1866, 344, as cited in Gallacher, 114.
14. Ibid., 6 Nov. 1869.
15. *Nanaimo Free Press*, 9 July 1975.
16. Bate, Box 3, 1997, original document appointing Mark Bate manager of business and affairs of the VCML.
17. Reksten, (1991), 39.
18. Jackman, 148.
19. Forrester.
20. Nanaimo Community Heritage Commission.
21. Zu Erpen, 31.
22. Hendrickson, vol II.
23. Hendrickson, vol II, 105.
24. *Daily British Colonist*, 15 Oct. 1861: 2.
25. *Colonist*, 9 May 1862: 2.
26. Mackie, 205.
27. Lyons (1958), 170-1.
28. *Colonist*, 31 Jan. 1863: 3.
29. Audain, 41.
30. *Colonist*, 22 Oct. 1964: 3.
31. *British Columbia Historical News*, Sum. 1993 edition.
32. Hayman, 102.
33. Akrigg, 356.
34. Ormsby, 223.
35. Captain William Hales Franklyn family history file.
36. Hendrickson, vol V.

Chapter Twelve
1. Hendrickson, vol I, 104.
2. Hayman, 8-11.
3. Ibid. 102.
4. Bowen, 124.
5. Hayman, 104

6. Crosby, 167.
7. HBC Nanaimo Memoranda 1855-1859, 1992 38 M, 9 Oct. 1855.
8. Hayman, 16.
9. Nicholls.
10. Crosby. All of the information regarding Crosby's stay in Nanaimo is from this source. See pages 24, 30-35, 42, 63, 117, 170, 206, 209, 241.
11. Pethick (1978), 19.
12. Ibid., 22.
13. Robin, 42. Source BCA (H/A/So2), S.P.G. Papers, 1858-1861, Good to Hills, January 6, 1862. Information in this section comes from this source unless otherwise stated. See pages 46-50, 51, 56, and 57.
14. Norcross (1979), 49.
15. Macfie, 468-69.
16. Tennant, 42.

Chapter Thirteen
1. *Victoria Colonist*, 8 May 1867.
2. Bate, Box 3, 1997, Political Papers, series #4, letter from Robert Dunsmuir to Hon. H.L.Langevin, 20 Sept. 20, 1871.
3. Reksten (1991), 28.
4. Ibid., 30.
5. Nanaimo City Directory: Wellington 1882-83.
6. Swanson, 3, Transportation Box, Code 31, Box 1. All information about this small railway comes from this source unless otherwise stated.
7. Reksten (1991), 3.
8. Ibid, 106
9. Ibid.
10. Ibid, Family chart.
11. MacDonald, 369.
12. Merilees, 53-60.
13. Nicolls, vol. 3, Hawkes family.
14. Bate, "Reminiscences of Early Nanaimo," *Nanaimo Free Press,* 16 Mar. 1907.
15. Jesse Sage family history file.
16. Zu Erpen, 39.
17. *Daily British Colonist*, 23 Sept.1865.
18. Hendrickson, 345
19. Zu Erpen, 211.
20. Hendrickson, vol.III, 507.
21. Ibid.
22. Hendrickson, 345-6.
23. Ibid. 348.
24. *Nanaimo Free Press,* 1924 Jubilee Edition.
25. *Colonist*, 20 Apr. 1866: 2.
26. Hendrickson, 356.
27. *Nanaimo Gazette*, 19 May 1866.
28. Ibid, 10 July 1865.
29. Akrigg, 393, citing C.M.Tate, "Autosketch," United Church Archives, Toronto, G6i, Box 22, #13.

Chapter Fourteen
1. Ormsby, 219.

2. Shelton, 78.
3. *British Columbian*, 18 May 1867.
4. Hardy, 251.
5. Ormsby, 250.
6. Ibid., 252.

Chapter Fifteen
1. *Columns, Cornices, & Coal*, 15.
2. *Nanaimo Free Press*, 18 Dec. 1874.
3. Bate.
4. Zu Erpen, 44.
5. Ibid.
6. Nanaimo History, Box 1, Code 5. Paper: "Ownership of Gordon St., Commercial Inlet," 9, citing *Gazette*, 26 Dec. 1875: 303.
7. Nanaimo History, Box 1, Code 5.
8. Ibid.
9. Nicolls, vol. 4, "The Sage Descendants."
10. Zu Erpen, 81.
11. *Nanaimo Free Press*, 19 April 1909.
12. Zu Erpen, Appendix H, Nanaimo: Municipal Officers and employees until 1900.
13. Mike Manson family history file.
14. Ibid.
15. Nicolls, vol. 2, Samuel Gough.
16. Bate, Speech about early Nanaimo.
17. Norcross (1979), 76.
18. *Nanaimo Free Press*, 24 Mar. 1878.
19. Nicolls, vol. 4, "The Ganner Descendants."
20. Duncan, 146-7.
21. Nanaimo City By-law No. 18, Public Moral Amendment by-law 1895, A-03-01/Box 1
22. File 1992 003 C City Clerk's Office Box 2, Bylaws.
23. Duncan, 145.
24. Bate, "A Stroll Around Nanaimo in 1874."
25. See *Columns, Cornices, & Coal*, 44.
26. Nanaimo Directory 1881, Water Works.
27. *Nanaimo Free Press*, 19 June 1901.
28. Nanaimo and District Museum Society, *The Story of a City*, 36.

Chapter Sixteen
1. Bate, "A Stroll Around Nanaimo In 1874."
2. Ibid.
3. *British Columbia Biographical*, vol. IV, 304-6.
4. Stark family history file.
5. *Columns, Cornices, & Coal,* 31.
6. *Nanaimo Free Press*, "History of Convent Bound up with city." 15 Mar. 1962.
7. Code 20, Box 3, Education file: Sisters of St. Ann.
8. Lewis-Harrison, 64-7.
9. CJAV Pioneer Parade radio show script by Meg Trebett, subject "Alexander Shaw," Port Alberni, Sept. 14, 1947.
10. Norcross (1978), 44-45.

11. Begg, 473.
12. Peterson (1996), 100.
13. Martha A. Kenny file, "First Hospital."
14. Gordon Frith, "History of Hospitals in Nanaimo 1850-1967," March 28, 1968, pamphlet file. See also Nanaimo Museum Collection Public Service file, Code 4, Box 1. Brochure: Nanaimo's New Hospital.
15. British Columbia Directory 1882-83.
16. *Nanaimo Free Press*, 10 Apr. 1884.
17. Zu Erpen, 212-3.
18. Church information file: NCA
19. Box 11, code 22, Wilfred Nicholson writings.
20. Family History files, Hilbert family.
21. Robin 144-150.
22. Ibid., 123, 153, 159-60, 176.
23. Akrigg, 11.
24. Dodie Gogo, editor, *St. Peter's Church 1960-2000.*
25. Peterson (1996), 44.
26. Sabiston family history file.
27. *Nanaimo Gazette*, 5 May, 1866. See also article by Rhoda M. Beck "Brierly Hill by Boat to New Homes in Nanaimo."
28. Nicolls, vol 5, "The Richardson Descendants."
29. Begg, 492.
30. *Nanaimo Free Press*, 18 July 1893 and 11 Feb. 1894.
31. *St.Andrew's Presbyterian Church 125 Anniversary,* 1865-1990.
32. Nanaimo History miscellaneous, undated article "Nanaimo in 1871" by Arnold Olson.
33. Ibid. *Nanaimo Free Press*, Jubilee edition 1874-1934.
34. *Nanaimo Free Press*, 12 Apr. 1894 and 4 Jan. 1895.
35. Nicolls, vol. 4, "Sage family descendants."
36. Church information file.
37. G.W.Taylor, Pacific Biological Station, Nanaimo. Correspondence file. T.D.Sale, *St. Paul's Anglican Church, Nanaimo, B.C.* R.History, 1861-1986.
38. T.D. Sale.

Chapter Seventeen
1. British Columbia Directory 1882-3.
2. Narcross (1979), 81.
3. British Columbia Directory. 1882-3
4. Ibid., 1900.
5. Union Brewery Company Minute book 1892-1900.
6. City Directory 1892, 323.
7. Martha A. Kenny file.
8. John Hirst family history file.
9. *Nanaimo Free Press*, 10 Apr. 1884.
10. Ibid, 29 Jan. 1881.
11. Andersen, 10.
12. John Hilbert family file.
13. Code 22, Box 9, Martha Kenny Historical Notes.
14. Nicolls, vol. 3, Webb family.
15. Code 22, Box 9, Martha Kenny Historical Notes.
16. Alexander Mayer family history file.

17. Nicolls, vol. 3, "The Bevilockway Descendants."
18. *Nanaimo Free Press*, 30 July and 22 Nov. 1890. Also 15 Dec. 1896.
19. Norcross (1979), 45.
20. Tape NHSWB #17, A-08-95 Box 5 A-10-13 original, transcript A-05005 Box 7 #17.
21. Norris family history file.
22. Bate, "Stroll around Nanaimo in 1874."
23. Nicolls, vol. 2, Gough family.
24. *Nanaimo Free Press*, 19 Apr. 1879.
25. Nanaimo Board of Trade brochure. Act of incorporation and bylaws. Pamphlet file.
26. John Meakin family history file.
27. Bate Research Box 3, 1997, Nanaimo Literary Institute Report 1862.
28. Nanaimo History Box 1, Code 5.
29. Box 11, Code 22. Nicholson Writings.
30. Audain, 47.
31. Minute Book of the Silver Cornet Band 1893-1942.
32. Ibid.
33. Box 11, Code 22, Wilfred Nicholson Writings.
34. Nanaimo and District Museum Society, *Nanaimo, The Story of a City*, 53.
35. Box 11, Code 22, Nicholson Writings.
36. History Box 1, Code 5, undated article, "Trapeze artist plunge ends in Nanaimo waters."
37. City Directoy 1893, 327.
38. Code 26, Box 1, Nanaimo Opera House Program.
39. Keller, 95.
40. Martha Kenny file: Early buildings. See also *Nanaimo Free Press* 28 Sept. 1894.
41. *Nanaimo Free Press*, 21 May 1881.
42. Tully Boyce family history file. See also pamphlet file, Special Events, Labour Day.
43. Audain, 56.
44. Martha A. Kenny file, re Planta.

Chapter Eighteen
1. Turner, 40.
2. Province of British Columbia, *Crown Land Grants: A history of the Esquimalt and Nanaimo Railway Land Grant, the Railway Belt, the Peace River Block*, 1981. 2
3. Berton (1971), 305
4. Bate papers.
5. Canadian Pacific Ltd., Corporate Archives, Montreal, Quebec, March 24, 1875.
6. Ibid., April 10, 1875.
7. Bate papers, box 3, 1997.
8. Howay and Schoefield, vol. II, 410
9. *British Columbian*, 7 Oct. 1882.
10. Statues, B.C. 1883, C14.
11. Code 22, box 12, *Petitioners of Nanaimo & Comox Constituencies, 1884*. Contributed by Margaret Sharon. *The British Columbia Genealogist*, vol 16, No. 1 (1987).

12. Johnstone.
13. Turner, 41.
14. *The Resources of British Columbia, 1883/4/5,* shelf BL AR 5/33, vol.2, No.8, Oct.1, 1884, 2.
15. Littlefield 120.
16. Olsen, 87.
17. *Nanaimo Free Press* 25 July 1885.
18. Ormsby, 290.
19. Reksten (1991) 73.
20. Transportation Box, code 31, box 2: E & N Railroad.
21. Barraclough interview of Joseph E.L.Muir, Oral History Tape Transcripts, Box 6, Loc.A-0505.
22. Martha Kenny file, Part two (6).
23. Bate papers, box 3, 1997, Political Papers, series #4.
24. John Cass notes.
25. Transportation Box, code 31, box 2: E & N Railroad.
26. Begg, 509.
27. Ibid., 543

Epilogue
1. Newman, XXI.

BIBLIOGRAPHY

Books, Journals, and articles

Akrigg, G.P.V. and Helen B. Akrigg. *British Columbia Chronicle, 1847-1871*. Gold & Colonists. Vancouver: Discovery Press, 1977.

Andersen, Earl. *Hard Place To Do Time: The Story of Oakalla Prison*. New Westminster, BC: Hillpointe Publishing, 1993.

Arnett, Chris. 1999. *Terror of the Coast: Land Alienation and Colonial War on Vancouver Island and the Gulf Islands, 1849-1863*. Burnaby, BC: Talonbooks.

Audain, James. *From Coal Mine to Castle: The Story of the Dunsmuirs of Vancouver Island*. New York: Pageant Press. 1955.

Ball, Tim. "Company Town." *The Beaver* June-July (1988).

Barman, Jean. *The West Beyond the West: A History of British Columbia*. Toronto: U of Toronto Press. 1955.

Barnett, Homes G. *The Coast Salish of British Columbia*. Eugene: University of Oregon, 1955.

Barnett, Tom. "Alberni riding Member of Parliament." *Twin Cities Times* [Alberni, B.C.] 25 Oct. 1967: n.p.

Barraclough, William. "The Woolly White Dog of the Indians." Norcross, Nanaimo Retrospective.

Bartroli, Thomas. *Brief Presence, Spain's activity on American's Northwest Coast (1774-1796)*. Vancouver: Self- published, 1991.

Beck, Rhoda M. "Brierly Hill By Boat To New Homes In Nanaimo." Nanaimo Community Archives.

Begg, Alexander. *A History Of British Columbia From Its Earliest Discovery to the Present Time*. Toronto: William Briggs, 1894.

Bird, George. *Tse-wees-tah, One Man in a Boat*. 1971. Port Alberni, BC: Alberni District Museum and Historical Soc., 1972.

Boam, Henry, comp., and Ashley G. Brown, ed. *British Columbia, Its History, People, Commerce, Industries and Resources*. London: Sells, 1912.

Bowen, Lynne. *Three Dollar Dreams*. Lantzville, BC: Oolichan Books, 1987.

Bowering, George. *Bowering's B.C.: A Swashbuckling History*. Toronto. Penguin Canada, 1996.

Brazier, Graham. "On the Trail of the One-Armed Man." B.C. Historical News *33.4 (2000): 22-24.*

British Columbia Biographical. Vol. IV. S.J.Clarke Publishing, 1914.

Brown, Craig, ed. *The Illustrated History of Canada*. Toronto: Lester & Orpen Dennys, 1987.

Brown, Jennifer S.H. "A parcel of Upstart Scotchmen." *The Beaver* Feb – Mar. (1988).

Centennial Committee 1966-67. *Harewood — Land of Wakesiah*. Nanaimo, 1967.

Clearibue, Joyce. "Fort Victoria & H.B.Co. Doctors." BCHN 32.1 (1998-99): 33.

Colomba, John Robert. Colombo's Canadian References. Toronto: Oxford U.P., 1976.

Crosby, Thomas. Among the An-ko-me-nums of the Pacific Coast. Toronto: William Briggs 1907.

Currie, A.W. "The Vancouver Coal Mining Company, A source for Galsworthy's strife." Queen's Quarterly 70.1 (1963).

Douglas, James. "Report of a canoe expedition along the East Coast of Vancouver Island." Journal of the Royal Geographical Society 24 (1854): 247.

Duncan, Eric. From Shetland to Vancouver Island: Recollections of Seventy-Five Years. Edinburgh: Oliver and Boyd, 1937.

Province of British Columbia. Electorial History of British Columbia 1871-1986. Victoria, BC: Legislative Library, 1988.

Fisher, Robin. Contact and Conflict: Indian-European Relations in British Columbia, 1774-1890. Vancouver: UBC Press, 1977.

Forbes, Elizabeth. Wild Roses at their feet: Pioneer Women on Vancouver Island. Vancouver: B.C.Centennial '71 Committee, 1971.

Gale, Charles. First Mate. "Log of the Princess Royal 1854-55" File NCA Families. Code 22, box 12. Voyage of the Princess Royal.

Gogo, Dodie, ed. St. Peter's Church 1960-2000. Nanaimo, B.C., 2000.

Gough, Barry M. "Fort Rupert, Its Coal and Its Spar Trad." Norcross, Company on the Coast.

Goult, Barrie H.E. "First and last Days of the Princess Royal." Nanaimo Community Archives.

Graham, Donald. Keepers of the Light. Madeira Park, BC: Harbour, 1985.

Hardy, W.G. From Sea Unto Sea, The Road to Nationhood 1850-1910. New York: Doubleday, 1959.

Hayman, John, ed. Robert Brown and the Vancouver Island Exploring Expedition. Vancouver: UBC Press, 1989.

Helgeson, Marion, ed. Footprints, Pioneer Families of the Metchosin District Southern Vancouver Island 1851-1900. Metchosin, B.C.: Metchosin School Museum Society, 1983.

Hendrickson, James E, ed. Journals of the Colonial Legislatures of the Colonies of Vancouver Island and British Columbia 1851-1871. 5 vols. Victoria, BC: Provincial Archives, 1980.

Hodding, Bruce Alan. North Cowichan, A History in Photographs. Duncan, BC: District of North Cowichan, 1998.

Howay, F.W. and E.O.S.Scholefield. British Columbia from the Earliest Times to the Present. 4 vols. Vancouver, 1914.

Humphreys, Danda. "Memorial to a brief sojourn." Victoria Times Colonist, The Islander 15 Aug. 1999: 3.

———. "The Trail from the Bay." Victoria Times Colonist, "Islander" [Victoria] 8 Oct. 2000.

Jackman, S.W. Portraits of the Premiers: An informal History of British Columbia. Sidney, BC: Gray's Publishing, 1969.

Johnson, Patricia M. "Fort Rupert." Beaver 302 Spring (1972):4.

Johnson, Patricia M. "Teacher and Preacher CORNELIUS BRYANT." Beaver, Winter (1961): 34-39.

Johnstone, Bill. "The E & N Land Grant." Island Rail July – Aug. 1996: 41.

Karr, Clarence G. "James Douglas: The Gold Governor in the Context of His Times." Norcross, Company on the Coast.

Keller, Betty. Pauline: A Biography of Pauline Johnson. Vancouver: Douglas & McIntyre, 1981.

Kerr. J. B. Biographical Dictionary of Well-known British Columbians. Vancouver: Kerr & Begg, 1890.

Leduc, Joanne. ed. Overland from Canada to British Columbia. Vancouver: UBC Press, 1991.

Lewis-Harrison, June. The People of Gabriola. Cloverdale, BC: Friesen, 1982.

Lillard, Charles. "Douglas Was An Explorer, Too." Victoria Times Colonist, "Islander" 24 Apr. 1988.

Lyons, C.P. Milestones on Vancouver Island. Vancouver: Evergreen Press, 1958.

MacDonald, Duncan George Forbes. British Columbia and Vancouver Island. 2nd. ed. London, Eng.: Longman, Green, 1862.

Macfie, Matthew. Vancouver Island and British Columbia: Their History, Resources and Prospects. Ibid, 1865.

Mayne, Richard. Four Years in British Columbia and Vancouver Island. London, Eng.: John Murray, 1862.

McKelvie, B.A. "Founding of Nanaimo." B.C.Historical Quarterly 8.3 (1944): 168-188.

—. Pageant of B.C. Nanaimo, BC: Thomas Nelson, n.d.

Merilees, Bill. Newcastle Island, A Place of Discovery. Surrey, BC: Heritage House, 1998.

Nanaimo and District Museum Society. Nanaimo, The Story of a City. Nanaimo, BC, 1983.

Nanaimo Community Heritage Commission. Columns, Cornices & Coal. City of Nanaimo: 1999.

Newman, Peter. Caesars of the Wilderness. Markham, ON: Viking Books, 1987.

—. Company of Adventurers. Markham, ON: Penguin Books, 1985.

—. Empire of the Bay. Toronto: Madison Press, 1989.

Nicolls, Peggy. From the Black Country to Nanaimo 1854. Vols.1-5. Nanaimo Historical Society/Peggy Nicolls, 1991-1995.

—. A History of Nanoose Bay. Nanoose Centennial Committee, 1958.

Norcross, E. Blanche, ed. Company on the Coast. Nanaimo, B.C.: Nanaimo Historical Society, 1983.

—, ed. Nanaimo Retrospective: The First Century. Nanaimo Historical Society, 1979.

—. Not Just Pin Money. Essay. Victoria: Camosun College, 1984.

Olsen, W.H. Water Over the Wheel. 1963. Chemainus, BC: Schultz Industries, 1981.

Olson, Arnold. "Nanaimo in 1871" Nanaimo Community Archives, n.d.

Orford, Emily-Jane. "J.D.Arrived At An Opportune Time." Victoria Times Colonist, "Islander" 3 July 1988.

Ormsby, Margaret A. British Columbia: A History. Toronto: Macmillan, 1958.

Ovanin, Thomas K. Island Heritage Buildings. 1984. Islands Trust, 1987.

Paterson, T.W. Ghost Towns and Mining Camps of British Columbia. Langley, B.C.: Stagecoach, 1979.

Peterson, Jan. The Albernis, 1860-1922. Lantzville, BC: Oolichan Books, 1992.

—. Cathedral Grove, MacMillan Park. Ibid, 1996.

Pethick, Derek. *British Columbia Disasters*. Langley, BC: Stagecoach Publishing, 1978.

——, and Susan Im Baumgarten. *British Columbia Recalled: A Picture History 1741-1871*. Saanichton, BC: Hancock House Publishers, 1974.

Pojar, Jim and Andy MacKinnon. *Plants of Coastal British Columbia*. Vancouver: Lone Pine Publishing, 1994.

Pritchard, Allan, ed. *Vancouver Island Letters of Edmund Hope Verney 1862-65*. Vancouver: UBC Press, 1996.

Province of British Columbia. Ministry of Lands, Parks and Housing. *Crown Land Grants: A history of the Esquimalt and Nanaimo Railway Land Grant, the Railway Belt, the Peace River Block*. Victoria, 1981.

Ray, Arthur J. *I Have Lived Here Since The World Began: An Illustrated History Of Canada's Native People*. Toronto: Lester Publishing and Key Porter Books, 1996.

Reksten, Terry. *More English Than The English*. Victoria: Orca Book Publishers, 1986.

——. *The Dunsmuir Saga*. Vancouver: Douglas & McIntyre, 1991.

Sale, T.D. *St. Paul's Anglican Church, Nanaimo 1861-1986*. Nanaimo Community Archives, n.d.

Shelton, W.G., ed. *British Columbia & Confederation*. Victoria: 1967.

Smith, Dorothy Blakey, ed. *The Reminiscences of Doctor John Sebastian Helmcken*. Vancouver: UBC Press, 1975.

Sproat, Gilbert Malcolm. *"History of British Columbia." British Columbia Archives*.

Strickland, Val. *"Petticoat Cargo." Victoria Times Colonist*, "Islander" 12 Sept. 1999: 7.

Swanson, R.E. *The History Of A Railway*. Victoria, BC: Dept. Commercial Transport Railways Branch, B.C., 1960.

Taylor, Edward Drummond. "A Very Gentle Man: The Reverend George William Taylor 1854-1912." 1990. Nanaimo Community Archives.

Tennant, Paul. *Aboriginal Peoples and Politics*. Vancouver: UBC Press, 1990.

Turner, Robert D. *Vancouver Island Railroads*. 1973. San Marino, CA: Golden West Books. Victoria: Sono Nis Press, 1997.

Walkem, W.W. *Stories of Early British Columbia*. Vancouver: News-Advertiser, 1914.

Manuscripts:

Forrester, Elizabeth Anne Marshall. "The Urban development of Central Vancouver Island." M.A.Thesis. University of British Columbia, 1966.

Frith, Gordon. "History of Hospitals in Nanaimo 1850-1967." Nanaimo Community Archives.

Gallacher, Daniel Thomas, "Coal Management in British Columbia, 1864-89." M.A. Thesis. University of Victoria, 1970.

Littlefield, Loraine, "Gender, Class and Community, The History of Sne-nay-muwx women's employment." Diss. U.B.C., 1995.

——. "The Goals of Nanaimo." 1954. Nanaimo Community Archives.

Manson, Mike. "Name of Manuscript. Date. Nanaimo Community Archives.

Nicholls, M.A. *"A History of Nanoose Bay." Compiled for the Nanoose Centennial Committee in 1958. Vancouver Island Regional Library, Northwest Collection*.

Owen, Olga Blanche. "Biography of Adam Grant Horne." 1980.(Courtesy Terry Simpson).
Robin, Peter William. *Beyond the Bounds of the West: The Life of John Booth Good 1833-1916*. M.A. Thesis. University of Victoria, 1991. BCA (H/A/So2), S.P.G.Papers, 1858-1861, Good to Hills, January 6, 1862.
Smith, Brian Ray Douglas. "A Social History of Early Nanaimo." M.A. Thesis. University of British Columbia, 1956.
Sproat, Gilbert Malcolm. "History of British Columbia." Transcript. BCA.
Underhill, Ruth. *A Place to Prosper, or Just Survive? Motivations for the Emigration of Scottish Labourers to Vancouver Island. 1848-1852*. M.Litt.Thesis. University of St. Andrews, Scot: 1997.
Zu Erpen, Walter J.Meyer. "Towards an understanding of the Municipal Archives of Nineteenth Century British Columbia. A case study of the Archives of the Corporation of the City of Nanaimo, 1875-1904." M.A. Thesis. University of British Columbia, 1985.

Articles located in Mark Bate Papers and NCA:
"Brierly Hill by boat to New Homes in Nanaimo." Rhoda Beck.
"Canoe, Boat Coaches all served well."
"Description of arrival at Nanaimo."
"Honey production dates to early Nanaimo days."
"Music in Nanaimo long ago."
"Nanaimo built Vessel Wrecked on West Coast."
"Recollections of a chief trader in the HBC." Joseph William McKay, 1878.
"Reminiscences of Early Days in Nanaimo." 1907.
"Speech in response to the toast of the pioneers."
"Speech to Native Sons and Daughters."
"Story of Olden Days Graphically Told by One Who Knows."
"Stroll around Nanaimo in 1874."
"The Photographer." Frances G. Claudet.
"Toasting the Pioneers."
"Trapeze artist plunge ends in Nanaimo waters." N.d.

Diaries, Journals, Lectures, Letters, Minute Books, Notes, Audio Tapes, Papers
(Listings are from the Nanaimo Community Archives unless otherwise stated.)
Cartwright, William. Diary.
Cass, John. Research notes.
——. "The History of Nanaimo City Parks." 1967
CJAV "Pioneer Parade." Radio script. 14 Sept. 1947. Alberni District Historical Society Archives.
Douglas Private Papers, British Columbia Archives.
Douglas, James. "To John Henry Pelly, Fort Victoria." 5 Dec. 1848. Bowsfield, Fort Victoria Letters.
Franklyn, William Hales Papers, BCA.
Horne, Adam Grant. Exploration stories.
Hudson's Bay Company Correspondence.
Kenny, Martha. Historical notes.
Labour Day Pamphlet.
McKay, Joseph William. Nanaimo Day Book. 1852-1854.

Memoranda 1855-1859
Minute Book Silver Cornet Band 1893-1942.
Muir, Andrew. Diary. Nanaimo Community Archives.
Muir, Joseph E.L. Interview by William Barraclough. Audio tape transcripts Box 6, Loc. A-0505.
Muir, Joseph E.L. Interview by William Barraclough. Mark Bate Fonds, Series 1, File 40.
Nanaimo Board of Trade brochure 1889.
Nicholas, Wilfred writings.
Princess Royal Log.
St. Peter's Church 1960-2000 brochure.
St.Andrew's Presbyterian Church, 125 Anniversary booklet: 1865-1990.
Stuart, Captain Charles Edward. Journal.
Stuart, Charles Edward. "To W.G.Young, Victoria." 1860. HBC archives.

Government Records
British Columbia: Hon. H. L. Langevin Report, Ottawa 1872.
Ministry of Mines Reports 1875 - 1900
Nanaimo City Directory
Nanaimo: Ownership of Gordon Street, Commercial Inlet.
Nanaimo: Public Moral Amendment by-law 1895. By-law No. 18.
Passenger Act - British Columbia Courthouse Library Society.

Newspapers & Magazines

Beaver, The
British Colonist [Victoria, B.C.]
British Columbia Historical News
British Columbian [New Westminster, B.C.]
Colonist [Victoria, B.C.]
Daily British Colonist [Victoria, B.C.]
Daily/Weekly Herald [Nanaimo, B.C.]
Island Rail – Successful Senior Magazine [City]
Nanaimo Free Press [Nanaimo, B.C.]
Nanaimo Gazette [Nanaimo, B.C.]
Queen's Quarterly: A Canadian Review
Resources of British Columbia 1883-85
Royal Geographical Society Journal
Shale, Journal of the Gabriola Historical and Museum Society [Garbriola Island, B.C.]
Times Colonist, "The Islander." [Victoria, B.C.]
Twin City Times [Alberni, B.C.]
Victoria Colonist [Victoria, B.C.]
West Coast Advocate [Port Alberni, B.C.]
Western People Magazine

Photo Credits

B.C. Parks Branch Library: p 138;
Heritage House collection: p 136 (private collection);
Ministry of Lands, Parks & Housing, p 208 (1992-032-A Map 1981);
Murphy Family: p 52;
Nanaimo City Hall: p 150;
Nanaimo Community Archives: p 12; p 106; p 111; p 157 (989.29 B5/135); p 168 (989.29 B5/135);
Nanaimo District Museum: p 208 (12–280); p 69 (11–6); p 70 (HI-1); p 79 (Terry Simpson photo); p 82 (J1-2); p 86 (11–251); p 109 (11–250); p 117 (12–280); p 149 (J1–2); p 153 (12-26); p 166 (K1–19); p 174 (C1–82); p 175 (C1–23); p 176 (C1–15); p 161 (S.B. Sutton photo F1-2); p 171 lower (C2–12); p 182 (1893-1918) (Q1-7); p 183 (C3–111); p 185 (12–30); p 188: (1890) (13–74); p 194 (L1–14); p 198 (Elite Studio) (L1–36); p 199 (Q3–114); p 200 (12–276); p 212 (Q2-2);
Darlene Nickull: p 135;
Jan Peterson: p 38;
William Rayner: p 114;

Map Designs:
Ian Wilson: p 13;
John Peterson: p 10;

Drawings and sketches:
By Jan Peterson, including, p 47; p 134; p 156; p 197; p 171 top; p 180.

Front cover image: Old postcard of Nanaimo Harbour and Bastion, British Columbia.
Back cover photographs (clockwise from left): Ki-et-sa-kun (Coal Tyee) bronze bust situated at the Mark Bate Memorial Tree Plaza, Nanaimo; the Haliburton Street Methodist Church, known as the Tillicum Haus Society, Nanaimo; and the Nanaimo railway station. (Jan Peterson Photographs)

Index

The Author

Jan Peterson was born in Scotland and immigrated with her family to Kingston, Ontario in 1957. In 1972 she moved to the Alberni Valley with her husband Ray and their three children. Painting and writing have been lifelong interests. She has worked as a reporter for *The Alberni Valley Times* and won a Jack Wasserman Award for investigative journalism on social and environmental affairs.

Jan's record of community service is long: she served as director of the Alberni Valley Museum Advisory Board, the Alberni District Historical Society, the Alberni Valley Chamber of Commerce, and was president of the Alberni Valley Community Arts Council and Friends of North Island College. She is a life member of the Community Arts Council. Jan was honoured with a Canada 125 medal for community service, and received a Certificate of Appreciation for historical research from the City of Port Alberni.

During her tenure as president of the Community Arts Council she undertook the renovation of an old heritage building which became the Rollin Art Centre. Provincially she served on the British Columbia Arts Board and was part of a committee that studied visual arts in the province. Since retiring to Nanaimo in 1996, she has continued her community involvement as a director of the Nanaimo Historical Society, a member of the Nanaimo Community Archives Society, and Nanaimo District Museum Society.

Since her health failed in 1987 Jan has been researching and writing history and has published four books on the Port Alberni area; *The Albernis: 1860-1922*; *Twin Cities: Alberni–Port Alberni*; *Cathedral Grove: MacMillan Park*, and *Journeys down the Alberni Canal to Barklay Sound*. *Black Diamond City* is the first of an historical trilogy on the City of Nanaimo.